Secrets of Fat-Free Italian Cooking

Over 200 low-fat and fat-free, traditional & contemporary recipes—from antipasto to ziti

SANDRA WOODRUFF, RD

Avery Publishing Group
Garden City Park, New York

Text Illustrator: John Wincek
Interior Color Photographs: Victor Giordano
Photo Food Styling: BC Giordano
Front Cover Photograph: Amy Reichman
Back Cover Photographs: Victor Giordano
Cover Design: William Gonzalez
Typesetting: Bonnie Freid
In-House Editor: Joanne Abrams

Cataloging-in-Publication Data

Woodruff, Sandra L.
    Secrets of fat-free Italian cooking: over 200 low-fat and
fat-free, traditional and contemporary recipes—from antipasto to
ziti / Sandra Woodruff.
    p. cm.
    ISBN 0-89529-748-5

    1. Cookery, Italian.   2. Low-fat diet—Recipes.   I. Title.
TX723.W66 1996   641.5'945
                                                         QBI96-40145

Printed in the United States of America

10 9 8 7 6 5 4 3 2 1

Contents

This book is dedicated to my favorite taste testers, Wiley and C.D.

Acknowledgments

It has been a great pleasure to produce this book with the talented and dedicated professionals at Avery Publishing Group, who have so generously lent their support and creativity at every stage of production. Special thanks go to Rudy Shur and Ken Rajman for providing the opportunity to publish this book, and to my editor, Joanne Abrams, whose hard work, endless patience, and diligent attention to detail have added so much.

Thanks also go to my dear friends and family members for their enduring support and encouragement, and to my clients and coworkers, whose questions and ideas keep me learning and experimenting with new things. Last, but not least, I would like to thank my husband, Tom Maureau, for his long-term support and encouragement, and for always being there for me.

Preface

Who doesn't love Italian food? The crusty pizzas, creamy sauces, satisfying pastas, savory soups, spicy entrées, and alluring desserts unique to Italian cuisine are loved the world over. Unfortunately, many of these favorites are also loaded with a staggering amount of fat. Pools of butter, cream, and olive oil; gobs of high-fat cheeses; and piles of pork-filled sausages just won't do these days. As everyone now knows, these are the very foods that compromise our health, leading to diet-related diseases like obesity, heart disease, and cancer.

As a nutritionist, I have long been aware of the need to help people eliminate the fat from their diet. I also know the importance of creating nutrient-rich dishes made from whole grains, fresh vegetables, and other ingredients that are as close as possible to their natural state. At the same time, I appreciate the fact that foods must be more than just healthy. They must be visually appealing and absolutely delicious, and they must be quick and easy to prepare. If they are

not the former, people simply will not eat them. If they are not the latter, people simply will not make them.

Secrets of Fat-Free Italian Cooking was written specifically for people who want to reduce the fat in their diet, maximize their nutrition, and treat family and friends to delicious home-style Italian meals. From Sausage and Ricotta Pan Pizza, to Penne With Spinach Cream Sauce, to Almost Veal Marsala, to Fudge Marble Cheesecake, every recipe has been designed to reduce fat and boost nutrition. Just as important, every recipe has been kitchen-tested to make sure you enjoy success each and every time you make it, and people-tested to make sure that each dish you create is a sure-fire hit.

Secrets of Fat-Free Italian Cooking begins by explaining just why dietary fat should be reduced, and just how much fat is allowable in a healthy diet. You will also learn about the many nonfat and low-fat ingredients that will help you reduce fat without sacrificing taste, and you will learn about the nutritional analysis that accompanies each and every recipe in this book.

Following this important information, each chapter focuses on a specific meal of the day or a specific type of dish made with healthful low-fat and fat-free products. Looking for guilt-free egg dishes that not only are tempting enough to lure family members out of bed, but also can double as quick and easy dinners? Chapter 3, "Eggstraordinary Omelettes and Frittatas," presents a wide selection of Italian-style egg dishes, including Sausage, Pepper, and Onion Frittata and Bacon and Tomato Omelette. Or perhaps you are looking for an assortment of palate-pleasing hot and cold hors d'oeuvres that will not wreak havoc on your healthy lifestyle. "Antipasti and Appetizers With Appeal" will lead the way with fabulous selections such as Gorgonzola Party Pizzas and Baked Spinach and Artichoke Dip. Still other chapters will show you how to create steaming soups, like Savory Italian Sausage Soup; refreshing salads, like Slim Caesar Salad; savory pasta dishes, like Tempting Turkey Tetrazzini; hot and hearty polentas and risottos, like Polenta Lasagna and Shrimp and Asparagus Risotto; deliciously light pizzas, like Primavera Pan Pizza; savory sauces, like Roasted Tomato Sauce; and easy but elegant entrées, like Almost Veal Parmesan and Chicken Rollatini. And because for some of us, the meal isn't complete until we've enjoyed a taste of something sweet, there's a tempting selection of deceptively decadent desserts—including cheesecakes, tortes, puddings, pies, cookies, and other treats designed to provide a sweet but light conclusion to your low-fat meal.

It is my hope that *Secrets of Fat-Free Italian Cooking* will prove to you, your family, and your friends, that Italian cuisine can be delicious and satisfying without being rich and fattening. So eat well and enjoy! As you will see, it is possible to do both—at every meal, and on every day of the year.

Introduction

During the past few years, people have become aware of the relationship between diet and health as never before. Most especially, they have focused on the health benefits of reducing dietary fat. As a result, counting fat grams has become a national pastime.

At the same time, Italian cuisine has enjoyed ever-increasing popularity throughout the country. Rather than having familiarity with just a few Italian dishes, Americans have become more sophisticated in their knowledge of the many delights of the Italian table, and have integrated a variety of these foods—from pizza to pasta to risotto—into their everyday menus.

Unfortunately, as many fat counters have discovered, it is all too easy to blow your fat budget when enjoying Italian cuisine. In fact, even a moderate portion of fettuccini Alfredo or a single wedge of white pizza can have no place in a low-fat eating plan . . . or couldn't, until now. Because of the nation's focus on fat, manufacturers have been prompted to produce a multitude of low- and no-fat products. Supermarket shelves are now filled with a dazzling variety of such products, from nonfat mozzarella to light and healthy tomato sauces. Similarly, everyone from weekend cooks to world-renowned chefs has been inspired to explore new ways of making and eating food. So now low-fat and fat-free Italian food is not only possible to make, but actually *easy* to make.

Still, it is important to be aware that not all low- and no-fat cookbooks are alike. While every one of these books does provide low-fat recipes, many reduce fat by using artificial fat substitutes and chemical-laden, highly processed ingredients. Extra salt is frequently added to recipes to make up for the flavor lost when fat is removed. And fat-free desserts may include so much extra sugar that, when compared with their full-fat counterparts, they offer little or no actual savings in calories. The result? In an effort to reduce or eliminate fat, nutrition is often greatly compromised.

Secrets of Fat-Free Italian Cooking is a very different kind of cookbook. It was designed to help you create delicious low- and no-fat foods that are as high in nutrition as they are in flavor.

As a nutritionist, I began looking for ways to reduce or totally eliminate the fat in foods long before anyone heard the term "fat-free." Through years of experimentation and kitchen testing, I developed simple ways to do just this. But the recipes in this book are more than just low-fat. I have further improved the nutritional value of these recipes by using natural sweeteners like fruits and juices whenever possible to reduce the need for added sugar. Whole grains and whole grain flours have also been incorporated into these recipes for fiber and extra nutritional value. As an added bo-nus, the use of herbs, spices, and other season-ings, as well as minimal reliance on processed foods, has helped keep sodium under control.

Perhaps the best part of these recipes, though, is their simplicity. Every effort has been made to keep the number of ingredients, pots, pans, and utensils to a minimum. This will save you time and make cleanup a breeze—important consid-erations for most people today.

As you will see, watching your fat intake does not have to mean dieting and deprivation. This book is filled with easy-to-follow recipes for deli-cious dishes that your whole family will enjoy, as well as plenty of ideas for getting the fat out of your own Italian specialties. I wish you the best of luck and health with all your fat-free cooking!

1

Mastering Fat-Free Italian Cooking

Who says you can't have your pizza and eat it too? If you know the secrets of fat-free Italian cooking, you can have just about anything you want—creamy fettuccine Alfredo, cheese-layered lasagna, crisp-crusted pizzas, deceptively rich cheesecake, and much more.

For too many years, eating healthfully has meant limited choices, deprivation, and extra hours spent shopping and cooking. "If it's good for you, it probably tastes awful," was the attitude that emerged. Fortunately, this is far from true. *Secrets of Fat-Free Italian Cooking* introduces you to a variety of innovative fat-free cooking techniques, and shows you how to use the latest nonfat and low-fat products, as well as many traditional ingredients. The result? Italian favorites that are never bland or boring, that are simple to prepare, and that your whole family will love.

In these pages you will find recipes for a wide variety of delicious low-fat and fat-free Italian dishes. You will be delighted by "defatted" versions of old favorites, as well as tempting new creations that will let you eat the foods you love without guilt. Perhaps just as important, this book will show you that contrary to popular belief, changing to a low-fat lifestyle does not have to be an ordeal. As you will see, the recipes in this book will not save you just fat and calories, but time and effort, too. Most of these recipes are very simple to prepare, even for beginners, and are designed to create as little mess as possible, saving you cleanup time.

This chapter will explain why your dietary fat should be reduced, and will guide you in budgeting your daily fat intake. In addition, you will learn about the best ingredients to use in your low-fat and no-fat Italian dishes, and you will discover how to use these foods to create great-tasting, sure-fire family favorites.

WHY FIGHT FAT?

There are plenty of good reasons to fight fat, but the most common one is the desire to lose weight. How does fighting fat help with weight loss? With more than twice the calories of carbohydrates or protein, fat is a concentrated source of calories. Compare a cup of butter or margarine (almost pure fat) with a cup of flour (almost pure carbohydrates). The butter has 1,600 calories and the flour has 400 calories. It's easy to see where most of our calories come from.

Besides being high in calories, fat is also readily converted into body fat when eaten in excess. Carbohydrate-rich foods eaten in excess are also stored as fat, but they must first be converted into fat—a process that burns up some of the carbohydrates. The bottom line is that a high-fat diet will cause 20 percent more weight gain than will a high-carbohydrate diet, even when the two diets contain the same number of calories. So a high-fat diet is a double-edged sword for the weight-conscious person. It is high in calories, and it is the kind of nutrient that is most readily stored as body fat.

But high-fat diets pose a threat to much more than our weight. When fatty diets lead to obesity, diseases like diabetes and high blood pressure can result. And specific types of fats present their own unique problems. For example, eating too much saturated fat—found in meat, butter, and margarine, among other foods—raises blood cholesterol levels, setting the stage for heart disease. Polyunsaturated fat, once thought to be the solution to heart disease, can also be harmful when eaten in excess. A diet overly rich in certain vegetable oils—corn, sunflower, and safflower, and products made from these oils—can alter body chemistry to favor the development of blood clots, high blood pressure, and inflammatory diseases. Too much polyunsaturated fat can also promote free-radical damage to cells, contributing to heart disease and cancer.

Where do monounsaturated fats fit in? Monounsaturated fats—abundant in olive oil, canola oil, avocados, cashews, almonds, and peanuts—have no known harmful effects other than being a concentrated source of calories, like all fats.

One other kind of fat needs to be considered—especially if you are concerned about heart disease. Trans-fatty acids, also called trans fats, are chemically altered fats that are produced by adding hydrogen to liquid vegetable oils. This process, called hydrogenation, transforms the liquid vegetable oils into solid margarines and shortenings, giving these products a butter-like consistency. While hydrogenation improves the cooking and baking qualities of oils, and extends their shelf life as well, it also creates trans fats. And trans fats, it has been found, act much like saturated fats to raise levels of LDL, or "bad" cholesterol, and at the same time lower levels of HDL, or "good" cholesterol.

Considering the problems caused by excess fat, you may think it would be best to completely eliminate fat from your diet. But the fact is that we do need some dietary fat. For instance, linoleic acid, a polyunsaturated fat naturally abundant in oils such as corn, soy, and safflower, and in walnuts, pine nuts, sunflower seeds, and sesame seeds, is essential for life. The average adult needs a minimum of 3 to 6 grams of linoleic acid per day—the amount present in one to two teaspoonfuls of polyunsaturated vegetable oil or one to two tablespoonfuls of nuts or seeds. Linolenic acid, a fat present mainly in fish, flax seeds, and green plants, is also essential for good health. Some fat is also needed in the diet so that we may absorb fat-soluble nutrients like vitamin E.

Unfortunately, many people are getting too much of a good thing. The liberal use of mayonnaise, oily salad dressings, margarine, and cooking oils has created an unhealthy overdose of linoleic acid in the American diet. And, of course, most people also eat far too much saturated fat. How can we correct this? We can minimize the use of refined vegetable oils and table fats, and eat a diet rich in whole grains, legumes, vegetables, and fruits, with moderate amounts of nuts and seeds, fish, and, if desired, lean meats.

HOW TO FIGHT FAT

Now that you understand some of the reasons you should get the fat out of your diet, it's time to do just that. In the remainder of this chapter, you will discover how to develop your own personal fat budget, and you will become acquainted with the healthful foods that can help you prune the fat from your diet and maximize the nutrients. Throughout the rest of the book, you will learn how to use these foods to create delicious Italian fare that you will be proud to serve, and family and friends will love to eat.

Budgeting Your Fat

For most Americans, about 34 percent of the calories in their diet come from fat. However, currently it is recommended that fat calories constitute no more than 30 percent of the diet, and, in fact, 20 to 25 percent would be even better in most cases. So the amount of fat you should eat every day is based on the number of calories you need. Because people's calorie needs depend on their weight, age, gender, activity level, and metabolic rate, these needs vary greatly among people. Most adults, though, must consume 13 to 15 calories per pound to maintain their weight. Of course, some people need even fewer calories, while very physically active people need more.

Once you have determined your calorie requirements, you can estimate a fat budget for yourself. Suppose you are a moderately active person who weighs 150 pounds. You will probably need about 15 calories per pound to maintain your weight, or about 2,250 calories per day. To limit your fat intake to 20 percent of your caloric intake, you can eat no more than 450 calories derived from fat per day (2,250 x .20 = 450). To convert this to grams of fat, divide by 9, as one gram of fat has 9 calories. Therefore, you should limit yourself to 50 grams of fat per day (450 ÷ 9 = 50).

The following table shows two recommended maximum daily fat gram budgets—one based on 20 percent of calorie intake, and one based on 25 percent of calorie intake. If you are overweight, go by the weight you would like to be. This will allow you to gradually reach your goal weight. And keep in mind that although you have budgeted X amount of fat grams per day, you don't *have* to eat that amount of fat—you just have to avoid going over budget.

Recommended Maximum Daily Fat and Calorie Intakes

Weight (pounds)	Recommended Daily Calorie Intake (13–15 calories per pound)	Fat Grams Allowed (20% of Calorie Intake)	Fat Grams Allowed (25% of Calorie Intake)
100	1,300–1,500	29–33	36–42
110	1,430–1,650	32–37	40–46
120	1,560–1,800	34–40	43–50
130	1,690–1,950	38–43	47–54
140	1,820–2,100	40–46	51–58
150	1,950–2,250	43–50	54–62
160	2,080–2,400	46–53	58–67
170	2,210–2,550	49–57	61–71
180	2,340–2,700	52–60	65–75
190	2,470–2,850	55–63	69–79
200	2,600–3,000	58–66	72–83

How Low Should You Go?

If you are like most people, you have discovered that for maximum health, you must reduce your daily fat intake. How low should you go? As discussed earlier, some fat is necessary for good health. Therefore, you should not try to consume less than 20 grams of fat per day. Of course, if you eat a balanced diet rich in whole, natural foods, it would be almost impossible to eat less than this, anyway. On the other hand, if you eat a diet rich in fat-free refined and processed foods, you could be at risk for a deficiency of essential fats, as well as deficiencies of other nutrients. This is why the recipes in this book so often include whole grains and other natural foods, and minimize the use of refined and processed foods.

Realize, too, that a very low-fat diet is not for everyone. If you have a specific medical problem, be sure to check with your physician or nutritionist before making any dramatic dietary changes.

Remember That Calories Count, Too

As you know by now, weight loss is the number-one reason that most people are trying to reduce their fat intake. And over the past decade, Americans have been able to reduce their fat consumption from 40 percent of calories to about 34 percent of calories. Yet during this same time, the rate of obesity has actually increased. Now, one out of three Americans is considered obese—compared with one out of four in 1980. How can this be? It's simple. People tend to forget that calories count too. The fact is that people now eat more calories than they did a decade ago—and exercise less.

In a way, the fat-free food frenzy has contributed to an expanding national waistline by creating a false sense of security. Many people mistakenly think that if a food is low in fat or fat-free, they can consume unlimited quantities of it. They may start their day with a jumbo fat-free muffin, keep a jar of jelly beans on their desk to nibble on throughout the day, snack on low-fat cookies at break time, and eat a bowl of fat-free ice cream for an evening snack. Although all of these foods are better choices than their full-fat counterparts, they are loaded with sugar and provide few or no nutrients. Moreover, some of these items have just as many calories as the full-fat versions. The truth is that any foods eaten in excess of calories burned in a day will be converted to body fat. And this is just as true of fat-free foods as it is of high-fat foods.

Does this mean that you should forget about using fat-free foods to lose weight? Not by any means. Chosen wisely, these foods can help you reach and maintain a healthy body weight. Setting up a fat budget is the best place to start, since a low-fat diet is generally low in calories, too—unless you eat too many fat-free junk foods. If you then stay within the bounds of your fat budget and choose mostly nutrient-rich foods, you should be able to reach your weight-management goals. But if you find that you are still having trouble losing or maintaining weight, you must consider whether you are staying within the bounds of your calorie budget, as well.

ABOUT THE INGREDIENTS

Never before has it been so easy to eat healthfully. Nonfat and low-fat alternatives are available for just about any ingredient you can think of. This makes it possible to create a dazzling array of healthful and delicious foods, including low-fat versions of many of your favorite dishes. In the pages that follow, we'll take a look at low-fat and nonfat cheeses, fat-free spreads and dressings, fat-free egg substitutes, ultra-lean meats, and many other ingredients that will insure success in all your light Italian cooking adventures.

Low-Fat and Nonfat Cheeses

From antipasto platters to ultra-rich cheesecakes, cheese is a star ingredient in Italian cooking. For many years, though, people who wanted to reduce the fat in their diet had to also reduce the cheese, or even eliminate cheese entirely. Fortunately, a wide range of nonfat and low-fat products is now available, making it possible to have your cheese and eat it too. Let's learn about some of the cheeses that you'll be using in your fat-free recipes.

Cottage Cheese. Although often thought of as a "diet food," full-fat cottage cheese has 5 grams of fat per 4-ounce serving, making it far from diet fare. Instead, choose nonfat or low-fat cottage cheese. When puréed until smooth, these versatile products make a great base for dips, spreads, and salad dressings. Cottage cheese also adds richness and body to casseroles, cheesecakes, and many other dishes. Select brands with 1 percent or less milkfat. Most brands of cottage cheese are quite high in sodium, with about 400 milligrams per half cup, so it's best to avoid adding salt when this cheese is a recipe ingredient. As an alternative, use unsalted cottage cheese, which is available in some stores.

Another option when buying cottage cheese is dry curd cottage cheese. This nonfat version is made without the "dressing" or creaming mixture. Minus the dressing, cottage cheese has a drier consistency; hence its name, "dry curd." Unlike most cottage cheese, dry curd is very low in sodium. Use dry curd cottage cheese as you would nonfat cottage cheese in casseroles, dips, spreads, salad dressings, and cheesecakes.

Cream Cheese. Regular full-fat cream cheese contains 10 grams of fat per ounce, making this popular spread a real menace if you're trying to reduce dietary fat. A tasty alternative is light cream cheese, which has only 5 grams of fat per ounce. Another reduced-fat alternative is Neufchâtel cheese, which contains 6 grams of fat per ounce. And, of course, nonfat cream cheese contains no fat at all. Like light cream cheese and Neufchâtel, nonfat cream cheese may be used in dips, spreads, and cheesecakes. Look for brands like Philadelphia Free and Healthy Choice, and use the block-style cheese for best results in all of your fat-free recipes.

When substituting nonfat cream cheese for the full-fat version in cheesecakes, you may find that the texture of the cake is softer—more pudding-like—than that of a traditional cheesecake. If this occurs, try adding a tablespoon of flour to the batter for each 8-ounce block of nonfat cream cheese used. This should produce a firm, nicely-textured cheesecake that is remarkably low in fat and calories.

Gorgonzola Cheese. This variety of blue cheese is a favorite of Italian cooks. Like other kinds of blue cheese, Gorgonzola is high in fat, with 9 grams per

ounce. However, since it is so flavorful, a little bit goes a long way. As you will see, when you use this product moderately in recipes like Gongonzola Dressing (page 53) and Gorgonzola Party Pizzas (page 38), you can still enjoy the flavor you love without a fat overload.

Mozzarella Cheese. One of the most commonly used cheeses in Italian cuisine is mozzarella. Fortunately, this versatile ingredient is now widely available in both low-fat and nonfat versions. Reduced-fat mozzarella generally has 3 to 5 grams of fat per ounce, while the nonfat product contains no fat at all. Compare this with whole milk varieties, which contain 8 to 10 grams of fat per ounce, and you'll realize your savings in fat and calories. When purchasing mozzarella, look for brands like Healthy Choice nonfat, Kraft Free, Polly-O Free, and Sargento Light.

How do nonfat and reduced-fat mozzarellas work in your favorite Italian recipes? Both versions work nicely in lasagna and casseroles, although any cheese used to top a casserole should be added only during the last ten minutes of baking—just long enough to allow the cheese to melt, but not so long that it gets dry and rubbery. Nonfat and low-fat mozzarella can also be used for pizza toppings, although low-fat brands like Sargento Light will have more "stretch" than will a nonfat brand. As for topping salads, any of the nonfat or low-fat shredded brands will give delicious results. Only your waistline will know the difference!

Parmesan Cheese. Parmesan typically contains 8 grams of fat and 400 milligrams of sodium per ounce. As with most cheeses, reduced-fat and nonfat versions—such as Kraft Free and Weight Watchers—are available. A little bit of this flavorful cheese goes a long way, so even if you used the "real thing" in any of the recipes in this book, the total fat per serving would still be quite low. In fact, in a few instances, the recipes do call for regular Parmesan instead of its nonfat counterpart.

While nonfat Parmesan works beautifully in sauces, soups, dressings, and casseroles, and as a topping for pasta, it is too dry to be used as a topping on focaccia bread, bread sticks, and casseroles. In these instances, a few tablespoons of regular Parmesan will produce the best results.

Provolone Cheese. With a subtle flavor and a pale yellow color, provolone is widely used in Italian cooking. Like reduced-fat mozzarella, reduced-fat provolone—which works in both cooked and cold dishes—will save you up to 5 grams of fat per ounce when compared with the full-fat product. Look for a brand like Alpine Lace.

Ricotta Cheese. Ricotta is a mild, slightly sweet, creamy cheese that may be used in dips, spreads, and traditional Italian dishes like lasagna and manicotti. As the name implies, nonfat ricotta contains no fat at all. Low-fat and light ricotta, on the other hand, have 1 to 3 grams of fat per ounce, while whole milk ricotta has 4 grams of fat per ounce. Look for brands like Frigo Fat-Free, Polly-O Free, Maggio Nonfat, Sorrento Fat-Free, and Sargento Light.

Soft Curd Farmer Cheese. This soft, spreadable white cheese makes a good low-fat substitute for cream cheese. Brands made with skim milk have about 3 grams of fat per ounce compared with cream cheese's 10 grams. Soft curd farmer cheese may be used in dips, spreads, and cheesecakes. Some brands are made with whole milk, so read the labels before you buy. Look for a brand like Friendship Farmer cheese. Similar products, hoop cheese and baker's cheese, can be used in the same ways. Typically fat-free and low in sodium, these two cheeses are usually found only in specialty shops.

Yogurt Cheese. A good substitute for cream cheese in dips, spreads, and cheesecakes, yogurt cheese can be made at home with any brand of plain or flavored yogurt that does not contain gelatin. Simply place the yogurt in a funnel lined with cheesecloth or a coffee filter, and let it drain into a jar in the refrigerator for eight hours or overnight. When the yogurt is reduced by half, it is ready to use. The whey that collects in the jar may be used in place of the liquid in bread and muffin recipes.

Nondairy Cheese Alternatives. If you choose to avoid dairy products because of a lactose intolerance or for another reason, you'll be glad to know that low-fat cheeses made from soymilk, almond milk, and Brazil nut milk are now available in a variety of flavors. Look for brands like Almondrella, Veganrella, and Tofurella.

Measuring Cheese

Throughout the recipes in this book, I have usually expressed the amount of cheese needed in cups. For instance, a recipe may call for 1 cup of cottage cheese or $\frac{1}{4}$ cup of grated Parmesan. Since you will sometimes buy cheese in chunks and grate it in your own kitchen, or buy packages marked in ounces when the recipe calls for cups, it is useful to understand that the conversion of cheese from ounces (weight) to cups (volume) varies, depending on the texture of the cheese. When using the recipes in *Secrets of Fat-Free Italian Cooking,* the following table should help take the guesswork out of these conversions.

Cheese Equivalency Amounts

Cheese	Weight	Equivalent Volume
Cottage Cheese	8 ounces	1 cup
Cream Cheese	8 ounces	1 cup
Farmer Cheese	8 ounces	1 cup
Baker's Cheese	8 ounces	1 cup
Hoop Cheese	8 ounces	1 cup
Mozzarella	8 ounces	2 cups shredded
Parmesan	8 ounces	$2\frac{1}{4}$ cups grated
Provolone	8 ounces	2 cups shredded
Ricotta	8 ounces	1 cup

Other Low-Fat and Nonfat Dairy Products

Of course, cheese isn't the only dairy product we use in our everyday cooking. How about the sour cream in dips, dressings, and sauces, and the buttermilk in your favorite cake? Fortunately, there are low-fat and nonfat versions of these and other dairy products as well.

Buttermilk. Buttermilk adds a rich flavor and texture to baked goods like breads and cakes, and lends a "cheesy" taste to sauces, cheesecakes, and casseroles. Originally a by-product of butter making, this product should perhaps be called "butterless" milk. Most brands of buttermilk contain from 0.5 to 2 percent fat by weight, but some brands contain as much as 3.5 percent fat.

If you cannot find nonfat buttermilk in your grocery store, 1 percent low-fat buttermilk is your next best choice. If this, too, is not available, a good substitute can be made by mixing equal parts of nonfat yogurt and skim milk. Alternatively, place a tablespoon of vinegar or lemon juice in a one-cup measure, and fill to the one-cup mark with skim milk. Let the mixture sit for five minutes, and use as you would nonfat buttermilk.

Evaporated Skimmed Milk. This ingredient can be substituted for cream in sauces, cream soups, custards, puddings, and other dishes, where it adds creamy richness but no fat.

Milk. Whole milk, the highest-fat milk available, is 3.5 percent fat by weight and has 8 grams of fat per cup. Instead, choose skim (nonfat) milk, which—with all but a trace of fat removed—has only about a 0.5 gram of fat per cup. Another good choice is 1-percent milk, which, as the name implies, is 1 percent fat by weight and contains 2 grams of fat per cup.

Nonfat Dry Milk. Like evaporated skimmed milk, instant nonfat dry milk powder adds creamy richness to cream soups, sauces, custards, and puddings, while boosting nutritional value. One cup of skim milk mixed with one-third cup of nonfat dry milk powder can replace cream in most recipes. Just be sure to use *instant* dry milk powder, as this product will not clump.

Sour Cream. As calorie- and fat-conscious people know, full-fat sour cream can contain almost 500 calories and about 48 grams of fat per cup! Use nonfat sour cream, though, and you'll save 320 calories and 48 grams of fat. Made from cultured nonfat milk thickened with vegetable gums, this product successfully replaces its high-fat counterpart in dips, spreads, and sauces.

All brands of nonfat sour cream can be substituted for the full-fat version in dips, dressings, and other cold dishes. However, some brands will separate when added to hot dishes like sauces and gravies. For these recipes, use a brand like Land O Lakes No-Fat, Breakstone's Free, or Sealtest Free, all of which hold up well during cooking.

Yogurt. Yogurt adds creamy richness and flavor to sauces, baked goods, and casseroles. And, of course, it is a perfect base for many dips and dressings. In your low-fat cooking, select brands with 1 percent or less milkfat. Like some brands of nonfat sour cream, yogurt will curdle if added to hot sauces or gravies. To prevent this, let the yogurt warm to room temperature, and stir in 2 tablespoons of unbleached flour or 1 tablespoon of cornstarch for each cup of yogurt used. The yogurt may then be added to the sauce without fear of separation. (For directions on using yogurt to make yogurt cheese, see page 8.)

Low-Fat and Fat-Free Spreads and Dressings

Like cheeses, spreads and dressings were long a major source of fat and calories. Happily, many low-fat and nonfat alternatives to our high-fat favorites are now available. Let's learn a little more about these fat-saving products.

Butter-Flavored Sprinkles. This product, which comes in handy shaker containers, can be added to sauces, pastas, casseroles, and other dishes in which a buttery flavor is desired. Butter sprinkles may also be shaken over foods like steamed vegetables and baked potatoes. Made mostly from cornstarch and natural butter flavor, this product is fat-free and contains only 4 calories per serving. Two widely available brands are Molly McButter and Butter Buds. Butter Buds is also available in packets that can be mixed with water to make a liquid butter substitute. While the resulting buttery liquid cannot be used for frying or sautéing, it is delicious when tossed with pasta or incorporated into sauces.

Margarine. If you are used to spreading foods with margarine, you can easily reduce your dietary fat by switching to a nonfat or reduced-fat margarine, and using it sparingly. Every tablespoon of nonfat margarine that you substitute for the full-fat version will save you 11 grams of fat.

You may be surprised to learn that you can also bake with reduced-fat margarine—and with light butter, too. Crisp cookies, light and tender cakes, and other goodies can easily be prepared with half the fat by substituting reduced-fat margarine or butter for the full-fat products, and by making a simple adjustment in the recipe. (For details on using these products in your baked goods, see the Low-Fat Cooking Tip on page 210.)

Mayonnaise. Nonfat mayonnaise is highly recommended over regular mayonnaise, which is almost pure fat. How can mayonnaise be made without all that oil? Manufacturers use more water and vegetable thickeners. Some commonly available nonfat brands are Kraft Free, Miracle Whip Free, Smart Beat, and Weight Watchers Fat-Free. In the low-fat category, you will find Hellmann's (Best Foods) Low-Fat, with only 1 gram of fat per tablespoon, and Weight Watchers Light, with 2 grams of fat. A variety of reduced-fat brands are also available, with half to two-thirds less fat than regular mayonnaise. Look for brands like Hellmann's Light, Kraft Light, Miracle Whip Light, and Blue Plate Light.

Salad Dressings. Low- and no-fat salad dressings are now available in a variety of flavors, including Italian, creamy Parmesan, red wine vinaigrette, roasted garlic, and raspberry vinaigrette. These new products make it easy to create tempting Italian-style salads that can complement virtually any entrée.

How do these lighter dressings stack up against their full-fat counterparts? Fat-free dressings contain either no oil or so little oil that they have less than 0.5 gram of fat per 2-tablespoon serving, while low-fat brands contain no more than 3 grams of fat per serving. Compare these products with their full-fat versions, which provide 12 to 18 grams of fat in the same size serving, and your savings are clear.

Brands like Good Seasons, Hidden Valley Ranch, Knott's Berry Farm, Kraft, Marie's, Pritikin, Seven Seas, Walden Farms, and Wishbone offer a wide variety of nonfat and reduced-fat dressings. Beware, though—many fat-free dressings are quite high in sodium, so compare brands and flavors and choose those that are on the lower end of the sodium range.

Oils and Cooking Sprays

Even in a low-fat kitchen, a little bit of oil is sometimes necessary to enhance flavor, prevent sticking, or promote browning. The following products will be invaluable in many of your low-fat Italian cooking adventures.

Nonstick Cooking Spray. Available unflavored and in butter and olive oil flavors, cooking sprays are pure fat. But because the amount produced in a one-second spray is quite small, these products add an insignificant amount of fat to a recipe. For the low-fat cook, nonstick cooking sprays are very useful to encourage the browning of foods and to prevent foods from sticking to pots and pans.

Olive Oil. This flavorful oil is a central ingredient in Italian cuisine, where it is traditionally used in liberal amounts. Olive oil is considered to be a "healthful" oil because it is low in saturated fat and does not promote heart disease. However, like all oils, olive oil is pure fat, and contains 120 calories per tablespoon. Some of the recipes in this book do include small amounts of olive oil—just enough to enhance flavor without blowing your fat budget.

Always be sure to use extra virgin olive oil, which is the least processed and most flavorful kind available. What about "light" olive oil? In this case, light refers to flavor, which is mild and bland compared with that of extra virgin oils. This means you would have to use more oil for the same amount of flavor—not a good bargain.

Egg Whites and Egg Substitutes

Everyone who cooks knows the value of eggs. Eggs are star ingredients in omelettes and frittatas, add richness to puddings and custards, and are indispensable in a wide range of baked goods. Of course, eggs are also loaded with cholesterol, and they contain some fat as well. For this reason, the recipes in this book call for egg whites or fat-free egg substitute. Just how great are your savings in cholesterol and fat when whole eggs are replaced with one of these ingredients? One large egg contains 80 calories, 5 grams of fat, and 210 milligrams of cholesterol. The equivalent amount of egg white or fat-free egg substitute contains 20 to 30 calories, no fat, and no cholesterol. The benefit of these substitute ingredients is clear.

You may wonder why some of the recipes in this book call for egg whites while others call for egg substitute. In some cases, one ingredient does, in fact, work better than the other. For instance, egg substitute is the best choice when making frittatas, omelettes, custards, and puddings. In addition, because they have been pasteurized (heat treated), egg substitutes are safe to use uncooked in salad dressings. On the other hand, when recipes require whipped egg whites, egg substitutes will not work.

In most recipes, egg whites and egg substitutes can be used interchangeably. Yet even in these recipes, one may sometimes be listed instead of the other due to ease of measuring. For example, while a cake made with three tablespoons of fat-free egg substitute would turn out just as well if made with three tablespoons of egg whites, this would require you to use one and a half large egg whites, making measuring something of a nuisance.

Whenever a recipe calls for egg whites, use large eggs. When selecting an egg substitute, look for a fat-free brand like Egg Beaters, Scramblers, Better'n Eggs, or Nu Laid. If you choose another brand, be sure to check the label carefully, as some egg substitutes contain vegetable oil. When replacing egg whites with egg substitute, or whole eggs with egg whites or egg substitute, use the following guidelines:

1 large egg = 1$\frac{1}{2}$ large egg whites
1 large egg = 3 tablespoons egg substitute
1 large egg white = 2 tablespoons egg substitute

Ultra-Lean Poultry, Meat, and Vegetarian Alternatives

Because of the high fat and cholesterol contents of meats, many people have sharply reduced their consumption of meat, have limited themselves to white meat chicken or turkey, or have totally eliminated meat and poultry from their diets. The good news is that whether you are a sworn meat eater, someone who only occasionally eats meat dishes, or a confirmed vegetarian, plenty of lean meats, lean poultry, and excellent meat substitutes are now available. All of these products can deliciously replace their high-fat counterparts in your favorite Italian dishes.

The most important point to remember when including meat in meals is to keep portions to a modest 6 ounces or less per day. For perspective, 3 ounces of meat is the size of a deck of cards. Here are some suggestions for choosing the leanest possible poultry and meat.

Turkey

Although both chicken and turkey have less total fat and saturated fat than beef and pork, your very best bet when buying poultry is turkey. What's the difference between the fat and calorie contents of chicken and turkey? While 3 ounces of chicken breast without skin contain 139 calories and 3 grams of fat, the same amount of turkey breast without skin contains only 119 calories and 1 gram of fat.

Your best defense when preparing and eating poultry is removing the skin and any underlying visible fat. Doing just this eliminates over half the fat. Is there any advantage to removing the skin *before* cooking? A slight one. Poultry cooked without the skin has about 20 percent less fat than poultry that has the skin removed after cooking. And, of course, when the skin is removed after cooking, so is the seasoning. For this reason, the recipes in this book all begin with skinless pieces.

All of the leanest cuts of turkey come from the breast, so that all have the same amount of fat and calories per serving. Here is what you're likely to find at your local supermarket:

Turkey Cutlets. Turkey cutlets, which are slices of fresh turkey breast, are usually about $\frac{1}{4}$-inch thick and weigh about 2 to 3 ounces each. These cutlets may be used as a delicious and ultra-lean alternative to boneless chicken breast, pork tenderloin slices, or veal.

Turkey Medallions. Sliced from turkey tenderloins, medallions are about 1 inch thick and weight 2 to 3 ounces each. Turkey medallions can be substituted for pork or veal medallions in any recipe.

Turkey Steaks. Cut from the turkey breast, these steaks are about $\frac{1}{2}$ to 1 inch in thickness. Turkey steaks may be baked, broiled, grilled, cut into stir-fry pieces or kabobs, or ground for burgers.

Turkey Tenderloins. Large sections of fresh turkey breast, tenderloins usually weight about 8 ounces each. Tenderloins may be sliced into cutlets, cut into stir-fry or kabob pieces, ground for burgers, or grilled or roasted as is.

Whole Turkey Breast. Perfect for people who love roast turkey but want only the breast meat, turkey breasts weigh 4 to 8 pounds each. These breasts may be roasted with or without stuffing.

Ground Turkey. Ground turkey is an excellent ingredient for use in meatballs, meat loaf, pasta sauces, burgers—in any dish that uses ground meat. When shopping for ground turkey, you'll find that different products have different percentages of fat. Ground turkey breast, which is only 1 percent fat by weight, is the leanest ground meat you can buy. Ground dark meat turkey made without the skin is 8 to 10 percent fat by weight. Brands with added skin and fat usually contain 15 percent fat. The moral is clear. Always check labels before making a purchase!

Chicken

Although not as low in fat as turkey, chicken is still lower in fat than most cuts of beef and pork, and therefore is a valuable ingredient in low-fat cooking. Beware, though: Many cuts of chicken, if eaten with the skin on, contain more fat than some cuts of beef and pork. For the least fat, choose the chicken breast, and always remove the skin—preferably, before cooking.

Does ground chicken have a place in low-fat cooking? Like ground turkey, ground chicken often contains skin and fat. Most brands contain at least 15 percent fat, in fact, so read the labels carefully before you buy.

Beef and Pork

Although not as lean as turkey, beef and pork are both considerably leaner today than in decades past. Spurred by competition from the poultry industry, beef and pork producers have changed breeding and feeding practices to reduce the fat content of these products. In addition, butchers are now trimming away more of the fat from retail cuts of meat. The result? On average, grocery store cuts of beef are 27 percent leaner today than in the early 1980s, and retail cuts of pork are 43 percent leaner.

Choosing the Best Cuts and Grades. Of course, some cuts of beef and pork are leaner than others. Which are the smartest choices? The following table will guide you in selecting those cuts that are lowest in fat.

The Leanest Beef and Pork Cuts

Cut (3 ounces, cooked and trimmed)	Calories	Fat
Beef		
Eye of Round	143	4.2 grams
Top Round	153	4.2 grams
Round Tip	157	5.9 grams
Top Sirloin	165	6.1 grams
Pork		
Tenderloin	139	4.1 grams
Ham (95% lean)	112	4.3 grams
Boneless Sirloin Chops	164	5.7 grams
Boneless Loin Roast	165	6.1 grams
Boneless Loin Chops	173	6.6 grams

While identifying the lowest-fat cuts of meat is an important first step in healthy cooking, be aware that even lean cuts have varying amounts of fat because of differences in grades. In general, the higher and more expensive grades of meat, like USDA Prime and Choice, have more fat due to a higher degree of marbling—internal fat that cannot be trimmed away. USDA Select meats have the least amount of marbling, and therefore the lowest amount of fat. How important are these differences? A USDA Choice piece of meat may have 15 to 20 percent more fat than a USDA Select cut, and USDA Prime may have even more fat. Clearly, the difference is significant. So when choosing beef and pork for your table, by all means check the package for grade. Then look for the least amount of marbling in the cut you have chosen, and let appearance be your final guide.

Ground Beef. While ground turkey breast is the leanest ground meat you can find, low-fat ground beef is also available, giving you another option. The leanest ground beef commonly sold in supermarkets is 95-percent lean. Some stores also carry brands that are as much as 96-percent lean. Can't find these products in your grocery store? Select a lean piece of top round, and ask the butcher to trim off the fat and grind the remaining meat. The resulting product will be about 95-percent lean. Your next best choice is 93-percent lean ground beef. Available in many stores, this beef, as the name implies, is only 7 percent fat by weight.

How different is the leaner ground beef from the more commonly sold product? Beef that is 95-percent lean contains 4.9 grams of fat and 132 calories per 3-ounce cooked serving. Compare this with regular ground beef, which is 73-percent lean and has 17.9 grams of fat and 248 calories per serving, and your savings are clear.

Lean Processed Meat

Because of our new fat-consciousness, low-fat sausages, hams, bacon, and lunchmeats are now available, with just a fraction of the fat of regular processed meats. Many of these low-fat products substitute beautifully for the high-fat hams, sausages, and bacons used in traditional Italian cooking. Here are some examples:

Bacon. Turkey bacon, made with strips of light and dark turkey meat, makes an excellent substitute for pork bacon in your Italian soups, sauces, pasta dishes, and other recipes. With 30 calories and 2 grams of fat per strip, turkey bacon has 50 percent less fat than crisp-cooked pork bacon, and shrinks much less during cooking.

Another kind of bacon often used in Italian cooking is pancetta. This unsmoked peppery bacon is shaped into a roll, and then thinly sliced and used in a wide variety of Italian recipes. Like pork bacon, pancetta is quite high in fat. To save fat and calories, try using a thinly shaved Canadian bacon, which is typically about 95-percent lean. Or try a thinly shaved brand of lean ham, such as Healthy Choice, Butterball, Oscar Mayer Free, or Louis Rich. These hams are 97-percent to 100-percent lean.

Italian Sausage. An essential part of many favorite Italian dishes, Italian sausage is generally very greasy. Just one ounce of this sausage—which is traditionally made with fatty cuts of pork—contains over 90 calories and 7 grams of fat! Fortunately, low-fat turkey Italian sausage is very easy to prepare at home using the recipe on page 182. With 33 calories and less than 1 gram of fat per ounce, this homemade product is a real boon to the low-fat cook. Many stores also sell ready-made turkey Italian sausage. When buying these foods, always check the package and choose the leanest mixture available.

Another trick for adding Italian sausage flavor to your dishes, without adding any meat at all, is to toss in some fennel seeds. Fennel seeds give Italian sausage its characteristic flavor. So a sprinkling of these seeds in your pasta sauce or over the top of your pizza will add Italian sausage flavor, but no fat or calories.

Lunchmeats. Many varieties of ultra-lean lunchmeats are now available, including ham, roast beef, pastrami, and bologna. These meats make ideal substitutes for high-fat cold cuts in sandwiches and antipasto platters. Like all processed meats, though, they should be used in moderation due to their high sodium content.

Some processed meats are now labelled "fat-free." Since all meats naturally contain some fat, how can this be? The manufacturer first starts with a lean meat such as turkey breast, and then adds enough water to dilute the fat to a point where the product contains less than 0.5 gram of fat per serving. Though more and more "fat-free" meat products are becoming available, you will be happy to know that meats labelled 96- to 99-percent lean are also lean enough to fit into a low-fat diet, since they contain only 0.3 to 1 gram of fat per ounce.

Vegetarian Alternatives

Nonmeat alternatives to ground meat can be substituted for ground beef or ground poultry in many of the recipes in this book. Two good choices are Green Giant's Harvest Burger for Recipes, and Morningstar Farms Ground Meatless. Made from soybeans and other vegetable proteins, these products are rich in protein and fat-free. Both products are available in the freezer case of the grocery store, and can be substituted for ground meat in spaghetti sauce or as a pizza topping.

Texturized vegetable protein (TVP) is yet another alternative to ground meat. Made from defatted soy flour, TVP has about 0.3 gram of fat per ounce. TVP is packaged as dry nuggets that you rehydrate with water, and then use in the same way as Harvest Burger for Recipes and Morningstar Farms Ground Meatless.

Fish and Seafood

Of the many kinds of fish that are available, some types are almost fat-free, while others are moderately fatty. However, the oil that fish provides contains an essential substance known as omega-3 fatty acids—a substance that most people do not eat in sufficient quantities. Omega-3 fatty acids are valuable because they can help reduce blood cholesterol, lower blood pressure, and prevent deadly blood clots from forming. This means that all kinds of fish, including the higher-fat varieties, are considered healthful.

Many fish are now raised on "farms." Do these fish offer the same health benefits as do fish caught in their natural habitats? No. Farm-raised fish are fed grains instead of a fish's natural diet of plankton and smaller fish. As a result, farm-raised fish contain as much or more fat than wild fish, but are much lower in the beneficial omega-3 fatty acids.

What about the cholesterol content of shellfish? It may not be as high as you think it is. With the exception of shrimp, a 3-ounce serving of most shellfish contains about 60 milligrams of cholesterol, placing it well under the upper limit of 300 milligrams per day. An equivalent serving of shrimp has about 160 milligrams of cholesterol—just over half the recommended daily limit. Keep in mind, though, that all seafood, including shellfish, is very low in saturated fat, which has a greater cholesterol-raising effect than does cholesterol.

Fish is highly perishable, so it is important to know how to select a high-quality product. First, make sure that the fish is firm and springy to the touch. Second, buy fish only if it has a clean seaweed odor, rather than a "fishy" smell. Third, when purchasing whole fish, choose those fish whose gills are bright red in color, and whose eyes are clear and bulging, not sunken or cloudy. Finally, refrigerate fish as soon as you get it home, and be sure to cook it within forty-eight hours of purchase.

Grains and Flours

Just because a food is fat-free does not mean it is good for you. Fat-free products made from refined white flour and refined grains provide few nutrients, and can actually deplete nutrient stores if eaten in excess. Whole grains and whole grain flours, on the other hand, contain a multitude of nutrients such as vitamin E, zinc, magnesium, chromium, potassium, and many other nutrients that are lacking in refined grains. Whole grain products also add fiber to our diets, making our meals more satisfying. You see, fiber—like fat—provides a feeling of fullness. Fiber also helps maintain blood sugar levels, which helps keep hunger at bay. Adequate fiber is, in fact, an important part of a successful low-fat eating plan, as a diet of fat-free and low-fat refined foods is sure to leave you hungry.

Fortunately, once accustomed to the heartier taste and texture of whole grains, most people prefer them over tasteless refined grains. Following is a description of some whole grain products used in the recipes in this book. Many of these products are readily available in grocery stores, while others may be found in health foods stores and gourmet shops. If you are unable to locate a particular grain or flour in your area, it is probably available by mail order. (See the Resource List on page 219.)

Arborio Rice. This starchy short grain rice is the preferred rice for making a true Italian risotto. Arborio rice is refined, so it contains less fiber and nutrients than brown rice does. However, arborio rice is fat-free and rich in complex carbohydrates, so it can be enjoyed as part of a healthful low-fat diet.

Barley. This grain has a nutty light flavor, making it a great substitute for rice in pilafs, soups, casseroles, and other dishes. Hulled barley, like brown rice, cooks in about 50 minutes. Quick-cooking barley, which retains most of the fiber and nutrients of the long-cooking variety, can be prepared in only 10 to 12 minutes.

Barley Flour. Made from ground barley kernels, this flour is rich in cholesterol-lowering soluble fiber. Slightly sweet-tasting, barley flour adds a cake-like texture to baked goods, and can be used interchangeably with oat flour in any recipe.

Bread Flour. Made from high-gluten wheat flour, this product is designed especially for use in yeast breads. Bread flour also contains dough conditioners, such as ascorbic acid (vitamin C), that make the dough rise better.

Brown Rice. Brown rice is whole-kernel rice, meaning that all nutrients are intact. With a slightly chewy texture and a pleasant nutty flavor, brown rice makes excellent pilafs and stuffings.

Brown Rice Flour. Brown rice flour is simply finely ground brown rice. With a texture similar to that of cornmeal, this product adds a mildly sweet flavor to baked goods. Use it in cookies for a crisp and crunchy texture.

Cornmeal. This grain adds a sweet flavor, a lovely golden color, and a crunchy texture to baked goods. Select whole grain (unbolted) cornmeal for the most nutrition. By contrast, bolted cornmeal is nearly whole grain, and degermed cornmeal is refined.

Italians cook coarsely ground yellow cornmeal, called polenta, in water or stock to make a thick cornmeal mush, which is also called polenta. The ground meal can be found in gourmet shops and some grocery stores. If you cannot find polenta, yellow corn grits, which are also coarsely ground cornmeal, will substitute nicely.

Oat Bran. Made of the outer part of the oat kernel, oat bran has a sweet, mild flavor and is a concentrated source of cholesterol-lowering soluble fiber. Oat bran helps retain moisture in baked goods, making it a natural for fat-free baking. This product also makes a fiber-rich substitute for bread crumbs in meat loaf and meatballs. Look for it in the hot cereal section of your grocery store, and choose the softer, more finely ground products, like Quaker Oat Bran. Coarsely ground oat bran makes excellent hot cereal, but is not the best choice for baking.

Oat Flour. This mildly sweet flour is perfect for cakes, muffins, and other baked goods. Like oat bran, oat flour retains moisture in baked goods, reducing the need for fat. To add extra fiber and nutrients to your own recipes, replace up to a third of the refined wheat flour in your own recipes with an equal amount of oat flour. If you can't find oat flour in your local stores, you can easily make it at home by grinding quick-cooking oats in a blender.

Oats. Loaded with cholesterol-lowering soluble fiber, oats add a chewy texture and sweet flavor to muffins, breads, cookies, and crumb toppings. They are also delicious in breakfast cereals and other dishes, and make an excellent filler for meat loaf and meatballs. The recipes in this book use quick-cooking rolled oats. (Look for oats that cook in one minute.) Old-fashioned oats, which are cut slightly thicker, cook in 5 minutes.

Unbleached Flour. This is refined white flour that has not been subjected to a bleaching process. Unbleached white flour lacks significant amounts of nutrients compared with whole wheat flour, but does contain more vitamin E than bleached flour. The unbleached flour that is widely available in supermarkets is a multipurpose flour that can be used for a variety of baking purposes—including any recipes in this book that call for unbleached flour.

If you can find an **unbleached pastry flour,** it will produce even better results in cakes, pie crusts, cookies, quick breads, and muffin recipes. However, you will need to substitute it for regular flour by using the guidelines on page 17. Made from a softer (lower-protein) wheat, unbleached pastry flour will produce a finer, softer texture in baked goods than will regular unbleached flour. Unfortunately, unbleached pastry flour is not widely available, but it can be purchased in some specialty shops and health food stores.

Wheat Bran. Unprocessed wheat bran—sometimes called miller's bran—is made from the outer portion of the whole wheat kernel. This product adds fiber and texture to breads, muffins, and other foods.

Wheat Germ. When toasted, this ingredient adds crunch and nutty flavor to baked goods. A supernutritious food, with 90 percent less fat than nuts, toasted wheat germ provides generous amounts of vitamin E and minerals.

Whole Grain Wheat. Available in many forms, this grain is perhaps easiest to use in the form of bulgur wheat. Cracked wheat that is precooked and dried, bulgur wheat can be prepared in a matter of minutes, and can be used to replace rice in just about any recipe.

Whole Wheat Flour. Made of ground whole grain wheat kernels, whole wheat flour includes the grain's nutrient-rich bran and germ. Nutritionally speaking, whole wheat flour is far superior to refined flour. Sadly, many people grew up eating refined baked goods, and find whole grain products too heavy for their taste. A good way to learn to enjoy whole grain flours is to use part whole wheat and part unbleached flour in recipes, and gradually increase the amount of whole wheat used over time.

When muffin, quick bread, cake, and cookie recipes call for whole wheat flour, **whole wheat pastry flour** will produce the best results. Whole wheat pastry flour produces lighter, softer-textured baked goods than regular whole wheat flour because it is made from a softer (lower-protein) wheat and is more finely ground. Look for a brand like Arrowhead Mills whole grain pastry flour, which can be found in health food stores and some grocery stores. Be aware that while whole wheat pastry flour should be your first choice when making muffins, quick breads, cakes, and cookies, it does not contain enough protein to perform well in most yeast breads.

White whole wheat flour is another option for baking. Made from hard white wheat instead of the hard red wheat used to make regular whole wheat flour, white whole wheat flour is sweeter and lighter tasting than its red wheat counterpart. However, unless the label specifically states that your white whole wheat flour is a soft or pastry flour, it will produce baked goods with a heavier, coarser texture than those made from whole wheat pastry flour. Unlike whole wheat pastry flour, white whole wheat flour can be used for baking yeast breads.

As you can see, there is a wide variety of flours available for use in baking. Experiment with various flours to see which kinds you like best. Here are some general guidelines that will allow you to substitute various flours for refined wheat flour in your own favorite recipes.

1 cup refined wheat flour equals:

❑ 1 cup unbleached flour
❑ 1 cup plus 2 tablespoons unbleached pastry flour
❑ 1 cup plus 2 tablespoons cake flour
❑ 1 cup minus 2 tablespoons regular whole wheat flour
❑ 1 cup whole wheat pastry flour
❑ 1 cup minus 1 tablespoon white whole wheat flour
❑ 1 cup brown rice flour
❑ 1 cup barley flour
❑ 1 cup oat flour

Sweeteners

Refined white sugar contains no nutrients. In fact, when eaten in excess, refined sugar can actually deplete the body's stores of essential nutrients like chromium and the B vitamins. Of course, a moderate amount of sugar is usually not a problem for people who eat an otherwise healthy diet. What's moderate? No more than 10 percent of your daily intake of calories should come from sugar. For an individual who needs 2,000 calories to maintain his or her weight, this amounts to an upper limit of 12.5 teaspoons (about $\frac{1}{4}$ cup) of sugar a day. Naturally, a diet that is lower in sugar is even better.

The baked goods and dessert recipes in this book contain 25 to 50 percent less sugar than traditional recipes do. Ingredients like fruit juices, fruit purées, and dried fruits; flavorings and spices like vanilla extract, nutmeg, and cinnamon; and mildly sweet oats and oat bran have often been used to reduce the need for sugar.

The recipes in this book call for moderate amounts of white sugar, brown sugar, and different liquid sweeteners. However, a large number of sweeteners are now available, and you should feel free to substitute one sweetener for another, using your own tastes, your desire for high-nutrient ingredients, and your pocketbook as a guide. (Some of the newer less-refined sweeteners are far more expensive than traditional sweeteners.) For best results, replace granular sweeteners with other granular sweeteners, and substitute liquid sweeteners for other liquid sweeteners. You can, of course, replace a liquid with granules, or vice versa, but adjustments in other recipe ingredients will have to be made. (For each cup of liquid sweetener substituted for granulated sweetener, reduce the liquid by $\frac{1}{4}$ to $\frac{1}{3}$ cup.) Also be aware that each sweetener has its own unique flavor and its own degree of sweetness, making some sweeteners better suited to particular recipes.

Following are descriptions of some of the sweeteners commonly available in grocery stores, health foods stores, and gourmet shops.

Brown Sugar. This granulated sweetener is simply refined white sugar that has been coated with a thin film of molasses. Light brown sugar is lighter in color than regular brown sugar, but not lower in calories, as the name might imply. Because this sweetener contains some molasses, brown sugar has more calcium, iron, and potassium than white sugar. But like most sugars, brown sugar is no nutritional powerhouse. The advantage to using this sweetener over white

sugar is that it is more flavorful, so less can generally be used.

Date Sugar. Made from ground dried dates, date sugar provides copper, magnesium, iron, and B vitamins. With a distinct date flavor, date sugar is delicious in breads, cakes, and muffins. Because it does not dissolve as readily as white sugar does, it's best to mix date sugar with the recipe's liquid ingredients and let it sit for a few minutes before proceeding with the recipe. Date sugar is less dense than white sugar, and so is only about two-thirds as sweet. However, date sugar is more flavorful, and so can often be substituted for white sugar on a cup-for-cup basis.

Fruit Juice Concentrates. Frozen juice concentrates add sweetness and flavor to baked goods while enhancing nutritional value. Use the concentrates as you would honey or other liquid sweeteners, but beware—too much will be overpowering. Always keep cans of frozen orange and apple juice concentrate in the freezer just for cooking and baking. Pineapple and tropical fruit blends also make good sweeteners, and white grape juice is ideal when you want a more neutral flavor.

Fruit Source. Made from white grape juice and brown rice, this sweetener has a rather neutral flavor and is about as sweet as white sugar. Fruit Source is available in both granular and liquid forms. Use the liquid as you would honey, and the granules as you would sugar. The granules do not dissolve as readily as sugar does, so mix Fruit Source with the recipe's liquid ingredients, and let it sit for a few minutes before proceeding with the recipe.

Fruit Spreads, Jams, and Preserves. Available in a variety of flavors, these products make delicious sweeteners. For best flavor and nutrition, choose a brand made from fruits and fruit juice concentrate, with little or no added sugar, and select a flavor that is compatible with the baked goods you're making. Use as you would any liquid sweetener.

Honey. Contrary to popular belief, honey is not significantly more nutritious than sugar, but it does add a nice flavor to baked goods. It also adds moistness, reducing the need for fat. The sweetest of the liquid sweeteners, honey is generally 20 to 30 percent sweeter than sugar. Be sure to consider this when making substitutions.

Maple Sugar. Made from dehydrated maple syrup, granulated maple sugar adds a distinct maple flavor to baked goods. Powdered maple sugar is also available, and can be used to replace powdered white sugar in glazes.

Maple Syrup. The boiled-down sap of sugar maple trees, maple syrup adds a delicious flavor to all baked goods, and also provides some potassium and other nutrients. Use it as you would honey or molasses.

Molasses. Light, or Barbados, molasses is pure sugarcane juice boiled down into a thick syrup. Light molasses provides some calcium, potassium, and iron, and is delicious in spice cakes, muffins, breads, and cookies. Blackstrap molasses is a by-product of the sugar-refining process. Very rich in calcium, potassium, and iron, it has a slightly bitter, strong flavor and is half as sweet as refined sugar. Because of its distinctive taste, more than a few tablespoons in a recipe is overwhelming.

Sucanat. Granules of evaporated sugarcane juice, Sucanat tastes similar to brown sugar. This sweetener provides small amounts of potassium, chromium, calcium, iron, and vitamins A and C. Use it as you would any other granulated sugar.

Vinegars

Vinegars play an important role in Italian cuisine by adding a unique dimension to a wide variety of dishes. Besides adding a flavor of their own, vinegars, because of their acidity, reduce the need for salt in many dishes. The following vinegars are used in this book.

Balsamic Vinegar. Made from grapes aged in wooden casks, traditional balsamic vinegar is reddish brown in color and has an intense sweet-and-sour flavor. Just a little of this vinegar goes a long way toward enhancing the taste of meats and poultry, salads, and even fresh fruit. Also available is white balsamic vinegar, which has a lighter flavor that is perfect in light dressings and sauces.

Wine Vinegar. Wine vinegar, as the name implies, is made from wine—either white or red. Both red and white wine vinegars can be used to add zip to salad dressings, marinades, soups, and many other dishes.

Wines

Wines—both white and red—have an important place in the Italian pantry. A splash of red wine added to a sauce or marinade or used to braise meat adds a delightful depth of flavor. White wines are perfect for sautéing vegetables, adding flavor to light sauces, and cooking poultry or fish. If you would rather not cook with alcoholic beverages, try substituting tomato juice or beef broth for red wine, and chicken or vegetable broth for white wine.

Most of the wines called for in this book are dry, rather than sweet. When a recipe calls for a dry red wine, a wide variety of wines will work nicely. Try a Barolo, Bardolino, Chianti, Cabernet Sauvignon, Merlot, or Valpolicella. When you need a dry white wine, try a Chablis, Chardonnay, Pino Grigio, or Soave. Many of these are available in your grocery store, while others can be found in liquor stores, where the merchant will be able to guide you towards other wines that will work well in your recipes. Avoid buying any products that are labelled "cooking wine," as these are typically loaded with salt.

Marsala is also a favorite of Italian cooks. Similar to sherry, this wine adds a slightly sweet and nutty flavor to dishes like Veal Marsala, and is a delicious addition to vegetables, soups, and sauces.

Liqueurs

These sweet alcoholic beverages come in a variety of flavors, and are best known for their use in after-dinner coffee drinks. Liqueurs can also be used to add a special flavor to fruit desserts, mousses, trifles, cheesecakes, fruit salads, and sauces. Italian cuisine often features liqueurs such as amaretto (almond), Frangelico (hazelnut), Grand Marnier (orange), and Chambord (raspberry). If you don't want to use alcoholic beverages in your cooking, simply substitute an appropriate fruit juice for the suggested liqueur.

Herbs, Spices, and Flavorings

Herbs, spices, and condiments play an essential role in low-fat cooking. Proper use of these ingredients adds so much flavor that you will never miss the fat.

If you have never used fresh herbs before, be aware that a little careful handling is needed to keep these valuable ingredients at their best. Rinse the herbs with cool water, shake off the excess moisture, wrap in paper towels, and seal in a plastic bag. The herbs will then keep for seven to ten days. For longer storage, remove the paper towel and place the sealed bag in the freezer. Then simply break off and crumble the desired amount, and add to sauces, soups, and other cooked dishes.

Anchovies. These small fish are usually salted and packed in olive oil. Anchovies are typically mashed or chopped, and then added to sauces and dressings or used as a pizza topping. Since only small amounts of anchovies are needed to enhance the flavors of foods, even oil-packed products may be used in low-fat cooking. Anchovy paste, a convenient mixture of mashed anchovies and olive oil, can be substituted for mashed anchovies in any recipe.

Anise Seeds. These greenish-gray seeds of the anise plant have a licorice-like flavor, and are a popular addition to biscotti—Italian twice-baked cookies. Anise seeds can be found in the spice section of your supermarket.

Basil. A popular Italian herb, basil has a distinctly pungent aroma and flavor that go exceptionally well with tomatoes. Basil is also the classic herb for making pesto sauce. Available both fresh and dried in supermarkets, basil is easily grown at home.

Bay Leaves. These leaves of the bay laurel shrub are available in dried form in the spice section of supermarkets. Sharp and pungent, whole bay leaves are frequently used to add richness to meat and poultry dishes; stocks, soups, and stews; and tomato sauces. Be sure to remove bay leaves from the dish before serving.

Capers. These small round green buds are picked from a Mediterranean bush and then packed in brine, where they develop their characteristic piquant flavor. Sold in jars, capers vary in size, depending on the variety. Large capers may be coarsely chopped before being added to recipes. Just a few capers are all that is needed to add a characteristic flavor to Puttanesca Sauce and many other Italian dishes.

Crushed Red Pepper. Sold as dried flakes, crushed red pepper is made from the seeds and membranes of the red chili pepper. Just a little of this seasoning enhances the flavor of sauces and reduces the need for salt. Heat releases the power of red pepper, so use it with discretion in cooked dishes.

Fennel. Fennel seeds, available in the spice section of your supermarket, add a distinctive licorice-like flavor to Italian sausage, and are also used to season stuffings and meat dishes.

Garlic. This pungent herb is an essential ingredient in many Italian recipes. Garlic is generally peeled and then crushed or minced to release its flavors. The flavor of fresh garlic is so superior to that of jarred minced garlic and garlic powder, that it should be the only garlic of choice for your low-fat recipes. For convenience, you can peel the cloves from several heads of garlic and freeze them in plastic bags. When ready to use, simply remove the desired number of garlic cloves from the freezer and let them sit for a few minutes at room temperature before using.

When browning garlic, be very careful not to burn it, as this will give your dish a bitter, acrid taste. Brown the garlic only until it begins to turn a light golden color and smells fragrant.

Raw garlic has a very strong flavor that becomes sweeter and milder the longer it cooks. For this reason, roasted garlic is often used to add delicious flavor to soups, dressings, sauces, and many other dishes. (Read more about roasting garlic on page 62.)

Italian Parsley. A flat-leaf parsley that is available fresh in many grocery stores, Italian parsley has a more pronounced flavor than the curly variety of the herb. Like curly parsley, though, Italian parsley is easy to grow both indoors and outdoors.

Italian Seasoning. A dried blend of several Italian herbs—including basil, oregano, thyme, and rosemary—this seasoning is a convenient means of adding Italian flavor to a wide variety of dishes.

Olives. Ripe black olives are frequently used to add flavor and texture to Italian sauces, salads, and many other dishes. Should the fat-conscious cook avoid olives? Not necessarily. One large olive has only 5 calories and a half-gram of fat. And since the fat in olives is olive oil—a monoun-saturated fat—a few sliced or chopped olives added to a recipe will not blow your fat budget or raise your cholesterol.

Oregano. This powerful herb is frequently used to season tomato sauces, pizzas, bean soups, and stews. Oregano is available both fresh and dried in supermarkets, and is easily grown at home.

Rosemary. This herb resembles short, thick pine needles, and has a characteristic flavor that goes well with most meats, potatoes, and bean soups. Rosemary is available both fresh and dried in supermarkets, and is easily grown at home.

Sage. This herb has a pale green fuzzy leaf and a strong distinctive flavor that complements stuffings, bean soups, and pork dishes. Rubbed (crumbled) dried sage is commonly available in supermarkets.

Shallots. A member of the onion family, shallots resemble garlic, with clustered bulbs wrapped in a papery bronze skin. Shallots have a mild onion flavor with a hint of garlic. They are a delicious addition to sauces, dressings, salads, and many other dishes.

Thyme. This warm, pungent herb enhances the flavors of many foods, including dried beans, stuffings, most meats, tomato dishes, eggplant, onions, and green beans. Thyme is available both fresh and dried in supermarkets, and is easily grown at home.

Vegetables

Italian cuisine features plenty of fresh vegetables in salads, side dishes, and pasta dishes, and also makes good use of some canned produce. The following vegetables, which have a prominent place in Italian cooking, may already have a place in your menu planning, or may be new to you.

Artichokes. These green globes have fleshy leaves that emerge from the base in a layered fashion, enclosing the artichoke heart. The leaves, heart, and bottom of the artichoke are all edible. Whole artichokes can be steamed and served with a dip as an appetizer. To eat the leaves, pull them off with your fingers, dip the wide base of the leaf into the sauce, and use your teeth to scrape the meat off each leaf. Once the leaves have been eaten, the heart and bottom can be exposed and eaten as well.

Artichoke hearts are used in a variety of dishes, from salads to pizzas and entrées. To save time, you can purchase the hearts frozen or in cans. A 10-ounce package of frozen artichoke hearts will contain the same amount as a 14-ounce can after draining. To limit your sodium intake, consider using the frozen hearts.

Artichoke bottoms can be stuffed, baked, and served as an appetizer. Like the hearts, the bottoms can also be sliced or diced and used in a range of recipes. Ready-to-use artichoke bottoms are available in cans.

Arugula. Also known as rocket and Italian cress, arugula is a popular Mediterranean salad green. When young, arugula's tender, narrow green leaves have a nutty, subtle peppery flavor. Mature arugula has a hot mustard-like flavor. Arugula is most often used in salads, but can also be added at the last minute to soups and pasta dishes.

Eggplant. Typically oblong with shiny purple skins and greenish-white flesh, two main varieties of eggplant are commonly available. The larger of the two, the Western eggplant, has more moisture and is more bitter than the smaller Asian eggplant. Some recipes require that Western eggplants be sliced, sprinkled with salt, and left to stand for at least thirty minutes. The vegetables are then rinsed and patted dry before being cooked. This procedure extracts some of the bitter juices.

Escarole. With its ragged, broad leaves, this salad green has a firm, crisp texture and a slightly bitter flavor. Escarole is delicious mixed with other greens in both crisp chilled salads and wilted salads. It also makes a flavorful addition to soups.

Fennel. This bulb-shaped vegetable with celery-like stems and feathery leaves has a licorice-like flavor. Raw fennel adds crunch and flavor to salads. Cooked fennel may be served as a side dish or used in soups and stews.

Leeks. Resembling large scallions, leeks have a sweet, mild onion flavor. Serve leeks raw in salads or cooked in sauces, soups, side dishes, frittatas, and other dishes. A thorough cleaning of leeks is essential to remove all of the soil that gets lodged between the shoots as the plant is cultivated.

Mushrooms. Italian cuisine uses several different species of mushrooms to add a meaty flavor and texture to foods.

Button mushrooms are the type most commonly found in supermarkets. Use small button mushrooms in salads, soups, and sauces, and larger ones for stuffing.

Often marketed as Italian brown mushrooms, **Crimini mushrooms** are similar to button mushrooms, but are slightly larger with a light brown cap.

Usually packaged in dried form, **porcini mushrooms** have a nutty, woodsy flavor and a meaty texture. Before using the dried porcini in your recipes, rehydrate them by soaking them in warm water or broth for twenty to thirty minutes. The soaking liquid, which picks up the flavor of the mushrooms, is generally strained and added to the recipe, as well.

Sometimes referred to as a "grown-up" version of the Crimini mushroom, the **Portabella mushroom** is very large-capped, with a meaty texture and flavor.

Tomatoes. Tomatoes are central to Italian cuisine, where they are used in a wide range of dishes.

Canned whole or diced tomatoes make a convenient base for soups, sauces, and other dishes. Look for brands like Hunt's No Salt Added tomatoes, Eden No Salt Added tomatoes, and Muir Glen No Salt Added Organic tomatoes. When canned whole tomatoes must be crushed for use in a recipe, simply transfer the tomatoes to a bowl and crush them with a wooden spoon or potato masher.

Canned tomato purée also makes a convenient base for pizza sauces, pasta sauces, and other dishes. Look for brands like Progresso tomato purée, which contains no added salt.

With just a little added seasoning and minimal cooking time, **canned crushed tomatoes** can be transformed into a flavorful sauce. Look for a brand like Cento crushed tomatoes, which is unsalted. Progresso Recipe Ready Crushed Tomatoes With Added Purée and Muir Glen Organic Ground Peeled Tomatoes are other good brands that have less than half the salt of most canned tomatoes.

As for fresh tomatoes, two kinds are commonly available in supermarkets. Medium to large round tomatoes, known as **slicing tomatoes**, are best suited to eating raw. Slicing tomatoes are also popular ingredients in salads and sandwiches. **Plum tomatoes**, also known as Roma, Italian, sauce, and paste tomatoes, are egg-shaped with a meaty texture and few seeds. Be sure to use only the very best vine-ripened plum tomatoes when making fresh tomato sauces.

Plum tomatoes that have been dried to remove most of the moisture, **sun-dried tomatoes** have a very intense tomato flavor and a chewy texture. Dried tomatoes must be plumped in water before being added to recipes. Simply place the tomatoes in an equal amount of boiling water, reduce the heat to low, cover, and simmer for 2 minutes; then drain. Or pour some boiling water over the tomatoes and let them sit for about 10 minutes before draining. Sun-dried tomatoes make a delicious addition to salads, sauces, entrées, and side dishes. The recipes in this book call for plain sun-dried tomatoes, not the kind that's packed in oil.

Radicchio. This salad ingredient somewhat resembles a small head of purple cabbage. When chopped and added to salad greens, radicchio adds a beautiful contrasting color and a slightly bitter but pleasant flavor.

Other Ingredients

Aside from the ingredients already discussed, a few more items may prove useful as you venture into fat-free cooking.

Barley Nugget Cereal. Crunchy, nutty cereals like Grape-Nuts make a nice addition to crumb toppings, cookies, muffins, and other baked goods when you want to reduce or eliminate high-fat nuts.

Bread Crumbs. Bread crumbs are essential ingredients for stuffings, coatings, and many other uses. The recipes in this book call for both soft and dried bread crumbs. Soft bread crumbs are easily made by tearing slices of stale bread and processing them into crumbs in a blender or food processor. One slice of bread makes about $\frac{1}{2}$ cup of soft crumbs. Dried bread crumbs are available in your grocery store in both plain and seasoned varieties.

Canned Stocks. Like dry bouillons, ready-to-use canned stocks are convenient substitutes for homemade stocks. And these days, chicken, beef, and vegetable flavors are available in many low-fat and fat-free brands. Look for Campbell's Healthy Request, Swanson Natural Goodness, Health Valley No Salt Added, and Pritikin.

Dry Bouillons. Dry bouillons are great to have on hand for those days when there's no time to make soup stock from scratch. Available in beef, ham, chicken, vegetable, and onion flavors, bouillons can also add flavor to vegetable side dishes, casseroles, and many other culinary creations.

While bouillons are fat-free, sodium can be a real problem, with most brands containing close to 1,000 milligrams per teaspoon. To keep so-dium under control, look for a brand like Maggi instant bouillon granules, which contains about 30 percent less sodium than the average brand. Brands of low-sodium bouillons, such as Feath-erweight and Lite Line Low-Sodium, are also available. These products are made with potas-sium chloride instead of sodium chloride (salt), and so should be avoided by people on potas-sium-restricted diets.

Other products that can help you reduce your salt intake are Vogue soup bases. Made mostly of powdered vegetables, Vogue chicken, beef, vege-table, and onion bases contain about 60 percent less sodium than most dry bouillons. Simply add to water for a great reduced-sodium stock.

When shopping for bouillons, keep in mind that most products do contain monosodium glu-tamate or the related substances, hydrolyzed vegetable protein and autolyzed yeast extract. If these are ingredients you are trying to avoid, read the label carefully before tossing the product into your shopping cart.

Low-fat Graham Crackers. Graham crackers have always been fairly low in fat, usually with less than 3 grams of fat per cracker. Now some brands of both traditional and chocolate gra-hams have less than half the fat of regular gra-ham crackers, giving you an even better option. This ingredient is especially useful for making low-fat graham cracker pie crusts.

Nuts. It may surprise you to learn that the recipes in this book sometimes include nuts as an ingredient, or suggest them as an optional addition. Although nuts are high in fat, used in the small amounts called for in this book, nuts will not blow your fat budget, and will provide some of the essential fats necessary for good health.

Oat Flake-and-Almond Cereal. Ready-to-eat cereals like General Mills Oatmeal Crisp with Almonds and Quaker Honey Nut Toasted Oat-

meal can be ground into crumbs just like graham crackers, and used to make crisp almond-fla-vored crusts for cheesecakes and tarts, to add texture to cookies, or as a sweet and crunchy crumb topping.

A Word About Salt

Salt, a combination of sodium and chloride, en-hances the flavors of many foods. However, most health experts recommend a maximum of 2,400 milligrams of sodium per day, the equivalent of about one teaspoon of salt. For this reason, very little salt is added to the recipes in this book. A minimal use of salt-laden processed ingredients, as well as the wise use of herbs and spices, keeps the salt content under control without compro-mising taste.

ABOUT THE NUTRITIONAL ANALYSIS

The Food Processor II (ESHA Research) com-puter nutrition analysis system, along with prod-uct information from manufacturers, was used to calculate the nutritional information for the reci-pes in this book. Nutrients are always listed per one piece, one slice of pizza, one cookie, one serving, etc.

Sometimes recipes give you options regard-ing ingredients. For instance, you might be able to choose between nonfat mozzarella and re-duced-fat mozzarella, nonfat mayonnaise and reduced-fat mayonnaise, 95-percent lean ground beef or ground turkey, or raisins and nuts. This will help you create dishes that suit your tastes. Just keep in mind that the nutritional analysis is based on the first ingredient listed.

In your quest for fat-free eating, you might be inclined to choose fat-free cheese over reduced-fat cheese, and to omit any optional nuts. Be aware, though, that if you are not used to nonfat cheeses, it might be wise to start by using re-duced-fat products. Similarly, if you like nuts, you should feel free to use them in baked goods and other foods. In very low-fat recipes like the ones in this book, you can afford to add a few nuts or to sometimes choose the higher-fat ingredient.

The nutritional analysis for each recipe also provides an estimate of the calories and fat grams you save by using low- and no-fat products. This analysis is based on a comparison of the low-fat recipe with a standard recipe that uses full-fat ingredients. The comparison becomes even more meaningful when you consider that for every 100 calories you trim from your diet on a daily basis, you can lose ten pounds in a year!

WHERE DOES THE FAT COME FROM IN FAT-FREE RECIPES?

You may notice that even though a recipe may contain no oil, butter, margarine, nuts, or other fatty ingredients, it still may contain a small amount of fat (less than one gram). This is because many natural ingredients contain some fat. Whole grains, for example, store a small amount of oil in their germ, the center portion of the grain. This oil is very beneficial because it is loaded with vitamin E, an antioxidant. Products made from refined grains and refined flours—ingredients that have been stripped of the germ—do have slightly less fat than whole grain versions, but also have far less nutrients.

Other ingredients, too, naturally contain some fat. For instance, even fruits and vegetables, like grains, contain small amounts of oil. Ingredients like olives, nuts, and lean meats also contribute fat to some recipes. However, when these ingredients are used in moderation, the amount of fat in the total recipe is still well within the bounds of a healthful low-fat diet. In fact, the majority of recipes in this book contain less than 2 grams of fat per serving.

This book is filled with creative Italian dishes that can make any meal of the day special. The recipes not only are simple, satisfying, and delicious, but also are foods that you can feel good about serving to your family and friends. So get ready to create some new family favorites and to experience the pleasures and rewards of fat-free Italian cooking.

Having It Your Way at Italian Restaurants

As the recipes in this book show, just about any Italian dish can be made at home with little or no fat. Unfortunately, when you eat in a restaurant, it's a different story. Greasy sausages, gobs of cheese, and pools of olive oil and cream are a standard part of Italian restaurant fare. The good news is that there is plenty you can to do avoid a fat overload when dining out. Some Italian restaurants now include special low-fat selections for health-conscious diners. These are great, as they take the guesswork out of ordering. But even when such selections aren't offered, there are many strategies you can use to make sure you get what you want. Below you will find some general guidelines, followed by a list of dishes that will help you stay within your fat budget, and a list of dishes that should be avoided at all costs.

GENERAL DINING GUIDELINES

❑ Call ahead to ask about the menu, or review the menu posted on the outside window before going inside. Find out if special requests—such as broiling without butter—are honored.

❑ Look for menu items that are broiled, grilled, roasted, stewed, braised, or cooked in their own juices. Then, when placing your order, ask questions about the amount of fat used in cooking. (Broiled foods have been known to come drenched in butter or olive oil.)

❑ Avoid items that are served in butter sauce, marinated in oil, fried, or served in a cream or cheese sauce. Also beware of items described as "flaky," "crispy," "creamy," "battered," or "breaded." These terms often indicate the use of a high-fat ingredient.

❑ Request that dressings, sauces, and margarine or butter be served on the side so that you can control the amount used.

❑ If portions are large—as they tend to be in Italian restaurants—split an entrée with a friend, or take half of the order home. If the restaurant offers pasta dishes in half-portions, try combining a half-portion of pasta with soup or salad for a satisfying meal.

❑ Budget ahead for restaurant splurges. Then spend the calories on foods you really want.

❑ If you can't resist the tiramisu or cheesecake, share it with a friend.

FOODS TO CHOOSE

❑ Vegetable- or bean-based soups, like minestrone and pasta e fagioli.

❑ Steamed clams or mussels.

❑ Pasta with tomato-based sauces (marinara, puttanesca, and arrabbiata), or with tomato-seafood sauces.

❑ Broiled or grilled chicken and fish dishes. (Request that very little fat be used to prepare the dish.)

❑ Chicken cacciatore, chicken or veal piccata, or chicken or veal Marsala. (Request that very little fat be used to prepare the dish.)

❑ Seafood stews like cioppino.

❑ Thin-crust pizza with vegetable toppings. (Ask for less cheese and no olive oil splash.)

❑ Baked or broiled polenta with tomato sauce, or gnocchi with tomato sauce.

❑ Granita, poached fruits, biscotti, and cappuccino made with low-fat milk.

FOODS TO AVOID

❑ Meat and cheese antipasto platters, fried calamari, and fried mozzarella.

❑ Vegetables marinated in large amounts of olive oil.

❑ Pasta with creamy sauces, like Alfredo and carbonara.

❑ Cheese-laden dishes, like lasagna, manicotti, and cannelloni.

❑ Dishes like eggplant Parmesan and veal Parmesan, which are battered, fried, and blanketed with cheese.

❑ Dishes containing Italian sausage.

❑ Pasta tossed with oily pesto sauces.

❑ Pizza with extra cheese, olive oil, or meat toppings.

❑ Garlic bread.

❑ Cheesecake, tiramisu, Italian pastries, spumoni, and mousses.

2

Antipasti and Appetizers With Appeal

The first course in a traditional Italian dinner is known as antipasto, or "before the pasta." Antipasti—the plural of antipasto—include a wide range of food choices, some simple, and some elaborate. For instance, the first course might consist of some savory stuffed mushrooms, of crusty bruschetta topped with a tempting spread, or of an elaborate platter of cured meats, cheeses, seafood, marinated vegetables, and roasted peppers.

While many antipasto selections, such as roasted peppers, can be very low in fat, other choices, such as fatty cured meats and cheeses, can use up your entire fat budget for the meal! And traditional antipasti such as stuffed mushrooms, marinated vegetables, and fried zucchini are usually prepared with generous amounts of butter and oil. But as the recipes in this chapter will prove, all that fat is not essential for great taste. These dishes start out with ultra-lean meats, nonfat and reduced-fat cheeses, plenty of

fresh vegetables, flavorful herbs, wines, and fat-free broths. Then simple and innovative cooking techniques keep fat to a minimum. The result? Traditional Italian antipasti without the traditional fat.

While many antipasti are versatile and make delicious party fare, sometimes an occasion may call for dips and other pick-up foods rather than an antipasto. Fortunately, these foods, too, can be made with Italian flair, and with very little fat. In this chapter, you'll be delighted by appetizers like Gorgonzola Party Pizzas, Baked Spinach and Artichoke Spread, and Great Garbanzo Dip—palate-pleasing fare that is perfect for get-togethers.

So the next time you want a savory dish to whet the appetite or an appealing pick-up treat to keep hunger at bay, you need look no further. You'll find that even crispy zucchini sticks and cheese-topped mini-pizzas can be made low in fat and high in flavor—once you know the secrets of fat-free Italian cooking.

Clam-Stuffed Mushrooms

Yield: 24 appetizers

24 medium-large fresh mushroom caps

2 cans (6½ ounces each) chopped clams, undrained

½ cup finely chopped onion

½ cup finely chopped celery (include the leaves)

1 teaspoon crushed fresh garlic

¾ teaspoon dried oregano

⅛ teaspoon ground black pepper

1 cup soft whole wheat bread crumbs

¼ cup grated nonfat or reduced-fat Parmesan cheese

1 egg white, beaten

6–8 lemon wedges (garnish)

1. Wash the mushroom caps, pat dry, and set aside. Drain the clams, reserving the juice, and set aside.

2. Coat a large nonstick skillet with olive oil cooking spray, and preheat over medium-high heat. Add the onion, celery, garlic, oregano, and pepper, and stir-fry for about 3 minutes, or until the onion and celery begin to soften. Add a little of the reserved clam juice to the skillet if it becomes too dry. Remove the skillet from the heat, and set aside for a few minutes to cool slightly.

3. Add the bread crumbs and Parmesan to the skillet mixture, and toss to mix well. Gently toss in first the clams, and then the egg white. The mixture should be moist but not wet, and should hold together nicely. Add a little of the reserved clam juice if the mixture seems too dry.

4. Coat a 9-x-13-inch pan with nonstick cooking spray. Place a heaping teaspoonful of the stuffing in each mushroom cap, and arrange the mushrooms in the pan.

5. Cover the pan with aluminum foil, and bake at 400°F for 15 minutes. Remove the foil, and bake for 5 additional minutes, or until the mushrooms are tender and the stuffing is lightly browned. Serve hot accompanied by the lemon wedges.

NUTRITIONAL FACTS (PER APPETIZER)

Calories: 26   Carbohydrates: 3.1 g   Cholesterol: 5 mg
Fat: 0.3 g   Fiber: 0.6 g   Protein: 3.2 g   Sodium: 40 mg

You Save: Calories: 15   Fat: 2 g

Peppery Portabella Mushrooms

1. Arrange the arugula or spinach over the bottom of a medium-sized serving plate. Set aside.

2. Place the broth and cornstarch in a small dish. Stir to dissolve, and set aside.

3. Coat a large nonstick skillet with olive oil cooking spray, and preheat over medium-high heat. Add the mushrooms, and sprinkle with half of the salt and pepper. Sauté for $1\frac{1}{2}$ to 2 minutes, or until nicely browned.

4. Spray the tops of the mushrooms lightly with the cooking spray, and turn them over. Sprinkle with the remaining salt and pepper, and sauté for another minute or 2, or until nicely browned on the second side.

5. Arrange the mushrooms over the arugula or spinach on the serving plate, and cover to keep warm.

6. Reduce the heat under the skillet to medium, and add the garlic and wine. Cook, stirring frequently, for about 2 minutes, or until most of the wine has evaporated. Add the cornstarch mixture, and cook, stirring frequently, for a minute or 2, or until the mixture comes to a boil and thickens slightly.

7. Drizzle the sauce over the mushrooms and serve hot, accompanied by the bread.

Yield: 4 servings

$1\frac{1}{2}$ cups fresh tender arugula or spinach leaves

$\frac{1}{4}$ cup plus 1 tablespoon beef, chicken, or vegetable broth

$\frac{1}{4}$ teaspoon cornstarch

$\frac{1}{2}$ pound Portabella mushrooms, stems removed, and sliced $\frac{1}{2}$-inch thick

$\frac{1}{4}$ teaspoon salt

$\frac{1}{4}$ teaspoon coarsely ground black pepper

Olive oil cooking spray

1 teaspoon crushed fresh garlic

$\frac{1}{4}$ cup dry red or white wine

8 slices French or Italian bread, each $\frac{1}{2}$-inch thick

---

NUTRITIONAL FACTS (PER SERVING)

Calories: 89 Carbohydrates: 17 g Cholesterol: 0 mg
Fat: 1 g Fiber: 1.4 g Protein: 3.4 g Sodium: 283 mg

You Save: Calories: 119 Fat: 13.5 g

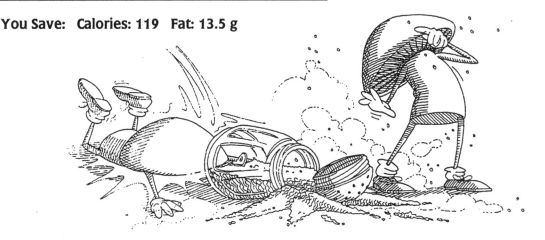

Shrimp-Stuffed Artichokes

Yield: *12 appetizers*

½ cup finely chopped onion

⅓ cup finely chopped green bell
pepper

⅓ cup finely chopped red bell
pepper

1 teaspoon crushed fresh garlic

½ teaspoon dried Italian
seasoning

¼ teaspoon ground black pepper

¾ cup cooked diced shrimp or
crab meat (about 4 ounces)

1 cup soft whole wheat or Italian
bread crumbs

3 tablespoons grated nonfat or
reduced-fat Parmesan cheese

2 tablespoons nonfat or
reduced-fat mayonnaise

12 canned artichoke bottoms
(about two 14-ounce cans,
drained)

Olive oil cooking spray

6 lemon wedges (garnish)

1. Coat a large nonstick skillet with olive oil cooking spray, and preheat over medium heat. Add the onion, green and red peppers, garlic, Italian seasoning, and pepper, and stir to mix well. Cook and stir over medium heat for about 4 minutes, or until the vegetables are soft. Remove the skillet from the heat, and allow to cool for several minutes.

2. Add first the shrimp or crab meat and then the bread crumbs and Parmesan to the skillet mixture, and toss to mix well. Add the mayonnaise, and toss gently to mix. The mixture should be moist, but not wet, and should hold together nicely. Add a little more mayonnaise if the mixture seems too dry.

3. Place a heaping tablespoonful of stuffing in the hollow of each artichoke bottom. Coat a 9-x-9-inch pan with nonstick cooking spray, and arrange the artichokes in the pan. Spray the tops of the stuffing lightly with the cooking spray.

4. Cover the pan with aluminum foil, and bake at 400°F for 15 minutes. Remove the foil, and bake for 5 additional minutes, or until the stuffing is lightly browned. Serve hot, accompanied by the lemon wedges.

NUTRITIONAL FACTS (PER APPETIZER)

Calories: 52   Carbohydrates: 8.1 g   Cholesterol: 19 mg
Fat: 0.6 g   Fiber: 2.9 g   Protein: 4.8 g   Sodium: 157 mg

You Save: Calories: 35   Fat: 4.5 g

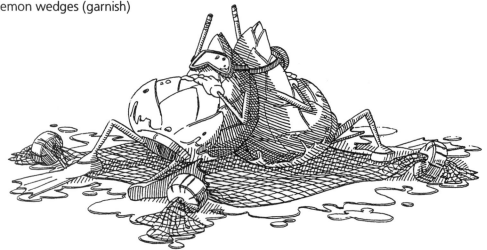

Bruschetta Pomodoro

1. To make the topping, place all of the topping ingredients in a medium-sized bowl, and toss to mix well. Let sit at room temperature for 10 minutes.

2. Arrange the bruschetta slices in a single layer on a serving platter. Top each slice with 2 tablespoons of the tomato mixture, and serve immediately.

Yield: 12 pieces

1 recipe Bruschetta (below)

TOPPING

1½ cups finely chopped seeded plum tomatoes (about 5 medium)

2 tablespoons bottled fat-free or reduced-fat Italian salad dressing

3 tablespoons chopped fresh basil

1 teaspoon crushed fresh garlic

¼ teaspoon coarsely ground black pepper

NUTRITIONAL FACTS (PER APPETIZER)

Calories: 58 Carbohydrates: 11 g Cholesterol: 0 mg
Fat: 0.7 g Fiber: 0.9 g Protein: 1.9 g Sodium: 132 mg

You Save: Calories: 49 Fat: 5.8 g

Bruschetta

This Italian garlic toast makes a delicious appetizer when topped with a chunky tomato sauce such as Roasted Tomato Sauce (page 169), Broiled Tomato-Basil Sauce (page 169), or Broiled Portabella and Plum Tomato Sauce (page 170). Bruschetta may also be served as an accompaniment to a dip, spread, soup, or salad.

Yield: 12 pieces

2 teaspoons crushed fresh garlic

12 slices Italian bread, each ¾-inch thick (about 8 ounces)

Olive oil cooking spray

1. Coat a large baking sheet with nonstick cooking spray, and spread the garlic evenly over the bottom of the pan. Arrange the bread slices in a single layer on the pan, and rub the slices over the bottom of the pan so that some of the garlic clings to the slices. Spray the tops of the slices lightly with the cooking spray.

2. Place the pan 6 inches under a preheated broiler, and broil for 30 to 60 seconds, or until lightly browned. Turn the slices, spray lightly with the cooking spray, and broil for 30 to 60 additional seconds to lightly brown the second side.

3. Serve immediately as an accompaniment to a dip, spread, soup, or salad, or use in recipes like Bruschetta Pomodoro (page 31).

NUTRITIONAL FACTS (PER APPETIZER)

Calories: 53   Carbohydrates: 9.4 g   Cholesterol: 0 mg
Fat: 0.7 g   Fiber: 0.6 g   Protein: 1.6 g   Sodium: 109 mg

You Save: Calories: 44 Fat: 5 g

Oven-Fried Zucchini Fingers

Yield: *32 appetizers*

4 medium zucchini (about 1½ pounds)

Olive oil cooking spray

1½ cups Basic Marinara Sauce (page 166) or bottled fat-free marinara sauce

BATTER

¼ cup plus 2 tablespoons unbleached flour

¼ cup plus 2 tablespoons fat-free egg substitute

¼ cup skim milk

CRUMB COATING

3¼ cups corn flakes

¼ cup plus 1 tablespoon grated nonfat or reduced-fat Parmesan cheese

1¼ teaspoons dried Italian seasoning

¼ teaspoon ground black pepper

1. Rinse the zucchini, pat dry, and trim and discard the ends. Quarter each zucchini lengthwise; then cut each piece in half crosswise. You should now have 32 zucchini fingers, each about 3½ inches long.

2. To make the batter, place all of the batter ingredients in a shallow dish, and stir to mix well. Set aside.

3. To make the coating, place the corn flakes in a food processor or blender, and process into crumbs. Measure the crumbs. There should be about ¾ cup plus 2 tablespoons. (Adjust the amount if necessary.)

4. Place the corn flake crumbs, Parmesan, Italian seasoning, and pepper in a shallow dish, and stir to mix well. Set aside.

5. Coat a large baking sheet with olive oil cooking spray. Dip the zucchini fingers, 1 at a time, first in the batter and then in the crumb coating mixture, turning to coat all sides. Arrange the zucchini fingers in a single layer on the sheet, and spray the tops lightly with the cooking spray.

6. Bake at 400°F for about 15 minutes, or until the zucchini is golden brown and crisp. While the zucchini is baking, place the sauce in a small pot and cook over medium heat until heated through. Transfer the zucchini to a serving plate, and serve with a bowl of the hot dipping sauce.

NUTRITIONAL FACTS (PER APPETIZER WITH SAUCE)

Calories: 28   Carbohydrates: 5 g   Cholesterol: 0 mg
Fat: 0.2 g   Fiber: 0.6 g   Protein: 1.4 g   Sodium: 74 mg

You Save: Calories: 37 Fat: 4.3 g

Sun-Dried Tomato and Scallion Spread

1. Place sun-dried tomatoes and water in small pot, and bring to boil over high heat. Reduce heat to low, cover, and simmer for 2 minutes, or until tomatoes have plumped. Remove pot from heat, and set aside.

2. Place the cream cheese in a small bowl, and beat with an electric mixer until smooth. Add the undrained tomatoes and scallions, and beat just until well mixed. Transfer the spread to a serving dish, cover, and chill for several hours.

3. Serve with sliced bagels, wedges of pita bread, whole grain crackers, or celery sticks, or use as a filling for hollowed-out cherry tomatoes or finger sandwiches.

Yield: 1 1/8 cups

3 tablespoons finely chopped sun-dried tomatoes (not packed in oil)

3 tablespoons water

1 block (8 ounces) nonfat or reduced-fat cream cheese, softened to room temperature

1/4 cup finely chopped scallions

NUTRITIONAL FACTS (PER TABLESPOON)
Calories: 13 Carbohydrates: 1.3 g Cholesterol: 1 mg
Fat: 0 g Fiber: 0.1 g Protein: 1.9 g Sodium: 72 mg

You Save: Calories: 33 Fat: 4.5 g

Roasted Eggplant Spread

1. Place the eggplant, tomatoes, vinegar, olive oil, garlic, oregano, salt, and pepper in a large bowl, and toss to mix well.

2. Coat a large roasting pan with nonstick cooking spray, and spread the eggplant mixture over the bottom of the pan. Bake at 425°F, stirring every 15 minutes, for about 1 hour, or until the eggplant is very soft. Remove the pan from the oven, stir in the broth, and allow the mixture to cool to room temperature.

3. When ready to serve, mound the spread in a serving bowl, and sprinkle with the olives. Serve at room temperature with whole grain crackers, fresh French or Italian bread, Bruschetta (page 31), or Parmesan Pita Crisps (page 36).

Yield: 2 1/2 cups

2 large eggplants (1 lb ea.), peeled and cut into 3/4-inch chunks

4 plum tomatoes, seeded and chopped

1 tablespoon balsamic vinegar

1 tablespoon extra virgin olive oil

6 cloves garlic, peeled and coarsely chopped

1 teaspoon dried oregano

1/2 teaspoon salt

1/4 teaspoon coarsely ground black pepper

1/4 cup vegetable or chicken broth

1/4 cup sliced black olives

NUTRITIONAL FACTS (PER TABLESPOON)
Calories: 11 Carbohydrates: 1.8 g Cholesterol: 0 mg
Fat: 0.5 g Fiber: 0.7 g Protein: 0.3 g Sodium: 45 mg

You Save: Calories: 18 Fat: 2 g

Baked Spinach and Artichoke Spread

Yield: 2¹/₂ cups

1 package (10 ounces) frozen chopped spinach, thawed and squeezed dry

1 package (9 ounces) frozen artichoke hearts, thawed, drained, and chopped, or 1 can (14 ounces) artichoke hearts, drained and chopped

¹/₂ cup nonfat or reduced-fat mayonnaise

2 tablespoons Dijon mustard

¹/₄ cup plus 3 tablespoons Parmesan cheese, divided

Use regular—not nonfat—Parmesan to make this hearty spread.

1. Place spinach, artichoke hearts, mayonnaise, mustard, and ¹/₄ cup plus 1 tablespoon of Parmesan in medium-sized bowl, and stir to mix well.

2. Coat a 1-quart casserole dish with nonstick cooking spray, and spread the mixture evenly in the dish. Sprinkle the remaining 2 tablespoons of Parmesan over the top.

3. Cover with aluminum foil, and bake at 350°F for 25 minutes, or until mixture is heated through. Remove foil, and bake for 5 additional minutes, or until top is lightly browned. Serve hot, accompanied by a loaf of Italian bread, Bruschetta (page 31), or Parmesan Pita Crisps (page 36).

NUTRITIONAL FACTS (PER TABLESPOON)

Calories: 12 Carbohydrates: 1.3 g Cholesterol: 1 mg
Fat: 0.4 g Fiber: 0.4 g Protein: 0.8 g Sodium: 50 mg

You Save: Calories: 30 Fat: 3.6 g

Great Garbanzo Dip

Yield: 1³/₄ cups

1 tablespoon extra virgin olive oil (optional)

1 tablespoon crushed fresh garlic

¹/₂ cup chopped onion

¹/₃ cup chopped red bell pepper

¹/₃ cup chopped green bell pepper

¹/₂ teaspoon dried oregano

1 can (15 ounces) garbanzo beans, rinsed and drained

1 tablespoon lemon juice

2 tablespoons chicken or vegetable broth

¹/₄ teaspoon ground black pepper

1. Coat a large nonstick skillet with olive oil cooking spray or the tablespoon of olive oil, and preheat over medium-high heat. Add the garlic, onion, red and green peppers, and oregano, and sauté, stirring frequently, for about 5 minutes, or until the vegetables begin to soften. Add a little chicken broth if the skillet becomes too dry.

2. Place the garbanzo beans, lemon juice, broth, and black pepper in the bowl of a food processor. Add the vegetable mixture, and process for about 2 minutes, scraping down the sides occasionally, until the ingredients are well mixed and the dip has reached the desired consistency. Add a little more broth if needed.

3. Serve at room temperature with whole grain crackers, raw vegetables, Parmesan Pita Crisps (page 36), or Bruschetta (page 31).

NUTRITIONAL FACTS (PER TABLESPOON)

Calories: 16 Carbohydrates: 2.7 g Cholesterol: 0 mg
Fat: 0.2 g Fiber: 0.8 g Protein: 0.8 g Sodium: 27 mg

You Save: Calories: 13 Fat: 1.4 g

Italian White Bean Dip

1. Place the sun-dried tomatoes in a bowl, and cover with the boiling water. Set aside for at least 30 minutes, or until the tomatoes have plumped.

2. Place the beans, roasted garlic cloves, Parmesan, lemon juice, rosemary, black pepper, and, if desired, the olive oil in the bowl of a food processor. Process for about 2 minutes, or until the mixture is smooth, scraping down the sides periodically. Drain any excess liquid from the tomatoes, and stir them into the dip.

3. Serve at room temperature with whole grain crackers, fresh-cut vegetables, Parmesan Pita Crisps (page 36), or Bruschetta (page 31).

NUTRITIONAL FACTS (PER TABLESPOON)

Calories: 21 Carbohydrates: 3.9 g Cholesterol: 0 mg
Fat: 0.1 g Fiber: 0.8 g Protein: 1.2 g Sodium: 38 mg

You Save: Calories: 19 Fat: 2.2 g

Yield: *1²/₃ cups*

2 tablespoons finely chopped sun-dried tomatoes (not packed in oil)

2 tablespoons boiling water

2 cups cooked cannellini or white beans, or 1 can (19 ounces) cannellini or white beans, rinsed and drained

2 heads garlic, separated into cloves and roasted (page 62)

2 tablespoons grated nonfat or reduced-fat Parmesan cheese

2 tablespoons lemon juice

1 teaspoon dried rosemary

⅛ teaspoon ground black pepper

2–3 teaspoons extra virgin olive oil (optional)

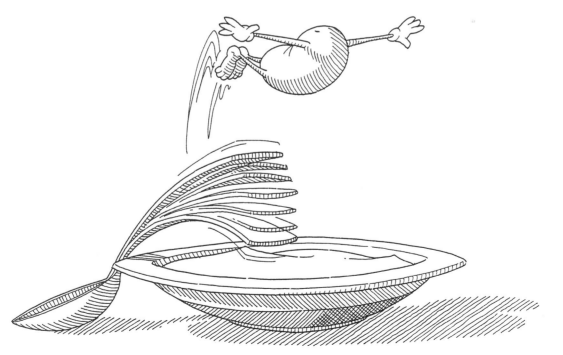

Parmesan Pita Crisps

Yield: *12 servings*

When preparing these savory crisps, use regular Parmesan cheese rather than a fat-free product

6 whole wheat or oat bran pita pockets (2 ounces each)

¼ cup plus 2 tablespoons grated Parmesan cheese

1½ teaspoons dried Italian seasoning

1. Using a sharp knife, cut each piece of pita bread around the entire outer edge to separate the bread into 2 rounds.

2. Arrange the pita rounds on a flat surface with the inside of the bread facing up. Sprinkle each round first with 1½ teaspoons of the Parmesan, and then with ⅛ teaspoon of the Italian seasoning.

3. Cut each round into 6 wedges. Arrange the wedges in a single layer on a large ungreased baking sheet, and bake at 375°F for 4 to 6 minutes, or until lightly browned and crisp. Serve with dips and spreads, or as an accompaniment to soups and salads.

NUTRITIONAL FACTS (PER 6 CHIPS)

Calories: 84   Carbohydrates: 15 g   Cholesterol: 2 mg
Fat: 1.2 g   Fiber: 2 g   Protein: 4.3 g   Sodium: 218 mg

You Save: Calories: 44   Fat: 4.8 g

Italian White Bean Dip

1. Place the sun-dried tomatoes in a bowl, and cover with the boiling water. Set aside for at least 30 minutes, or until the tomatoes have plumped.

2. Place the beans, roasted garlic cloves, Parmesan, lemon juice, rosemary, black pepper, and, if desired, the olive oil in the bowl of a food processor. Process for about 2 minutes, or until the mixture is smooth, scraping down the sides periodically. Drain any excess liquid from the tomatoes, and stir them into the dip.

3. Serve at room temperature with whole grain crackers, fresh-cut vegetables, Parmesan Pita Crisps (page 36), or Bruschetta (page 31).

Yield: 1²/₃ cups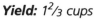

2 tablespoons finely chopped sun-dried tomatoes (not packed in oil)

2 tablespoons boiling water

2 cups cooked cannellini or white beans, or 1 can (19 ounces) cannellini or white beans, rinsed and drained

2 heads garlic, separated into cloves and roasted (page 62)

2 tablespoons grated nonfat or reduced-fat Parmesan cheese

2 tablespoons lemon juice

1 teaspoon dried rosemary

⅛ teaspoon ground black pepper

2–3 teaspoons extra virgin olive oil (optional)

NUTRITIONAL FACTS (PER TABLESPOON)

Calories: 21   Carbohydrates: 3.9 g   Cholesterol: 0 mg
Fat: 0.1 g   Fiber: 0.8 g   Protein: 1.2 g   Sodium: 38 mg

You Save: Calories: 19   Fat: 2.2 g

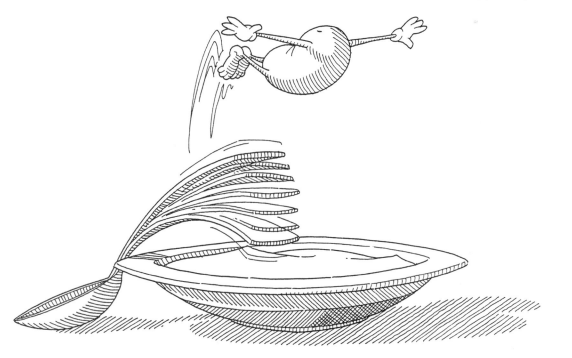

Parmesan Pita Crisps

Yield: *12 servings*

6 whole wheat or oat bran pita pockets (2 ounces each)

¼ cup plus 2 tablespoons grated Parmesan cheese

1½ teaspoons dried Italian seasoning

When preparing these savory crisps, use regular Parmesan cheese rather than a fat-free product

1. Using a sharp knife, cut each piece of pita bread around the entire outer edge to separate the bread into 2 rounds.

2. Arrange the pita rounds on a flat surface with the inside of the bread facing up. Sprinkle each round first with 1½ teaspoons of the Parmesan, and then with ⅛ teaspoon of the Italian seasoning.

3. Cut each round into 6 wedges. Arrange the wedges in a single layer on a large ungreased baking sheet, and bake at 375°F for 4 to 6 minutes, or until lightly browned and crisp. Serve with dips and spreads, or as an accompaniment to soups and salads.

NUTRITIONAL FACTS (PER 6 CHIPS)
Calories: 84   Carbohydrates: 15 g   Cholesterol: 2 mg
Fat: 1.2 g   Fiber: 2 g   Protein: 4.3 g   Sodium: 218 mg

You Save: Calories: 44   Fat: 4.8 g

Italian Roll-Ups

1. Arrange the tortillas on a flat surface, and spread each one with 3 tablespoons of cream cheese, extending the cheese to the outer edges. Lay 2 ounces of sliced turkey or ham over the *bottom half only* of each tortilla, leaving a 1-inch margin on each outer edge. Place one ounce of sliced cheese over the meat, and spread with 1 tablespoon of the dressing. Arrange 6 spinach or arugula leaves over the cheese, and sprinkle with 1 tablespoon of olives. Arrange 4 red pepper strips and a few onion rings over the olive layer. Finally, top with 3 tablespoons of artichoke hearts.

2. Starting at the bottom, roll each tortilla up tightly. Cut a $1\frac{1}{4}$ inch piece off each end and discard. Slice the remaining tortillas into six $1\frac{1}{4}$-inch pieces. Arrange on a platter and serve.

NUTRITIONAL FACTS (PER APPETIZER)

Calories: 61   Carbohydrates: 6.6 g   Cholesterol: 0 mg
Fat: 0.9 g   Fiber: 0.7 g   Protein: 6.2 g   Sodium: 159 mg

You Save: Calories: 41   Fat: 5.4 g

Time-Saving Tip

To avoid a last-minute rush, make Italian Roll-Ups up to 3 hours in advance. Cover the Roll-Ups with plastic wrap, and refrigerate until ready to serve.

Yield: 48 appetizers

8 fat-free flour tortillas (10-inch rounds)

$1\frac{1}{2}$ cups nonfat cream cheese (plain or garlic and herb flavor)

1 pound turkey breast or ham (at least 97% lean), thinly sliced

8 ounces nonfat or reduced-fat mozzarella cheese or reduced-fat provolone cheese, thinly sliced

$\frac{1}{2}$ cup bottled fat-free creamy Italian or roasted garlic salad dressing

48 fresh tender spinach or arugula leaves

$\frac{1}{2}$ cup coarsely chopped black olives

32 $\frac{1}{4}$-inch-thick strips of roasted red bell pepper (about 2 large) (page 57)

4 thin slices red onion, separated into rings

9 ounces frozen (thawed) artichoke hearts, or 1 can (14 ounces) artichoke hearts, drained and chopped

Gorgonzola Party Pizzas

Yield: *24 pieces*

2 medium plum tomatoes, seeded and finely chopped

1 tablespoon grated nonfat or reduced-fat Parmesan cheese

½ teaspoon crushed fresh garlic

1 recipe Parmesan-Polenta Pizza Dough (page 124)

¼ cup finely crumbled Gorgonzola cheese (about 1 ounce)

¾ teaspoon dried oregano or rosemary

1. Place the tomatoes, Parmesan, and garlic in a small bowl, and stir to mix well. Set aside.

2. Divide the dough into 4 equal pieces, and, using a rolling pin, roll each piece into an 8-inch circle to make 4 crusts. Coat a large baking sheet with nonstick cooking spray, and arrange the crusts on the sheet.

3. Spread a fourth of the tomato mixture over each crust, extending the filling to within ½ inch of the edge. Sprinkle first 1 tablespoon of the Gorgonzola and then a pinch of the oregano or rosemary over each pizza.

4. Bake at 450°F for 8 to 10 minutes, or until the cheese is melted and the crust is lightly browned. Cut each pizza into 6 wedges, arrange the wedges on a serving platter, and serve hot.

NUTRITIONAL FACTS (PER APPETIZER)

Calories: 40 Carbohydrates: 8 g Cholesterol: 2 mg
Fat: 0.5 g Fiber: 0.3 g Protein: 1.7 g Sodium: 65 mg

You Save: Calories: 26 Fat: 3 g

Artichoke Party Pizzas

Yield: *24 pieces*

¾ cup finely chopped frozen (thawed) or canned (drained) artichoke hearts

2 tablespoons grated nonfat or reduced-fat Parmesan cheese

2 teaspoons Dijon mustard

1 teaspoon crushed fresh garlic

1 recipe Parmesan-Polenta Pizza Dough (page 124) or Oatmeal Pizza Dough (page 126)

¾ cup shredded nonfat or reduced-fat mozzarella cheese

1. Place the artichoke hearts, Parmesan, mustard, and garlic in a small bowl, and stir to mix well. Set aside.

2. Divide the dough into 4 equal pieces, and, using a rolling pin, roll each piece into an 8-inch circle to make 4 crusts. Coat a large baking sheet with nonstick cooking spray, and arrange the crusts on the sheet.

3. Spread a fourth of the artichoke mixture over each crust, extending the filling to within ½ inch of the edge. Sprinkle 3 tablespoons of the mozzarella over each pizza.

4. Bake at 450°F for 8 to 10 minutes, or until the cheese is melted and the crust is lightly browned. Cut each pizza into 6 wedges, arrange the wedges on a serving platter, and serve hot.

NUTRITIONAL FACTS (PER APPETIZER)

Calories: 44 Carbohydrates: 8 g Cholesterol: 1 mg
Fat: 0.2 g Fiber: 0.6 g Protein: 2.8 g Sodium: 79 mg

You Save: Calories: 19 Fat: 2.4 g

Top: Bruschetta Pomodoro (page 31)

Center Right: Shrimp-Stuffed Artichokes (page 30)

Bottom: Oven-Fried Zucchini Fingers (page 32)

Top: *Sausage, Pepper, and Onion Frittata (page 40)*
Bottom Left: *Zucchini and Tomato Frittata (page 41)*
Bottom Right: *Italian Garden Salad (page 54)*

3

Eggstraordinary Frittatas and Omelettes

Eggs are an important part of Italian cuisine. The most well-known Italian egg dish is the frittata, which is basically an open-faced (unfolded) omelette. This simple and very versatile food is first cooked on top of the stove in a large skillet, and then whisked under the broiler just long enough to set the eggs. Frittatas often include cheeses such as Parmesan, mozzarella, and provolone; meats such as bacon, ham, and sausage; shrimp and other seafood; and a variety of vegetables and seasonings. Traditional folded omelettes, filled with these same flavorful ingredients, offer still another way to prepare eggs with Italian flair. This chapter features a wide range of quick-and-easy, great-tasting egg dishes made both ways.

If just the thought of eggs, meat, and cheese combined in one dish raises your cholesterol level, fear not. While a typical three-egg and cheese omelette can contain over 30 grams of fat and 600 milligrams of cholesterol, these slimmed-down versions provide less than 2 grams of fat and 30 milligrams of cholesterol per serving. How is it possible to so dramatically redúce the fat and cholesterol in an egg-based dish? The recipes start with fat-free, no-cholesterol egg substitutes. These products—which are 99 percent pure egg whites—are a major breakthrough for people who love eggs, but hate fat and cholesterol. Next, low-fat and nonfat Parmesan, mozzarella, and provolone are substituted for their high-fat counterparts. Then ultra-lean hams, bacon, and sausages add their own savor. Finally, the use of nonstick cooking sprays eliminates the need to coat the pan with heavy cooking oils. The result? Tempting guilt-free frittatas and omelettes that are perfect for a special breakfast, a satisfying lunch, or even a light dinner.

So whether you are in the mood for a frittata bursting with spinach and ham, or an omelette redolent with glazed onions, heat up the skillet, and get ready for an eggstraordinary delight. Though low in fat and cholesterol, you'll find these steaming dishes rich in the flavors of Italy.

Sausage, Pepper, and Onion Frittata

Yield: *4 servings*

2 cups fat-free egg substitute

¾ cup shredded nonfat or
   reduced-fat mozzarella cheese

8 ounces Turkey Italian Sausage
   (page 182)

1 small yellow onion, cut into thin
   wedges

½ medium red bell pepper, cut
   into thin strips

½ medium green bell pepper, cut
   into thin strips

1. Place the egg substitute and mozzarella in a medium-sized bowl. Stir to mix well, and set aside.

2. Coat a 10-inch ovenproof skillet with olive oil cooking spray, and preheat over medium heat. Add the sausage and cook, stirring to crumble, until the meat is no longer pink. (If the meat is very lean, there should be no fat to drain off.)

3. Add the onion and peppers to the skillet, and cook for 3 additional minutes, or until the vegetables are crisp-tender. Spread the mixture evenly over the bottom of the skillet.

4. Reduce the heat to low, and pour the egg mixture over the vegetables. Cook without stirring for 10 to 12 minutes, or until the eggs are almost set.

5. Remove the skillet from the heat, and place under a preheated broiler. Broil 6 inches from the heat for about 3 minutes, or until the eggs are set but not dry.

6. Cut the frittata into wedges, and serve immediately.

NUTRITIONAL FACTS (PER SERVING)

Calories: 170 Carbohydrates: 6 g Cholesterol: 37 mg
Fat: 1.6 g Fiber: 0.7 g Protein: 32 g Sodium: 365 mg

You Save: Calories: 271 Fat: 30.7 g

Spinach and Ham Frittata

Yield: 4 servings

2 cups fat-free egg substitute

2 teaspoons Dijon mustard

1 teaspoon crushed fresh garlic

2 cups (packed) chopped fresh
   spinach

4 ounces ham (at least 97% lean)
   or Canadian bacon, diced

1 cup shredded nonfat or
   reduced-fat mozzarella cheese

1. Place the egg substitute in a small bowl. Whisk in the mustard, and set aside.

2. Coat a 10-inch ovenproof skillet with olive oil cooking spray, and preheat over medium heat. Add the garlic, and stir-fry for about 30 seconds, or just until the garlic begins to turn color.

3. Add the spinach and ham to the skillet, and stir-fry for about 1 minute, or until the spinach begins to wilt. Spread the mixture evenly over the bottom of the skillet.

4. Reduce the heat to low, and pour the egg mixture over the spinach mixture. Cook without stirring for 10 to 12 minutes, or until the eggs are almost set.

5. Remove the skillet from the heat, and place under a preheated broiler. Broil 6 inches from the heat for about 3 minutes, or until the eggs are set but not dry.

6. Sprinkle the mozzarella over the frittata, and broil for an additional minute, or until the cheese has melted. Cut the frittata into wedges, and serve immediately.

NUTRITIONAL FACTS (PER SERVING)

Calories: 141 Carbohydrates: 5.5 g Cholesterol: 20 mg
Fat: 0.9 g Fiber: 0.8 g Protein: 26.5 g Sodium: 641 mg

You Save: Calories: 280 Fat: 32.4 g

Zucchini and Tomato Frittata

1. Place the egg substitute and Parmesan in a medium-sized bowl. Stir to mix well, and set aside.

2. Coat a 10-inch ovenproof skillet with nonstick cooking spray, and preheat over medium heat. Add the zucchini, onions, tomatoes, basil, and pepper, and stir-fry for about 4 minutes, or until the zucchini and onions are crisp-tender. Spread the mixture evenly over the bottom of the skillet.

3. Reduce the heat to low, and pour the egg mixture over the vegetables. Cook without stirring for 10 to 12 minutes, or until the eggs are almost set.

4. Remove the skillet from the heat, and place under a preheated broiler. Broil 6 inches from the heat for about 3 minutes, or until the eggs are set but not dry.

5. Sprinkle the mozzarella over the frittata, and broil for an additional minute, or until the cheese has melted. Cut the frittata into wedges, and serve immediately.

Yield: 4 servings

2 cups fat-free egg substitute

¼ cup grated nonfat Parmesan cheese

1 medium zucchini, halved lengthwise and sliced ¼-inch thick

1 medium yellow onion, cut into thin wedges

2 plum tomatoes, seeded and chopped

1 teaspoon dried basil

¼ teaspoon ground black pepper

¾ cup shredded nonfat or reduced-fat mozzarella cheese

NUTRITIONAL FACTS (PER SERVING)

Calories: 131 Carbohydrates: 10 g Cholesterol: 6 mg
Fat: 0.2 g Fiber: 1 g Protein: 22 g Sodium: 443 mg

You Save: Calories: 245 Fat: 28.7 g

Potato and Leek Frittata

Yield: *4 servings*

2 cups fat-free egg substitute

2 tablespoons grated nonfat Parmesan cheese

2 leeks

1 teaspoon crushed fresh garlic

1 teaspoon dried thyme

1/4 teaspoon ground black pepper

2 cups sliced cooked potatoes (about 2 medium)

3/4 cup shredded nonfat or reduced-fat mozzarella cheese

1. Place the egg substitute and Parmesan in a medium-sized bowl. Stir to mix well, and set aside.

2. Cut the leeks in half lengthwise, and rinse well. Thinly slice the white and light green parts, discarding the remainder. Set aside.

3. Coat a 10-inch ovenproof skillet with olive oil cooking spray, and preheat over medium heat. Add the garlic, leeks, thyme, and pepper to the skillet, and stir to mix well. Cover the skillet and cook, stirring occasionally, for about 2 minutes, or until the leeks are crisp-tender. Add a little broth or water if the skillet becomes too dry.

4. Add the potatoes to the skillet, and stir to mix well. Spread the mixture evenly over the bottom of the skillet.

5. Reduce the heat to low, and pour the egg mixture over the potato mixture. Cook without stirring for 10 to 12 minutes, or until the eggs are almost set.

6. Remove the skillet from the heat, and place under a heated broiler. Broil 6 inches from the heat for about 3 minutes, or until the eggs are set, but not dry.

7. Sprinkle the mozzarella over the frittata, and broil for an additional minute, or until the cheese has melted. Cut the frittata into wedges, and serve immediately.

NUTRITIONAL FACTS (PER SERVING)

Calories: 193   Carbohydrates: 26 g   Cholesterol: 5 mg
Fat: 0.2 g   Fiber 2.2 g   Protein: 22 g   Sodium: 399 mg

You Save: Calories: 241   Fat: 27.8 g

Glazed Onion Omelette

1. Coat an 8-inch nonstick skillet with olive oil cooking spray, and preheat over medium heat. Add the onions, thyme, salt, and pepper, and sauté for about 3 minutes, or until the onions are wilted and just starting to brown. (If the skillet becomes too dry, add a few teaspoons of broth as needed.) Transfer the onion mixture to a warm bowl, and cover to keep warm.

2. Coat the 8-inch nonstick skillet with olive oil cooking spray, and preheat over medium-low heat. Add the egg substitute, and cook without stirring for about 2 minutes, or until set around the edges.

3. Use a spatula to lift the edges of the omelette, and allow the uncooked egg to flow beneath the cooked portion. Cook for another minute or 2, or until the eggs are almost set.

4. Sprinkle the Parmesan over the top of the omelette. Then spread the onions over half of the omelette. Cover the onions with first the bacon, if desired, and then the mozzarella. Fold the other half over the filling and cook for another minute or 2, or until the eggs are set and the cheese is melted.

5. Slide the omelette onto a plate, and serve immediately.

Yield: 1 serving

1 small yellow onion, very thinly sliced

⅛ teaspoon dried thyme

Pinch salt

Pinch ground black pepper

¾ cup fat-free egg substitute

1½ teaspoons grated nonfat Parmesan cheese

1 slice turkey bacon, cooked, drained, and crumbled (optional)

2 tablespoons shredded nonfat or reduced-fat mozzarella cheese

---

NUTRITIONAL FACTS (PER SERVING)

Calories: 143   Carbohydrates: 10 g   Cholesterol: 4 mg
Fat: 0.1 g   Fiber: 0.1 g   Protein: 24.4 g   Sodium: 445 mg

You Save: Calories: 310   Fat: 34.1 g

Shrimp and Bacon Frittata

Yield: 4 servings

2 cups fat-free egg substitute

¾ cup grated nonfat or reduced-fat mozzarella cheese

1 medium yellow onion, cut into thin wedges

½ teaspoon dried Italian seasoning

⅛ teaspoon ground black pepper

4 ounces diced cooked shrimp (about 1 cup)

3 strips turkey bacon, cooked, drained, and crumbled

1. Place the egg substitute and mozzarella in a medium-sized bowl. Stir to mix well, and set aside.

2. Coat a 10-inch ovenproof skillet with olive oil cooking spray, and preheat over medium heat. Add the onion, Italian seasoning, and pepper, and stir-fry for about 4 minutes, or until the onion is crisp-tender.

3. Add the shrimp and bacon to the skillet. Stir to mix well, and spread the mixture evenly over the bottom of the skillet.

4. Reduce the heat to low, and pour the egg mixture over the onion mixture. Cook without stirring for 10 to 12 minutes, or until the eggs are almost set.

5. Remove the skillet from the heat, and place under a preheated broiler. Broil 6 inches from the heat for about 3 minutes, or until the eggs are set but not dry and the top is nicely browned.

6. Cut the frittata into wedges, and serve immediately.

NUTRITIONAL FACTS (PER SERVING)
Calories: 150 Carbohydrates: 5 g Cholesterol: 66 mg
Fat: 2.2 g Fiber: 0.3 g Protein: 26 g Sodium: 548 mg

You Save: Calories: 247 Fat: 26.1 g

Mushroom and Mozzarella Frittata

Yield: 4 servings

2 cups fat-free egg substitute

¼ cup grated nonfat Parmesan cheese

3 cups sliced fresh mushrooms

¼ teaspoon dried thyme

¼ teaspoon ground black pepper

¾ cup shredded nonfat or reduced-fat mozzarella cheese

1. Place the egg substitute and Parmesan in a medium-sized bowl. Stir to mix well, and set aside.

2. Coat a 10-inch ovenproof skillet with olive oil cooking spray, and preheat over medium-high heat. Add the mushrooms, thyme, and pepper, and stir-fry for about 4 minutes, or until the mushrooms start to brown and begin to release their juices. Spread the mushrooms evenly over the bottom of the skillet.

3. Reduce the heat to low, and pour the egg mixture over the mushrooms. Cook without stirring for 10 to 12 minutes, or until the eggs are almost set.

4. Remove the skillet from the heat, and place under a preheated broiler. Broil 6 inches from the heat for about 3 minutes, or until the eggs are set but not dry.

5. Sprinkle the mozzarella over the frittata, and broil for an additional minute, or until the cheese has melted. Cut the frittata into wedges, and serve immediately.

NUTRITIONAL FACTS (PER SERVING)

Calories: 128　Carbohydrates: 9 g　Cholesterol: 6 mg
Fat: 0.2 g　Fiber: 0.7 g　Protein: 22 g　Sodium: 441 mg

You Save:　Calories: 252　Fat: 29.4 g

Cottage Frittata

1. Place the egg substitute, cottage cheese, and pepper in a medium-sized bowl. Stir to mix well, and set aside.

2. Coat a 10-inch ovenproof skillet with olive oil cooking spray, and preheat over medium heat. Add the onions, and stir-fry for about 2 minutes, or until the onions are crisp-tender.

3. Add the garlic, spinach, and thyme to the skillet, and stir-fry for about 1 minute, or until the spinach wilts. Add the potatoes, and stir to mix well. Spread the mixture evenly over the bottom of the skillet.

4. Reduce the heat to low, and pour the egg mixture over the potato mixture. Cook without stirring for about 12 minutes, or until the eggs are almost set.

5. Remove the skillet from the heat, and place under a preheated broiler. Broil 6 inches from the heat for about 3 minutes, or until the eggs are set but not dry.

6. Sprinkle the cheese over the frittata, and broil for an additional minute, or until the cheese has melted. Let the frittata sit at room temperature for 5 minutes before cutting into wedges and serving.

Yield: 4 servings

1½ cups fat-free egg substitute

¾ cup nonfat cottage cheese

⅛ teaspoon ground black pepper

1 small yellow onion, cut into thin wedges

1 teaspoon crushed fresh garlic

2 cups (packed) chopped fresh spinach

½ teaspoon dried thyme

1½ cups diced cooked potato (about 1 large)

¾ cup shredded nonfat or reduced-fat mozzarella cheese or reduced-fat provolone cheese

---

NUTRITIONAL FACTS (PER SERVING)

Calories: 173　Carbohydrates: 20 g　Cholesterol: 5 mg
Fat: 0.3 g　Fiber: 2 g　Protein: 22 g　Sodium: 321 mg

You Save:　Calories: 226　Fat: 25.5 g

Bacon and Tomato Omelette

Yield: *1 serving*

¾ cup fat-free egg substitute

Pinch ground black pepper

¼ cup chopped seeded plum tomato (about 1 medium)

1 slice turkey bacon, cooked, drained, and crumbled

2 tablespoons shredded nonfat or reduced-fat mozzarella cheese

1 tablespoon finely chopped fresh Italian parsley (garnish)

1. Coat an 8-inch nonstick skillet with nonstick cooking spray, and preheat over medium-low heat. Add the egg substitute to the skillet, and cook without stirring for about 2 minutes, or until set around the edges. Sprinkle with the pepper.

2. Use a spatula to lift the edges of the omelette, and allow the uncooked egg to flow beneath the cooked portion. Cook for another minute or 2, or until the eggs are almost set.

3. Spread first the tomato and then the bacon and mozzarella over half of the omelette. Fold the other half over the filling and cook for another minute or 2, or until the eggs are set and the cheese is melted.

4. Slide the omelette onto a plate, sprinkle with the parsley, and serve immediately.

NUTRITIONAL FACTS (PER SERVING)
Calories: 160   Carbohydrates: 6 g   Cholesterol: 13 mg
Fat: 2.6 g   Fiber: 0.5 g   Protein: 27 g   Sodium: 637 mg

You Save: Calories: 275   Fat: 29.9 g

Ham and Mushroom Omelette

Yield: *1 serving*

1 ounce ham (at least 97% lean), thinly sliced and cut into thin strips

⅓ cup sliced fresh mushrooms

¾ cup fat-free egg substitute

Pinch ground black pepper

1 tablespoon finely chopped fresh Italian parsley (garnish)

1. Coat an 8-inch nonstick skillet with olive oil cooking spray, and preheat over medium-high heat. Add the ham and mushrooms, and stir-fry for about 3 minutes, or until nicely browned. Transfer the ingredients to a warm bowl, and cover to keep warm.

2. Coat the 8-inch nonstick skillet with olive oil cooking spray. Add the egg substitute, and cook without stirring for about 2 minutes, or until set around the edges. Sprinkle the pepper over the eggs.

3. Use a spatula to lift the edges of the omelette, and allow the uncooked egg to flow beneath the cooked portion. Cook for another minute or 2, or until the eggs are almost set.

4. Spread the ham and mushrooms over half of the omelette. Fold the other half over the filling and cook for another minute or 2, or until the eggs are set but not dry.

5. Slide the omelette onto a plate, sprinkle with the parsley, and serve immediately.

NUTRITIONAL FACTS (PER SERVING)

Calories: 128 Carbohydrates: 5 g Cholesterol: 15 mg
Fat: 0.9 g Fiber: 0.5 g Protein: 24 g Sodium: 498 mg

You Save: Calories: 339 Fat: 35.7 g

Artichoke and Roasted Red Pepper Omelette

1. Coat an 8-inch nonstick skillet with nonstick cooking spray, and preheat over medium-low heat. Add the egg substitute, and cook without stirring for about 2 minutes, or until set around the edges. Sprinkle with the pepper and Italian seasoning.

2. Use a spatula to lift the edges of the omelette, and allow the uncooked egg to flow beneath the cooked portion. Cook for another minute or 2, or until the eggs are almost set.

3. Sprinkle the Parmesan over the top of the omelette. Then spread first the artichokes and then the peppers and provolone over half of the omelette. Fold the other half over the filling and cook for another minute or 2, or until the eggs are set and the cheese is melted.

4. Slide the omelette onto a plate, and serve immediately.

Yield: 1 serving

^{3}/4 cup fat-free egg substitute

Pinch ground black pepper

Pinch dried Italian seasoning

1^1/2 teaspoons grated nonfat Parmesan cheese

^{1}/4 cup chopped frozen (thawed) or canned (drained) artichoke hearts

2 tablespoons chopped roasted red pepper (page 57)

2 tablespoons shredded reduced-fat provolone cheese

NUTRITIONAL FACTS (PER SERVING)

Calories: 154 Carbohydrates: 8 g Cholesterol: 9 mg
Fat: 2.6 g Fiber: 1.7 g Protein: 24.5 g Sodium: 407 mg

You Save: Calories: 254 Fat: 27.1 g

4

Sensational Salads

In Italy, salads are usually served as a separate course, rather than an accompaniment to the main dish. Some salads are so hearty, though, that you may be tempted to serve them as light entrées. And, of course, those of us who don't mind straying a bit from tradition will sometimes want to accompany our pasta with a light green salad. That's the beauty of salads. Depending on their ingredients, they can be light or substantial; sweet or savory; a protein-packed entrée, or a refreshing side dish. And because salads are portable, they are as much at home at picnics and pot-luck suppers as they are at multi-course Italian-style meals.

If you're watching your fat intake, though, beware. Despite the salad's reputation for being diet fare, many have no place on a low-fat menu. Fresh green Italian salads and marinated vegetable salads are typically drenched in olive oil. Other problem ingredients in Italian salads are high-fat cheeses like Gorgonzola and provolone, and fatty meats such as salami and ham. Just a

simple side salad made with these ingredients can exhaust your fat budget for the entire meal!

Made properly, though, Italian-style salads can be both light and delicious. Ingredients like non-fat and reduced-fat cheeses and ultra-lean meats make it possible to create a dazzling array of zesty salads with little or no fat, and with much fewer calories than their traditional counterparts. The recipes in this chapter combine these ingredients with crisp vegetables and salad greens, ripe fruits, satisfying pastas, and hearty beans. Then fat-free Italian-style dressings, ranging from a piquant Gorgonzola Dressing to Lite Balsamic Vinaigrette, add their spark. The result is a variety of garden-fresh dishes that will enhance your diet with nutrient-rich fruits and veggies in the most enjoyable way possible.

So whether you are looking for a classic Caesar Salad or a colorful medley of marinated vegetables, this chapter will delight you with dishes that are refreshingly light and healthful, yet brimming with the distinctive flavors of the Italian kitchen.

Slim Caesar Salad

Yield: *6 servings*

12 cups torn romaine lettuce

¼ cup grated nonfat Parmesan cheese

GARLIC CROUTONS

1 tablespoon plus 1 teaspoon Butter Buds liquid or chicken broth

1 tablespoon grated nonfat or reduced-fat Parmesan cheese

2 teaspoons crushed fresh garlic

¼ teaspoon dried Italian seasoning

2½ cups Italian or French bread cubes

DRESSING

¼ cup plus 2 tablespoons nonfat sour cream

¼ cup fat-free egg substitute

¼ cup grated nonfat Parmesan cheese

2 tablespoons white wine vinegar

2 tablespoons lemon juice

2 teaspoons chopped anchovy fillets

1 teaspoon crushed fresh garlic

1. To make the croutons, combine the Butter Buds liquid or broth, cheese, garlic, and Italian seasoning in a small dish, and stir to mix well. Rub the mixture over the inside of a medium-sized bowl. Place the bread cubes in the bowl, and toss gently to coat the cubes with the garlic mixture.

2. Coat a baking sheet with nonstick cooking spray, and arrange the cubes in a single layer on the sheet. Bake at 350°F for about 14 minutes, or until the croutons are lightly browned and crisp.

3. Turn the oven off, and let the croutons cool in the oven with the door ajar for 30 minutes. Store in an airtight container until ready to use.

4. To make the dressing, place all of the dressing ingredients in a blender, and blend for about 1 minute, or until smooth.

5. Place the lettuce in a large salad bowl. Pour the dressing over the lettuce, and toss to mix well. Add the croutons and Parmesan, and toss to mix well. Serve immediately.

NUTRITIONAL FACTS (PER 2-CUP SERVING)

Calories: 107   Carbohydrates: 16 g   Cholesterol: 5 mg
Fat: 0.7 g   Fiber: 2 g   Protein: 9 g   Sodium: 285 mg

You Save: Calories: 121   Fat: 15.9 g

Time-Saving Tip

To prepare Slim Caesar Salad in no time flat, substitute 2 cups of ready-made fat-free Caesar croutons for the homemade croutons.

Garden Salad With Gorgonzola Dressing

1. Arrange 1½ cups of the lettuce in each of six salad bowls. Using a potato peeler, shred the carrot into thin strips and place a sixth of the carrot on top of each salad. Top each salad with a few onion rings, 2 halves of an artichoke heart, and 2 halves of a cherry tomato.

2. Spoon 2 tablespoons of the dressing over each salad, and serve immediately.

NUTRITIONAL FACTS (PER SERVING)
Calories: 81   Carbohydrates: 15 g   Cholesterol: 5 mg
Fat: 2.2 g   Fiber: 3.8 g   Protein: 6.2 g   Sodium: 221 mg

You Save: Calories: 134   Fat: 16 g

Yield: 6 servings

9 cups torn romaine or buttercrunch lettuce

1 medium-large carrot, peeled

6 thin slices red onion, separated into rings

6 small canned (drained) or frozen (thawed) artichoke hearts, halved

6 cherry tomatoes, halved

¾ cup Gorgonzola dressing (page 53)

White Bean, Basil, and Tomato Salad

1. Place the beans, tomatoes, and basil in a large shallow bowl, and toss to mix well.

2. To make the dressing, place the dressing ingredients in a small bowl, and stir to mix well. Pour the dressing over the bean mixture, and toss to mix well.

3. Cover the salad and chill for 2 to 5 hours, stirring occasionally, before serving.

NUTRITIONAL FACTS (PER ⅔-CUP SERVING)
Calories: 106   Carbohydrates: 20 g   Cholesterol: 0 mg
Fat: 0.5 g   Fiber: 6.1 g   Protein: 6.2 g   sSodium: 117 mg

You Save: Calories: 79   Fat: 9 g

Yield: 8 servings

2 cans (15 ounces each) white beans or navy beans, rinsed and drained

1 pound fresh plum tomatoes, seeded and chopped (6–8 medium)

¼ cup plus 2 tablespoons coarsely chopped fresh basil

DRESSING

3 tablespoons white wine vinegar

1 tablespoon plus 1½ teaspoons Dijon mustard

2 teaspoons sugar

1 teaspoon crushed fresh garlic

⅛ teaspoon ground black pepper

The Well-Dressed Salad

Salads are among the most healthful foods you can add to your diet. But if you top your fresh salad with an oily dressing, you're probably taking a big bite out of your fat budget. Fortunately, these days most grocery stores stock nearly as many low-fat and nonfat dressings as they do high-fat dressings. However, many commercial salad dressings still contain far too much sodium—sometimes more than 200 milligrams per tablespoon. Make your own dressing, and the result will not only be low in sodium and fat, but also full of the fresh-made flavor that only homemade dressings have.

Roasted Red Pepper Dressing

Yield: 1 cup

½ cup chopped roasted red pepper (about 1 medium) (page 57)

½ cup white balsamic vinegar or white wine vinegar

¼ cup grated nonfat Parmesan cheese

2 tablespoons honey

1 tablespoon extra virgin olive oil

1 teaspoon crushed fresh garlic

½ teaspoon dried Italian seasoning

¼ teaspoon ground black pepper

¼ teaspoon salt

1. Place all of the ingredients in a blender, and process for about 1 minute, or until smooth.

2. Transfer the mixture to a covered container, and chill for several hours before serving.

NUTRITIONAL FACTS (PER TABLESPOON)

Calories: 23   Carbohydrates: 3.6 g   Cholesterol: 0 mg
Fat: 0.9 g   Fiber: 0.1 g   Protein: 0.8 g   Sodium: 58 mg

You Save: Calories: 60   Fat: 7.1 g

Roasted Garlic Italian Dressing

Yield: 1⅓ cups

½ cup nonfat or reduced-fat mayonnaise

¼ cup nonfat cottage cheese

¼ cup skim milk

¼ cup white wine vinegar

¼ cup grated nonfat Parmesan cheese

½ teaspoon dried Italian seasoning

⅛ teaspoon ground white pepper

Pulp from 2 to 3 heads of roasted garlic (page 62)

1. Place all of the ingredients in a blender or food processor, and process until smooth.

2. Transfer the dressing to a covered container, and chill for several hours before serving.

NUTRITIONAL FACTS (PER TABLESPOON)

Calories: 17   Carbohydrates: 3.3 g   Cholesterol: 1 mg
Fat: 0.1 g   Fiber: 0 g   Protein: 1.2 g   Sodium: 60 mg

You Save: Calories: 56   Fat: 7.2 g

Gorgonzola Dressing

1. Place ¼ cup of the Gorgonzola and all of the cottage cheese, mayonnaise, vinegar, lemon juice, and garlic in a blender or food processor, and process until smooth. Transfer the dressing to a small bowl, and stir in the remaining Gorgonzola and the pepper and oregano.

2. Transfer the dressing to a covered container, and chill for several hours before serving.

Yield: 1⅓ cups

½ cup crumbled Gorgonzola cheese, divided (about 2 ounces)

½ cup nonfat cottage cheese

½ cup nonfat or reduced-fat mayonnaise

¼ cup white wine vinegar

1 tablespoon lemon juice

1 teaspoon crushed fresh garlic

½ teaspoon coarsely ground black pepper

¼ teaspoon dried oregano

NUTRITIONAL FACTS (PER TABLESPOON)
Calories: 18 Carbohydrates: 1.6 g Cholesterol: 2 mg
Fat: 0.7 g Fiber: 0 g Protein: 1.4 g Sodium: 93 mg

You Save: Calories: 67 Fat: 8 g

Light Balsamic Vinaigrette

1. Place the broth and cornstarch in a small jar with a tight-fitting lid, and shake until smooth. Add the vinegars, honey, mustard, and pepper, and shake again. Set aside.

2. Place the olive oil in a small pot, and preheat over medium heat. Add the garlic, and sauté for a few seconds, or just until the garlic begins to turn color and smells fragrant.

3. Pour the broth mixture into the pot, and cook, stirring constantly, until the mixture comes to a boil and thickens slightly. Remove the pot from the heat, and pour the hot dressing over spinach or leaf lettuce for a wilted salad, or transfer the dressing to a covered container and chill for several hours before serving.

Yield: 1 cup

½ cup chicken or vegetable broth

1 teaspoon cornstarch

3 tablespoons balsamic vinegar

1 tablespoon white wine vinegar

2 tablespoons honey

1 tablespoon plus 1½ teaspoons Dijon mustard

¼ teaspoon ground black pepper

1 tablespoon extra virgin olive oil

1½ teaspoons crushed fresh garlic

NUTRITIONAL FACTS (PER TABLESPOON)
Calories: 18 Carbohydrates: 2.7 g Cholesterol: 0 mg
Fat: 0.9 g Fiber: 0 g Protein: 0 g Sodium: 34 mg

You Save: Calories: 66 Fat: 7.6 g

Italian Garden Salad

Yield: *6 servings*

6 cups torn romaine or iceberg lettuce

1½ cups coarsely chopped radicchio or coarsely shredded purple cabbage

2 thin slices red onion, separated into rings

1 cup sliced fresh mushrooms

2 plum tomatoes, sliced

¾ cup canned garbanzo beans, rinsed and drained

1 medium carrot, peeled

¼ cup grated nonfat or reduced-fat Parmesan cheese

1 teaspoon dried oregano

½ cup bottled fat-free red wine vinaigrette or Italian salad dressing

1 tablespoon extra virgin olive oil (optional)

1. Place the lettuce, radicchio or cabbage, onion, mushrooms, tomatoes, and garbanzo beans in a large salad bowl. Using a potato peeler, shred the carrot into thin strips and add it to the bowl. Add the Parmesan and oregano, and toss to mix well.

2. Drizzle the salad dressing and, if desired, the olive oil over the salad, and toss to mix well. Serve immediately.

NUTRITIONAL FACTS (PER 2-CUP SERVING)

Calories: 101 Carbohydrates: 18.3 g Cholesterol: 0 mg
Fat: 0.9 g Fiber: 3.2 g Protein: 6.2 g Sodium: 241 mg

You Save: Calories: 82 Fat: 10.7 g

LOW-FAT COOKING TIP

Adding Olive Oil Flavor to Your Salads

Want to enhance the flavor of your salad *without* blowing your fat budget? Just use a bottled fat-free Italian salad dressing, and then add a small amount of extra virgin olive oil to the recipe. A good-quality extra virgin olive oil has such an intense flavor that even two to three teaspoons will impart the desired taste to your dish, and yet add very little fat. For instance, in the Italian Garden Salad recipe found above, the optional tablespoon of olive oil will add only 20 calories and 2.2 grams of fat per serving.

Olive oils that are not marked "extra virgin" will be less flavorful, so that more oil will be needed to get the desired effect. What about "light" olive oil? In this case, light refers not to calorie content or color, but to flavor—which is the most mild and bland of all the olive oils. This means you would have to use a lot more oil for the same amount of flavor, making the ingredient a poor choice for the fat-free and low-fat cook.

Citrus Spinach Salad

1. To make the dressing, place all of the dressing ingredients except for the capers in a blender, and process for about 1 minute, or until smooth and creamy. Transfer the dressing to a small bowl, and stir in the capers. Cover and chill for several hours.

2. To assemble the salad, place the spinach, oranges, onions, and mushrooms in a large salad bowl, and toss to mix well. Pour the dressing over the salad, and toss to mix well. Serve immediately.

NUTRITIONAL FACTS (PER SERVING)

Calories: 84 Carbohyrates: 16 g Cholesterol: 0 mg
Fat: 1.9 g Fiber: 4.2 g Protein: 3.7 g Sodium: 194 mg

You Save: Calories: 100 Fat: 12 g

Yield: 6 servings

8 cups fresh spinach leaves

2 cups fresh orange sections, membranes removed (about 4 medium)

$\frac{1}{2}$ medium red onion, thinly sliced and separated into rings

$1\frac{1}{4}$ cups sliced fresh mushrooms

DRESSING

$\frac{1}{2}$ cup fresh orange sections, membranes removed (about 1 medium)

3 tablespoons white wine vinegar or white balsamic vinegar

2 tablespoons pine nuts or chopped walnuts

$2\frac{1}{2}$ teaspoons Dijon mustard

2 teaspoons honey

2 teaspoons crushed fresh garlic

$\frac{1}{4}$ teaspoon ground black pepper

$\frac{1}{8}$ teaspoon ground white pepper

1 tablespoon chopped capers

Minestrone Salad

Yield: 9 cups

8 ounces rotini pasta

1 cup 1-inch pieces fresh green beans (about 1/3 pound), or 1 cup frozen (unthawed) green beans

1 can (15 ounces) red kidney beans, rinsed and drained

1 small zucchini, quartered lengthwise, and thinly sliced (about 1 cup)

1 cup coarsely shredded cabbage

1 cup chopped seeded plum tomatoes (about 3 medium)

1/2 cup bottled fat-free Italian salad dressing

1 teaspoon dried basil

1/4 teaspoon ground black pepper

1/4 cup grated nonfat Parmesan cheese

1. Cook the pasta al dente according to package directions, adding the green beans to the pot during the last 5 minutes of cooking. Drain well, rinse with cool water, and drain again.

2. Place the pasta mixture in a large bowl. Add the kidney beans, zucchini, cabbage, and tomato, and toss to mix well. Add the salad dressing, basil, pepper, and Parmesan, and toss to mix well.

3. Cover the salad and chill for at least 2 hours before serving.

NUTRITIONAL FACTS (PER 1-CUP SERVING)

Calories: 163   Carbohydrates: 31 g   Cholesterol: 1 mg
Fat: 0.7 g   Fiber: 3.9 g   Protein: 7.9 g   Sodium: 213 mg

You Save: Calories: 98   Fat: 12.4 g

Marinated Roasted Peppers

1. Cut the peppers into 1 x 2-inch strips, and place in a shallow bowl. Add the dressing, and stir to mix well.

2. Cover the peppers and chill for several hours or overnight before serving.

Yield: 4 servings

2 large red peppers, roasted (below)

2 large green peppers, roasted (below)

3 tablespoons bottled fat-free or reduced-fat Italian salad dressing

---

NUTRITIONAL FACTS (PER SERVING)

Calories: 28 Carbohydrates: 6 g Cholesterol: 0 mg
Fat: 0.1 g Fiber: 1.4 g Protein: 0.7 g Sodium: 91 mg

You Save: Calories: 82 Fat: 10.2 g

Roasting Peppers

Great Italian cooks know that roasting adds an entirely new dimension to the bell pepper. Once roasted, this vegetable is frequently used to enhance the flavors of salads, sauces, side dishes, and entrées. It even makes a tasty pizza topping. And roasted peppers are a real boon to the fat-free cook, since they add depth and flavor but no fat.

When time is in short supply, you can purchase roasted red peppers in jars. This handy ingredient may be found near the jarred foods, like olives and capers, or in the imported foods or pasta section of the grocery store. Just make sure that the peppers are packed in water rather than oil.

If you have a little extra time, though, you'll find that fresh-roasted peppers are easy to make and lend a fresher taste to foods than do their jarred counterparts. And, of course, by roasting green and yellow peppers as well as red, you will be able to add a variety of flavors and colors to your dishes. Peppers can be roasted in just four easy steps:

1. Rinse the peppers, dry well, and cut in half lengthwise. Remove the stems, membranes, and seeds.

2. Coat a large baking sheet with nonstick cooking spray, and place the peppers, cut side down, on the sheet. Bake at 425°F for 25 minutes, or until the skins are blistered and charred.

3. Transfer the peppers to a bowl, cover tightly with a lid or plastic wrap, and allow to steam in the bowl for at least 15 minutes. Let the peppers sit until they are cool enough to handle.

4. Using a small paring knife or your fingers, gently peel the charred skins off the peppers (they should slip off easily). Dice or slice the roasted peppers, and use as desired.

Balsamic Three-Bean Salad

Yield: *8 servings*

4 cups 1-inch pieces fresh green beans (about 1¼ pounds)

1 cup canned red kidney beans, rinsed and drained

1 cup canned garbanzo beans, rinsed and drained

¼ cup plus 2 tablespoons chopped red onion

¾ cup Light Balsamic Vinaigrette (page 53) or bottled fat-free or reduced-fat red wine vinaigrette salad dressing

1. Place the green beans in a microwave or stove-top steamer. Add water, cover, and cook at high power or over medium-high heat for 6 to 8 minutes, or until tender. Rinse with cool water and drain.

2. Place the green beans in a large bowl. Add the kidney and garbanzo beans and the onion, and toss to mix well. Add the vinaigrette, and toss to mix well.

3. Cover the salad and chill for several hours or overnight, stirring occasionally, before serving.

NUTRITIONAL FACTS (PER ¾-CUP SERVING)

Calories: 113   Carbohydrates: 21 g   Cholesterol: 0 mg
Fat: 1.8 g   Fiber: 5.8 g   Protein: 5.4 g   Sodium: 138 mg

You Save: Calories: 80   Fat: 9.1 g

Country Potato Salad

Yield: *8 servings*

1¾ pounds small red potatoes, scrubbed

½ teaspoon salt

½ cup thinly sliced celery

½ cup diced red onion

3 slices turkey bacon, cooked, drained, and crumbled (optional)

¾ cup hot Light Balsamic Vinaigrette (page 53)

1. Slice the potatoes ¼-inch thick. Measure the potatoes. There should be 6 cups. (Adjust the amount if necessary.)

2. Place the potatoes in a 4-quart pot, and barely cover with water. Add the salt, and bring to a boil over high heat. Reduce the heat to medium and cover, leaving the lid slightly ajar. Cook for about 8 minutes, or until the potatoes are tender. Drain well, and return the potatoes to the pot.

3. Add the celery, onion, and, if desired, the bacon to the potatoes, and toss to mix well. Pour the vinaigrette over the mixture, and toss to mix well. Serve warm or at room temperature.

NUTRITIONAL FACTS (PER ¾-CUP SERVING)

Calories: 139   Carbohydrates: 26 g   Cholesterol: 0 mg
Fat: 1.4 g   Fiber: 2.7 g   Protein: 2.5 g   Sodium: 122 mg

You Save: Calories: 67   Fat: 7.7

Antipasto Salad

1. Arrange the lettuce over the bottom of a large serving platter. Lay first the tomato and then the onion slices over the lettuce. Arrange the mozzarella or provolone and ham strips over the onions. Arrange the kidney or garbanzo beans, artichoke hearts, peppers, and olives around the outer edges of the lettuce.

2. Serve immediately, topping each serving with 2 tablespoons of the dressing.

NUTRITIONAL FACTS (PER 1¾-CUP SERVING)

Calories: 134 Carbohydrates: 19 g Cholesterol: 10 mg
Fat: 1.5 g Fiber: 4.3 g Protein: 13 g Sodium: 382 mg

You Save: Calories: 172 Fat: 23 g

Yield: 6 servings

6 cups torn romaine lettuce

2 medium plum tomatoes, thinly sliced

6 thin slices red onion, separated into rings

3 ounces nonfat or reduced-fat mozzarella cheese or reduced-fat provolone, thinly sliced and cut into thin strips

3 ounces ham (at least 97% lean), thinly shaved and cut into thin strips

1 cup canned kidney or garbanzo beans, rinsed and drained

6 small canned (drained) or frozen (thawed) artichoke hearts, halved

6 cherry peppers or Greek salad peppers

6 large pitted black olives

¾ cup Roasted Garlic Italian Dressing (page 52) or bottled fat-free Italian salad dressing

Tuscan Tuna and Pasta Salad

Yield: *6 servings*

½ cup sun-dried tomatoes (not packed in oil}

10 ounces mostaccioli or penne pasta

2 cups 1-inch pieces fresh green beans (about ½ pound)

2 cans (6 ounces each) water-packed albacore tuna, drained

¼ cup plus 2 tablespoons sliced black olives

DRESSING

½ cup bottled fat-free or reduced-fat red wine vinegar salad dressing

1 tablespoon lemon juice

1 teaspoon crushed fresh garlic

1 teaspoon dried thyme

⅛ teaspoon ground black pepper

1. Place the tomatoes in a heatproof bowl, and add boiling water just to cover. Set aside for 10 minutes, or until the tomatoes have plumped. Drain well, and slice the tomatoes into thin strips. Set aside.

2. Cook the pasta al dente according to package directions. About 4 minutes before the pasta is done, add the green beans, and cook until the pasta is al dente and the beans are crisp-tender. Drain well, rinse with cool water, and drain again. Return the mixture to the pot.

3. Add the tuna, olives, and tomatoes to the pasta mixture, and toss to mix well.

4. To make the dressing, place all of the dressing ingredients in a small bowl, and stir to mix well. Pour the dressing over the pasta mixture, and toss to mix well.

5. Transfer the salad to a large bowl, cover, and chill for at least 2 hours before serving.

NUTRITIONAL FACTS (PER 1¾-CUP SERVING)

Calories: 284   Carbohydrates: 44 g   Cholesterol: 16 mg
Fat: 2.4 g   Fiber: 3.4 g   Protein: 21 g   Sodium: 571 mg

You Save: Calories: 122   Fat: 13.9 g

Orzo and Broccoli Salad

1. Place the tomatoes in a heatproof bowl, and add boiling water just to cover. Set aside for 10 minutes, or until the tomatoes have plumped. Drain well, and set aside.

2. Cook the orzo al dente according to package directions. About 1 minute before the pasta is done, add the broccoli, and cook until the pasta is al dente and the broccoli turns bright green and is crisp-tender. Drain well, rinse with cool water, and drain again. Return the mixture to the pot, tossing in the tomatoes and, if desired, the pine nuts.

3. To make the dressing, place all of the dressing ingredients in a small bowl, and stir to mix well. Pour the dressing over the pasta mixture, and toss to mix well.

4. Transfer the salad to a large bowl, cover, and chill for at least 4 hours before serving.

Yield: 6 servings

⅓ cup chopped sun-dried tomatoes (not packed in oil)

1 cup orzo pasta

2 cups chopped fresh broccoli

2 tablespoons pine nuts (optional)

DRESSING

¼ cup plus 2 tablespoons bottled fat-free or reduced-fat Italian salad dressing

½ teaspoon crushed fresh garlic

½ teaspoon dried basil

⅛ teaspoon ground black pepper

NUTRITIONAL FACTS (PER ⅔-CUP SERVING)
Calories: 131 Carbohydrates: 26 g Cholesterol: 0 mg
Fat: 0.6 g Fiber: 1.9 g Protein: 4.9 g Sodium: 192 mg

You Save: Calories: 57 Fat: 7.4 g

Roasting Garlic

Perhaps the most revered seasoning in Italian cuisine, garlic is well known for its uniquely pungent flavor. But garlic has another side, too. When roasted, garlic mellows and acquires a sweeter, richer character. Both healthful and aromatic, this ingredient is truly one of the secrets of fat-free Italian cooking. A spoonful of roasted garlic purée can add so much savor to sauces, soups, and dressings that you won't miss the fat.

You can roast garlic either in whole heads or in individual cloves. Whole roasted garlic heads make an outstanding appetizer—the soft, caramelized pulp can be squeezed onto warm, crusty bread instead of butter. As for roasted individual cloves, toss some into pasta or vegetable dishes, or add them to soups, sauces, and dressings for a new flavor dimension. Be sure to choose plump, fresh, solid heads of garlic for the best results.

To Roast Individual Garlic Cloves:

1. Peel the outer skin from the desired number of garlic heads. (To peel a garlic head easily, microwave it for 20 seconds at high power. This will loosen the husks and make peeling easier.) Separate the garlic heads into individual cloves.

2. Bring a small pot of water to a boil over high heat. Add the unpeeled cloves to the boiling water, and boil for 1 minute. (This makes the cloves easy to peel.) Drain well in a colander, and allow to cool. When cool enough to handle, peel.

3. For each head of garlic cloves being roasted, coat one 12-inch square of aluminum foil with nonstick olive oil cooking spray. Arrange the garlic cloves in a single layer over the center of one half of the foil. If desired, drizzle 1 teaspoon of extra virgin olive oil over the cloves. For extra flavor, sprinkle with $\frac{1}{4}$ teaspoon of dried rosemary or oregano.

4. Fold the foil over, and crimp the edges to form a sealed packet. Arrange the packets on a baking sheet, and bake at 350°F for 30 minutes, or until the garlic is very soft and sweet. Use the pulp in recipes, as desired. When a recipe calls for puréed roasted garlic pulp, simply place the cloves in a bowl, and mash the pulp with a fork until smooth.

Time-Saving Tip

When you have time, you may wish to roast extra garlic cloves and freeze them until needed. Simply allow the packets to cool to room temperature, and store in the freezer for up to 1 month. When ready to use, remove the desired number of cloves from a packet, and allow to sit at room temperature until thawed. Mash the cloves with a fork to make garlic purée, or use as your recipe directs.

To Roast Whole Heads of Garlic:

1. Peel the outer skin from the desired number of garlic heads, leaving just enough skin to keep the heads intact. Trim $\frac{1}{2}$ inch off the tops of the garlic heads to expose the cloves.

2. For each head of garlic being roasted, coat one 8-inch square of aluminum foil with nonstick olive oil cooking spray. Place 1 head in the center of each piece of foil. If desired, drizzle 1 teaspoon of olive oil over the garlic head, and/or sprinkle with $\frac{1}{4}$ teaspoon of dried rosemary or oregano. Bring the foil up to enclose the garlic head, and crimp or twist the edges to seal.

3. Arrange the packets on a baking sheet, and bake at 350°F for 50 minutes, or until the garlic is very soft and sweet. Remove the garlic from the foil, and let sit for a few minutes, or until cool enough to handle. Squeeze the garlic pulp onto bread or use it in recipes as desired.

Time-Saving Tip

When you have time, you may wish to roast extra garlic heads and freeze them until needed. Simply allow the packets to cool to room temperature, and store in the freezer for up to 1 month. When ready to use, remove the desired number of heads from the freezer, and allow to sit at room temperature for about 30 minutes, or until thawed. Squeeze out the pulp, and use as your recipe directs.

Antipasto Pasta Salad

1. Cook the pasta al dente according to package directions. About 2 minutes before the pasta is done, add the mushrooms, and cook until the pasta is al dente and the mushrooms are lightly cooked. Drain well, rinse with cool water, and drain again. Return the mixture to the pot.

2. Add the ham, cheese, artichoke hearts, red peppers, scallions or leeks, and, if desired, the olives to the pasta mixture, and toss to mix well. Add the dressing and oregano, and toss to mix well.

3. Transfer the salad to a large bowl, cover, and chill for at least 2 hours before serving. Add a little more salad dressing just before serving if the salad seems too dry.

Yield: *10 cups*

8 ounces penne or rotini pasta

1 cup sliced fresh mushrooms

4 ounces ham (at least 97% lean), thinly sliced and cut into thin strips

1 cup diced nonfat or reduced-fat mozzarella cheese

1 cup chopped frozen (thawed) or canned (drained) artichoke hearts

½ cup roasted red pepper cut into thin strips (page 57)

½ cup thinly sliced scallions or leeks

½ cup sliced black olives (optional)

½ cup bottled fat-free or reduced-fat red wine vinaigrette salad dressing

½ teaspoon dried oregano

NUTRITIONAL FACTS (PER 1-CUP SERVING)

Calories: 125   Carbohydrates: 20 g   Cholesterol: 8 mg
Fat: 0.7 g   Fiber: 0.8 g   Protein: 8 g   Sodium: 253 mg

You Save: Calories: 81   Fat: 10.1 g

Shrimp and Pasta Salad

Yield: 5 servings

10 ounces seashell pasta

1½ cups (about 8 ounces) cooked shrimp or crab meat

¾ cup chopped frozen (thawed) artichoke hearts or frozen (thawed) peas

½ cup finely chopped celery

½ cup diced red bell pepper

¼ cup chopped onion

DRESSING

½ cup nonfat or reduced-fat mayonnaise

3 tablespoons grated nonfat Parmesan cheese

1 tablespoon lemon juice

½ teaspoon dried Italian seasoning

⅛ teaspoon ground white pepper

1. Cook the pasta al dente according to package directions. Drain, rinse with cool water, and drain again.

2. Return the pasta to the pot, and add the seafood and vegetables. Toss to mix well.

3. To make the dressing, place all of the dressing ingredients in a small bowl, and stir to mix well. Pour the dressing over the pasta mixture, and toss to mix well.

4. Transfer the salad to a large bowl, cover, and chill for at least 2 hours before serving.

NUTRITIONAL FACTS (PER 1¾-CUP SERVING)

Calories: 302   Carbohydrates: 52 g   Cholesterol: 90 mg
Fat: 1.5 g   Fiber: 2.9 g   Protein: 19 g   Sodium: 353 mg

You Save: Calories: 146   Fat: 18.8 g

Primavera Pasta Salad

1. Cook the pasta al dente according to package directions. About 2 minutes before the pasta is done, add the broccoli, snow peas, or asparagus; carrots; and mushrooms. Cook until the pasta is al dente and the vegetables are crisp-tender. Drain well, rinse with cool water, and drain again. Return the mixture to the pot.

2. Add the red peppers and scallions to the pasta mixture, and toss to mix well. Add the dressing, Parmesan, and Italian seasoning, and toss to mix well.

3. Transfer the salad to a large bowl, cover, and chill for at least 2 hours before serving. Add a little more salad dressing just before serving if the salad seems too dry.

Yield: *8 servings*

8 oz. rotini or wagon wheel pasta

2 cups fresh broccoli florets, fresh snow peas, or fresh asparagus spears, cut into 1-inch pieces

1 cup sliced carrots

½ cup sliced fresh mushrooms

½ cup red bell pepper cut into matchstick-sized pieces

⅓ cup thinly sliced scallions

½ cup bottled fat-free or reduced-fat Italian salad dressing

¼ cup grated nonfat Parmesan cheese

½ teaspoon dried Italian seasoning

NUTRITIONAL FACTS (PER 1-CUP SERVING)

Calories: 141 Carbohydrates: 28 g Cholesterol: 1 mg
Fat: 0.6 g Fiber: 1.8 g Protein: 6 g Sodium: 181 mg

You Save: Calories: 94 Fat: 12.4 g

Spiked Fruit Salad

Many fruit salads are already fat-free, but this one also has half the added sugar of a traditional recipe.

1. To make the dressing, place the cornstarch and juice in a small saucepan, and stir to dissolve the cornstarch. Add the wine, honey, and orange rind, and stir to mix well. Cook over medium heat, stirring constantly, for several minutes, or until the mixture begins to boil and thickens slightly. Remove the pot from the heat, and allow to cool to room temperature.

2. Pour the dressing into a large bowl. Add the fruits, and toss to mix well. Cover and chill for 3 to 6 hours before serving.

Yield: *8 servings*

4 plums or peeled apricots, sliced

2 apples, peeled and sliced

2 pears, peeled and sliced

2 peaches or nectarines, peeled and sliced

1½ cups seedless red grapes

DRESSING

1 teaspoon cornstarch

½ cup orange juice

½ cup dry white wine

¼ cup honey

1 tablespoon freshly grated orange rind, or 1 teaspoon dried orange rind

---

NUTRITIONAL FACTS (PER ⅞-CUP SERVING)

Calories: 132 Carbohydrates: 31 g Cholesterol: 0 mg
Fat: 0.6 g Fiber: 2.5 g Protein: 0.8 g Sodium: 2 mg

You Save: Calories: 45 Fat: 0 g

5

Delightful Vegetable Side Dishes

Vegetables play an important part in any Italian meal. In some dishes, like Pasta Primavera, they are essential supporting players, adding color, flavor, and texture. When the Italian cook turns a hand to making savory side dishes, though, vegetables enjoy a starring role. This is good news, as vegetables are the most nutrient-dense of foods, providing a wealth of vitamins and minerals while adding very few calories and practically no fat.

Because of the many health benefits of vegetables, it is recommended that every diet contain at least three to five servings every day—and more would be even better. This goal isn't as difficult to reach as it may seem, as a serving is only half a cup of cooked vegetables, or one cup of leafy raw vegetables.

To get the most from your healthy, low-fat vegetables, it's important to keep them that way. Unfortunately, the Italian cuisine—like that of many other countries—often relies on a generous amount of fat for flavor. Butter and Italian ham or bacon are favorite additions to vegetables. These seasonings add not just calories, but also artery-clogging saturated fat. And while olive oil, another popular seasoning, is heart-healthy, it contains just as many calories as any other fat.

How do you add flavor without boosting fat? There are plenty of guilt-free options. As you will see, a splash of wine or balsamic vinegar, a clove of fresh or roasted garlic, a pinch of aromatic herbs, and a bit of imagination can make your vegetables rise to any occasion. In addition, techniques such as roasting, steaming, and stir-frying allow the natural flavors of the vegetables to shine through, reducing the need not just for fat, but also for salt.

So enjoy the distinctive flavors of Italy in these delightful vegetable side dishes. From Green Beans With Glazed Onions, to Mashed Potatoes With Roasted Garlic, to Oven-Fried Zucchini, these recipes provide a variety of healthful and delicious ways to make any meal a meal to remember.

Green Beans With Glazed Onions

Yield: *6 servings*

1 pound fresh green beans

1 cup chicken or vegetable broth

½ large Spanish onion, sliced into very thin wedges

¾ teaspoon dried thyme

¼ teaspoon salt

⅛ teaspoon ground black pepper

1 teaspoon sugar

1 tablespoon balsamic vinegar

1. Rinse the beans with cool water. Trim the ends, and snap the beans into 1½-inch pieces. Place the broth in the bottom of a stove top or microwave steamer, and add the beans. Cover and cook over high heat or on high power for 10 minutes, or until tender.

2. While the beans are cooking, coat a large nonstick skillet with olive oil cooking spray, and preheat over medium heat. Add the onions, thyme, salt, and pepper, and sauté for about 5 minutes, or until the onions are wilted and are just starting to brown. (If the skillet becomes too dry, add a few teaspoons of broth as needed.) Add the sugar, and sauté for another minute. Add the vinegar, and stir to mix well.

3. Add the beans, along with 2 tablespoons of the broth used for steaming, to the skillet. Toss the beans and onions together for a minute or 2 over medium heat, and serve hot.

NUTRITIONAL FACTS (PER ¾-CUP SERVING)
Calories: 35   Carbohydrates: 7 g   Cholesterol: 0 mg
Fat: 0.1 g   Fiber: 2.8 g   Protein: 1.6 g   Sodium: 94 mg

You Save: Calories: 70   Fat: 7.7 g

Spinach and Mushroom Sauté

1. Coat a large nonstick skillet with olive oil cooking spray, and preheat over medium-high heat. Add the garlic and mushrooms, and stir-fry for about 2 minutes, or just until the mushrooms start to brown and begin to release their juices.

2. Add the spinach, salt, and pepper to the skillet, and stir-fry for another 2 minutes, or just until the spinach is wilted. Add a little water or broth if the skillet becomes too dry. Serve hot.

Yield: 4 servings

1½ teaspoons crushed fresh garlic

2 cups sliced fresh mushrooms (about 8 ounces)

10 cups (packed) fresh spinach leaves (about 10 ounces)

¼ teaspoon salt

⅛ teaspoon ground black pepper

NUTRITIONAL FACTS (PER ¾-CUP SERVING)

Calories: 24 Carbohydrates: 4 g Cholesterol: 0 mg
Fat: 0.4 g Fiber: 2.4 g Protein: 2.8 g Sodium: 189 mg

You Save: Calories: 54 Fat: 6 g

Savory Sautéed Mushrooms

1. Coat a large nonstick skillet with olive oil cooking spray, and preheat over medium-high heat. Add the garlic, mushrooms, thyme, pepper, and salt, and stir-fry for several minutes, or until the mushrooms start to brown and begin to release their juices.

2. Add the wine to the skillet, and reduce the heat to medium. Cook and stir for several minutes, until all but a few tablespoons of the wine has evaporated.

3. Transfer the mushrooms to a serving dish, and sprinkle the parsley over the top. Serve hot.

Yield: 6 servings

1 teaspoon crushed fresh garlic

1 pound fresh mushrooms, sliced

¼ teaspoon dried thyme

¼ teaspoon ground black pepper

¼ teaspoon salt

¼ cup dry white wine

2 tablespoons finely chopped fresh Italian parsley

NUTRITIONAL FACTS (PER ½-CUP SERVING)

Calories: 22 Carbohydrates: 3.2 g Cholesterol: 0 mg
Fat: 0.3 g Fiber: 1 g Protein: 1.6 g Sodium: 92 mg

You Save: Calories: 80 Fat: 9 g

Zucchini With Roasted Red Peppers and Onions

Yield: *5 servings*

1 pound zucchini (about 3 medium), cut into 2-x-½-inch strips

1 small yellow onion, cut into thin wedges

½ teaspoon dried Italian seasoning

¼ teaspoon salt

⅛ teaspoon ground black pepper

1 large red bell pepper, roasted and cut into thin strips (page 57)

1. Coat a large nonstick skillet with olive oil cooking spray, and preheat over medium-high heat. Add the zucchini, onion, Italian seasoning, salt, and pepper, and stir-fry for about 4 minutes, or until the vegetables start to brown and become crisp-tender. (If the skillet becomes too dry, add a little white wine or chicken broth.)

2. Add the roasted red pepper strips to the skillet, and continue to stir-fry for another minute, or just until the peppers are heated through. Serve hot.

NUTRITIONAL FACTS (PER ¾-CUP SERVING)

Calories: 24 Carbohydrates: 4.1 g Cholesterol: 0 mg
Fat: 0.2 g Fiber: 1.7 g Protein: 1.4 g Sodium: 110 mg

You Save: Calories: 47 Fat: 5.4 g

Mashed Potatoes With Roasted Garlic

Yield: 7 servings

2 pounds white potatoes

2 heads garlic, roasted (page 62)

¼ cup plus 2 tablespoons instant nonfat dry milk powder

¼ teaspoon salt

⅛ teaspoon ground white pepper

1. Peel the potatoes, and cut them into chunks. Place the potatoes in a 2½-quart pot, add water just to cover, and bring to a boil over high heat. Reduce the heat to medium, cover, and cook for about 10 minutes, or until soft.

2. Drain all but about ½ cup of water from the pot, reserving the drained water. Squeeze the pulp from the roasted garlic heads, and add to the potatoes. Add the nonfat dry milk, salt, and pepper.

3. Using a potato masher, mash the mixture until smooth. If the potatoes are too stiff, add a little of the reserved cooking liquid. Serve immediately.

NUTRITIONAL FACTS (PER ¾-CUP SERVING)

Calories: 140 Carbohydrates: 30.2 g Cholesterol: 0 mg
Fat: 0.2 g Fiber: 2 g Protein: 4.3 g Sodium: 104 mg

You Save: Calories: 87 Fat: 9.8 g

Oven-Fried Zucchini

1. Place the egg substitute in a shallow bowl, and set aside. Place the bread crumbs, Parmesan, and Italian seasoning in another shallow dish. Stir to mix well, and set aside.

2. Diagonally slice the zucchini into $\frac{3}{8}$-inch-thick slices. Dip the zucchini slices, 1 at a time, first in the egg substitute, and then in the crumb mixture, turning to coat each side.

3. Coat a large baking sheet with olive oil cooking spray, and arrange the zucchini slices in a single layer on the sheet. Spray the tops lightly with the cooking spray.

4. Bake at 400°F for 8 minutes. Turn with a spatula, and bake for 7 additional minutes, or until golden brown. Serve hot.

Yield: 6 servings

$\frac{1}{2}$ cup plus 2 tablespoons fat-free egg substitute

$\frac{1}{2}$ cup dried bread crumbs

$\frac{1}{2}$ cup grated nonfat Parmesan cheese

1 teaspoon dried Italian seasoning

4 medium-large zucchini (about $1\frac{3}{4}$ pounds)

Olive oil cooking spray

NUTRITIONAL FACTS (PER SERVING)

Calories: 79 Carbohydrates: 13 g Cholesterol: 6 mg
Fat: 0.7 g Fiber: 2 g Protein: 7.3 g Sodium: 167 mg

You Save: Calories: 108 Fat: 14.2 g

Italian Squash and Onions

1. Coat a large nonstick skillet with nonstick cooking spray, and preheat over medium heat. Add the sausage, and cook, stirring to crumble, until the meat is no longer pink. (If the meat is very lean, there will be no fat to drain.)

2. Add the squash and onions to the skillet. Cover, and cook for about 7 minutes, stirring occasionally, until the vegetables are tender. Add a few tablespoons of water or chicken broth if the skillet becomes too dry. Serve hot.

Yield: 6 servings

4 ounces Turkey Italian Sausage (page 182)

4 medium pattypan or zucchini squash, sliced $\frac{1}{4}$-inch thick (about 5 cups)

1 medium yellow onion, sliced $\frac{1}{4}$-inch thick and separated into rings

---

NUTRITIONAL FACTS (PER $\frac{3}{4}$-CUP SERVING)

Calories: 44 Carbohydrates: 5 g Cholesterol: 12 mg
Fat: 0.7 g Fiber: 1.6 g Protein: 6 g Sodium: 82 mg

You Save: Calories: 66 Fat: 7.3 g

Green Beans Pomodoro

Yield: *6 servings*

1 pound fresh green beans

1 teaspoon crushed fresh garlic

1 can (14½ ounces) Italian-style stewed tomatoes

1. Rinse the beans with cool water. Trim the ends, and snap the beans into 2-inch pieces. Set aside.

2. Coat a large nonstick skillet with nonstick cooking spray, and preheat over medium-high heat. Add the garlic, and stir-fry for about 30 seconds, or just until the garlic begins to turn color.

3. Add the green beans and the tomatoes with their juice, and stir to mix. Bring the mixture to a boil, reduce the heat to low, and cover. Simmer, stirring occasionally, for about 25 minutes, or until the beans are tender. Serve hot.

NUTRITIONAL FACTS (PER ¾-CUP SERVING)

Calories: 43   Carbohydrates: 8 g   Cholesterol: 0 mg
Fat: 0.3 g   Fiber: 3.3 g   Protein: 2 g   Sodium: 176 mg

You Save: Calories: 79   Fat: 8.9 g

Carrots Marsala

Yield: *4 servings*

1 pound carrots (about 4 medium), peeled and cut into matchstick-sized pieces

½ cup chicken broth

¼ cup dry Marsala

1 tablespoon sugar

⅛ teaspoon ground black pepper

1. Place the carrots in a large nonstick skillet. Add the broth, Marsala, sugar, and pepper, and stir to mix well.

2. Bring the mixture to a boil over high heat. Reduce the heat to medium, cover, and cook for about 6 minutes, or until the carrots are tender.

3. Remove the cover from the skillet, and continue to cook for about 3 minutes, or until most of the liquid has evaporated. Serve hot.

NUTRITIONAL FACTS (PER SERVING)

Calories: 61   Carbohydrates: 14 g   Cholesterol: 0 mg
Fat: 0.2 g   Fiber: 2.7 g   Protein: 1.1 g   Sodium: 121 mg

You Save: Calories: 76   Fat: 8.6 g

Broccoli-Noodle Bake

For variety, try using spinach instead of broccoli. Always use regular Parmesan cheese rather than a fat-free brand to top this savory casserole.

1. Cook the noodles al dente according to package directions. Drain well, return to the pot, and cover to keep warm.

2. Coat a large nonstick skillet with nonstick cooking spray, and place over medium-high heat. Add the mushrooms, and sauté for 2 minutes, or until the mushrooms begin to brown and start to release their juices.

3. Remove the skillet from the heat. Add the noodles, broccoli, pepper, and sauce, and toss to mix well.

4. Coat an 8-inch square casserole dish with nonstick cooking spray, and spread the mixture evenly in the dish. Sprinkle the Parmesan over the top.

5. Cover the dish with aluminum foil, and bake at 350°F for 25 minutes. Remove the foil, and bake for 10 additional minutes, or until the casserole is bubbly and the top is lightly browned. Remove the dish from the oven, and let sit for 5 minutes before cutting into squares and serving.

Yield: *8 servings*

5 ounces yolk-free egg noodles (about 4 cups)

½ cup chopped fresh mushrooms

1 package (10 ounces) frozen chopped broccoli, thawed and drained

⅛ teaspoon ground black pepper

1 recipe Almost Alfredo Sauce (page 178)

3 tablespoons grated Parmesan cheese

NUTRITIONAL FACTS (PER ¾-CUP SERVING)
Calories: 155   Carbohydrates: 25 g   Cholesterol: 8 mg
Fat: 1.3 g   Fiber: 1.6 g   Protein: 12 g   Sodium: 251 mg

You Save: Calories: 132   Fat: 13.9 g

Rosemary Roasted Vegetables

Yield: *4 servings*

2 medium carrots, peeled and
   sliced ¾-inch thick

2 medium yellow onions, cut into
   ¾-inch-thick wedges

2 medium potatoes (unpeeled),
   cut into 1-inch cubes

8 ounces whole fresh
   mushrooms, cut in half

6 cloves garlic, peeled

1 tablespoon balsamic vinegar

1 tablespoon broth or water

1 tablespoon fresh rosemary, or 1
   teaspoon dried rosemary

¼ teaspoon coarsely ground
   black pepper

¼ teaspoon salt

1 tablespoon extra virgin olive oil
   (optional)

Olive oil cooking spray

1. Place the vegetables and garlic cloves in a large bowl, and toss to mix well. Add the vinegar, broth or water, rosemary, pepper, salt, and, if desired, the olive oil, and stir to mix well.

2. Coat a 9-x-13-inch nonstick pan with the cooking spray, and spread the vegetables in an even layer in the pan. If you did not use the olive oil, spray the tops of the vegetables with the cooking spray.

3. Cover the pan with aluminum foil, and bake at 450°F for 20 minutes. Remove the foil, and bake for 15 additional minutes. Turn the vegetables with a spatula, and bake for 15 minutes more, or until the vegetables are tender and nicely browned. Serve hot.

NUTRITIONAL FACTS (PER ¾-CUP SERVING)

Calories: 136 Carbohydrates: 30 g Cholesterol: 0 mg
Fat: 1 g Fiber: 3.7 g Protein: 4 g Sodium: 154 mg

You Save: Calories: 90 Fat: 10.2

FAT-FIGHTING TIP

Roasting Vegetables Without Oil

Italian cooks have long known that roasting brings out the best in vegetables. As they roast, vegetables become tender and their natural sugars rise to the surface, caramelizing into a slightly sweet, golden coating. A wide variety of vegetables can be roasted, including potatoes, carrots, parsnips, mushrooms, onions, winter squash, and many more.

   Most recipes for roasted vegetables call for a splash of vinegar, fresh or dried herbs, and a generous

Spinach-Stuffed Tomatoes

1. Cut each tomato in half crosswise, and scoop out and discard the pulp, leaving just the shell. Set aside.

2. Coat a nonstick skillet with nonstick cooking spray, and preheat over medium heat. Add the garlic, and stir-fry for about 30 seconds, or just until the garlic begins to turn color. Add the spinach, and stir-fry for another minute or 2, or just until the spinach is wilted.

3. Remove the skillet from the heat, and add the orzo, basil, Parmesan, and pepper. Toss to mix well.

4. Fill the hollowed-out tomatoes with the spinach mixture, mounding the tops slightly. Coat a 7-x-11-inch pan with nonstick cooking spray, and arrange the tomatoes in the pan.

5. Cover with aluminum foil, and bake at 350°F for 20 minutes, or just until the tomatoes are tender and the filling is heated through. Sprinkle 1 tablespoon of mozzarella over the top of each tomato, and bake uncovered for 5 additional minutes, or until the cheese is melted. Serve hot.

Yield: 8 servings

4 large tomatoes (about 8 ounces each)

1½ teaspoons crushed fresh garlic

3 cups (packed) chopped fresh spinach

2½ cups cooked orzo (about 1⅛ cups uncooked)

¼ cup finely chopped fresh basil

¼ cup grated nonfat Parmesan cheese

⅛ teaspoon ground black pepper

½ cup shredded nonfat or reduced-fat mozzarella cheese

NUTRITIONAL FACTS (PER SERVING)

Calories: 105 Carbohydrates: 19 g Cholesterol: 2 mg
Fat: 0.5 g Fiber: 1.6 g Protein: 7 g Sodium: 119 mg

You Save: Calories: 78 Fat: 8.6 g

---

amount of oil. For a healthier dish, omit all or part of the oil in the recipe, and instead toss the vegetables with a tablespoon of balsamic vinegar, some herbs, and a tablespoon of broth or wine. Coat a nonstick pan with nonstick cooking spray, and spread the vegetables out in a single layer. The pan should be just big enough to hold the vegetables in one layer. (If the pan is too large, the vegetables are likely to dry out, and may even burn during cooking.) If you omitted all of the oil from the recipe, spray the tops of the vegetables with some nonstick olive oil cooking spray.

Cover the vegetables with aluminum foil during the first twenty minutes of baking, as in the recipe for Rosemary Roasted Vegetables (page 74). Then remove the foil and finish roasting the vegetables, turning with a spatula about every 15 minutes until they are tender and golden. If the pan becomes too dry, add a little more broth, but be careful not to add too much liquid or the vegetables will steam instead of roast. This cooking method will keep the vegetables moist on the inside, yet allow their full flavors to develop.

Vegetables such as eggplant, zucchini, and asparagus can also be roasted, but since they require much shorter cooking times, there is no need to cover these vegetables during the first part of baking.

Polenta-Stuffed Peppers

Yield: *6 servings*

3 cups water

¾ cup coarsely ground cornmeal (polenta)

3 tablespoons grated nonfat Parmesan cheese

1½ cups Basic Marinara Sauce (page 166) or bottled fat-free marinara sauce

3 large red bell peppers

1 cup shredded nonfat or reduced-fat mozzarella cheese

1. To make the polenta, place the water in a 2-quart pot and bring to a boil over high heat. Slowly whisk in the cornmeal, and cook, stirring constantly, for about 2 minutes, or until the polenta starts to thicken. Reduce the heat to low, whisk in the Parmesan, and cook, still stirring, for about 20 minutes, or until the polenta begins to pull away from the sides of the pan. Remove the pot from the heat, and set aside.

2. Coat a 9-inch square pan with nonstick cooking spray, and pour the marinara sauce into the bottom of the pan.

3. Cut the peppers in half lengthwise. Remove the seeds and membranes and arrange the peppers, hollow side up, in the pan. Fill each pepper half with one-sixth of the polenta. Cover the dish with aluminum foil, and bake at 350°F for 45 minutes, or until tender.

4. Remove the foil, sprinkle some of the mozzarella over each pepper half, and bake for 10 additional minutes, or until the cheese is melted. Serve hot.

NUTRITIONAL FACTS (PER SERVING)

Calories: 132   Carbohydrates: 22 g   Cholesterol: 4 mg
Fat: 0.6 g   Fiber: 3.7 g   Protein: 10 g   Sodium: 221 mg

You Save: Calories: 75 Fat: 10.1 g

6

Hot and Hearty Soups

Hot and hearty, Italian soups are as satisfying as they are varied. Golden-brothed chicken and pasta soup, thick minestrone, creamy cauliflower soup—all are made deliciously in the Italian kitchen.

Naturally, when your kitchen is also low-fat, a little creativity is needed to keep your dishes healthy without sacrificing the flavors you love. Italian soups such as chicken and pasta soup, vegetable soup, and tomato soup tend to be lowest in fat to begin with—although most of these recipes can be further slimmed down by reducing oils and using fat-free broths. Cream soups and soups made with sausage and other high-fat ingredients pose more of a challenge. But with just a few tricks of the trade, these soups, too, can be prepared with little or no fat—and with a lot less salt than usual, too.

The recipes in this chapter start out with wholesome ingredients like fiber-rich beans, vegetables, and pasta. Then fat is kept to a minimum by substituting ultra-lean meats for fatty hams and sausages. The oil used for sautéing vegetables is also eliminated or greatly reduced. And evaporated skimmed milk and other nonfat and low-fat dairy products—as well as puréed vegetables—add creamy richness.

Will your low-salt, low-fat soups taste flat? Absolutely not! Vegetables like celery and onion; herbs like oregano and rosemary; a clove or two of garlic; a splash of balsamic vinegar; and other flavorful ingredients will make your soups so full-bodied that no one will miss the salt. Flavor can be enhanced further by using one of the rich homemade stocks presented on pages 92 through 94. Or, if you prefer, substitute one of the many fine low- or no-salt nonfat commercial stocks and broths now available. (See page 23 for details.)

This chapter presents a variety of heart-warming low-fat, reduced-sodium soups that are surprisingly simple to prepare. You'll even find fat-free cooking tips that will help you give your own favorite recipes a slimming makeover. So take out your kettle, and get ready to enjoy a dish that is as nutritious as it is delectable. It's easy, once you know the secrets of fat-free Italian cooking.

Chicken Capellini Soup

Yield: 8 servings

7 cups Savory Chicken or Turkey Stock (page 93)

4 cloves garlic, peeled

1$\frac{1}{2}$ teaspoons dried Italian seasoning or dried rosemary

1 tablespoon instant chicken bouillon granules

$\frac{1}{8}$ teaspoon ground white pepper

1 medium-large yellow onion, chopped

2 medium carrots, peeled, halved lengthwise, and sliced, divided

2 medium stalks celery, sliced (include the leaves), divided

2 cups diced cooked chicken breast

3 ounces capellini (angel hair) pasta, broken into 2-inch pieces (about 1 cup)

2 tablespoons finely chopped fresh Italian parsley

1. Place the chicken stock, garlic cloves, Italian seasoning or rosemary, bouillon granules, pepper, and onion in a 4-quart pot. Add half of the carrots and half of the celery, and bring to a boil over high heat. Reduce the heat to low, cover, and simmer for 20 minutes, or until the vegetables are tender.

2. Using a slotted spoon, transfer the vegetables and garlic cloves to a blender. Add 1$\frac{1}{2}$ cups of the hot broth, and place the lid on the blender, leaving the top slightly ajar to allow steam to escape. Carefully blend at low speed until the mixture is smooth. Return the puréed mixture to the pot, and stir to mix well.

3. Add the remaining carrots and celery to the pot, and bring to a boil over high heat. Reduce the heat to low, cover, and simmer for 15 minutes, or until the vegetables are tender. Add the chicken, and simmer for 5 additional minutes.

4. Add the capellini to the pot, and bring to a boil over high heat. Reduce the heat to medium, cover, and simmer for about 3 minutes, or until the pasta is al dente. (Be careful not to overcook, as the pasta will continue to soften in the hot soup.)

5. Stir the parsley into the soup. Ladle the soup into individual serving bowls, and serve hot.

NUTRITIONAL FACTS (PER 1-CUP SERVING)

Calories: 131   Carbohydrates: 18.7 g   Cholesterol: 25 mg
Fat: 1.1 g   Fiber: 1.1 g   Protein: 19 g   Sodium: 364 mg

You Save: Calories: 51   Fat: 5.8 g

Lentil Zuppa

1. Coat a 4-quart pot with nonstick cooking spray, and preheat over medium heat. Add the garlic, and sauté for about 30 seconds, or just until the garlic begins to turn color.

2. Add all of the remaining ingredients except for the Parmesan to the pot, and bring to a boil over high heat. Reduce the heat to low, cover, and simmer for about 45 minutes, or until the lentils are soft and the liquid is thick. Remove and discard the bay leaves.

3. Transfer 2 cups of the soup—including vegetables and hot broth—to a blender, and place the lid on the blender, leaving the top slightly ajar to allow steam to escape. Carefully blend at low speed until the mixture is smooth. Return the puréed soup to the pot, and stir to mix well.

4. Ladle the soup into individual serving bowls, and serve hot, topping each serving with a rounded teaspoon of the Parmesan if desired.

Yield: 8 servings

2 teaspoons crushed fresh garlic

1½ cups dried brown lentils, cleaned (page 80)

6 ounces ham (at least 97% lean), diced

1 medium yellow onion, chopped

2 medium stalks celery, chopped (include the leaves)

1 large carrot, peeled and chopped

7 cups Savory Chicken or Turkey Stock (page 93)

1 teaspoon chicken bouillon granules

1½ teaspoons dried oregano

2 bay leaves

½ teaspoon ground black pepper

¼ cup plus 2 tablespoons grated nonfat or reduced-fat Parmesan cheese (optional)

NUTRITIONAL FACTS (PER 1-CUP SERVING)
Calories: 186   Carbohydrates: 22.5 g   Cholesterol: 11 mg
Fat: 1.3 g   Fiber: 5.3 g   Protein: 21 g   Sodium: 315 mg

You Save: Calories: 84   Fat: 10.3

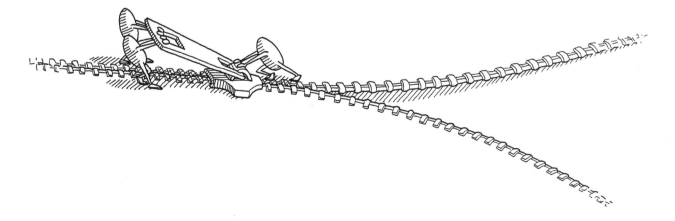

Bean Basics

If you really want to get the fat out of your diet, think beans—or *fagioli,* as the Italians say. A hearty and satisfying alternative to meat, beans are fat-free and rich in protein, complex carbohydrates, B vitamins, iron, zinc, copper, and potassium. As for fiber, no other food surpasses beans. Just a half cup of cooked beans provides 4 to 8 grams of fiber—up to four times the amount found in other plant foods.

The health benefits of eating beans are well established. Not only can beans help lower cholesterol, but they also stabilize blood sugar levels, making you feel full and satisfied long after the meal is over—a definite benefit if you're watching your weight.

Luckily, Italian cuisine makes good use of this versatile ingredient. From appetizers and soups to salads, side dishes, and entrées, beans are a prominent ingredient in a variety of flavorful dishes. The beans most commonly used in Italian dishes are cannellini, also known as white kidney beans; white beans such as Great Northern and navy; red kidney beans; garbanzos, also known as chickpeas; and lentils.

Some people avoid eating beans because of "bean bloat." What causes this problem? Complex sugars in beans, called oligosaccharides, sometimes form gas when broken down in the lower intestine. This side effect usually subsides when beans are made a regular part of the diet, and the body becomes more efficient at digesting them. The proper cleaning, soaking, and cooking of beans can also help prevent bean bloat. The following techniques will help you make beans a delicious and healthful part of your diet.

Cleaning

Because beans are a natural product, packages of dried beans sometimes contain shriveled or discolored beans, as well as small twigs and other items. Before cooking, sort through your beans and discard any that are discolored or blemished. Rinse the beans well, cover them with water, and discard any beans that float to the top.

Soaking

There are two methods used to soak beans in preparation for cooking. If you have time—if you intend to cook your dish much later in the day, for instance—you may want to use the long method, as this method is best for reducing the gas-producing oligosaccharides. If dinner is just a couple of hours away, though, the quick method is your best bet. Keep in mind that not all beans must be soaked before cooking. Black-eyed peas, brown and red lentils, and split peas do not require soaking.

The Long Method

After cleaning the beans, place them in a large bowl or pot, and cover with four times as much water. Soak for at least four hours, and for as long as twelve hours. If soaking the beans for more than four hours, place the bowl or pot in the refrigerator. After soaking, discard the water and replace with fresh water before cooking.

The Quick Method

After cleaning the beans, place them in a large pot, and cover with four times as much water. Bring the pot to a boil over high heat, and continue to boil for two minutes. Remove from the heat, cover, and let stand for one hour. After soaking, discard the water and replace with fresh water before cooking.

Cooking

To cook beans for use in salads, casseroles, and other dishes that contain little or no liquid, clean and soak as described above, discard the soaking water, and replace with two cups of fresh water for each cup of dried beans. When beans are to be cooked in soups or stews that include acidic ingredients—lemon juice or vinegar, for instance—add these ingredients at the end of the cooking time. Acidic foods can toughen the beans' outer layer, slowing the rate at which they cook. Large amounts of tomato products or salt can also slow the rate at which beans cook.

How do you know when beans are done? You will be able to mash them easily with a fork. Keep in mind that old beans may take longer to cook.

During long cooking times, periodically check the pot, and add more liquid—water or broth—if necessary.

The following table gives approximate cooking times for several different kinds of beans and legumes. Need a meal in a hurry? Lentils and split peas require no soaking and cook quickly. Lentils are the fastest cooking of all the beans—they can be ready in less than thirty minutes. Split peas cook in less than an hour.

Cooking Times for Dried Beans and Legumes

Bean or Legume	Cooking Time
Black, cannellini, garbanzo, Great Northern, kidney, navy, and pinto.	$1\frac{1}{2}$–2 hours
Black-eyed peas*	1–$1\frac{1}{4}$ hours
Lentils, brown*	25–30 minutes
Lentils, red*	15–20 minutes
Lima beans, baby	45 minutes–$1\frac{1}{4}$ hours
Lima beans, large	1–$1\frac{1}{2}$ hours
Split peas*	45–50 minutes

*These beans do not require soaking time.

Mama Mia Meatball Soup

Yield: *9 servings*

6 cups Hearty Beef Stock (page 92) or water

1 tablespoon instant beef bouillon granules

1 teaspoon dried Italian seasoning

¼ teaspoon ground black pepper

1 medium yellow onion, chopped

2 medium carrots, peeled, halved lengthwise, and sliced, divided

2 medium stalks celery, sliced, divided

1 can (14½ ounces) unsalted tomatoes, crushed

1 cup fresh or frozen (unthawed) cut green beans

4 ounces ziti pasta (about 1½ cups)

MEATBALLS

¾ pound 95% lean ground beef

¼ cup grated nonfat or reduced-fat Parmesan cheese

1 egg white

1 teaspoon dried Italian seasoning

¼ teaspoon ground black pepper

1. To make the meatballs, combine all of the meatball ingredients in a medium-sized bowl, and mix well. Shape the mixture into ¾-inch balls. Coat a baking sheet with nonstick cooking spray, and arrange the meatballs on the pan. Bake at 350°F for about 18 minutes, or until the meatballs are no longer pink inside. Set aside.

2. Place the stock or water, bouillon granules, Italian seasoning, pepper, and onion in a 4-quart pot. Add half of the carrots and half of the celery, and bring to a boil over high heat. Reduce the heat to low, cover, and simmer for 20 minutes, or until the vegetables are tender.

3. Using a slotted spoon, transfer the vegetables to a blender. Add 1½ cups of the hot broth, and place the lid on the blender, leaving the top slightly ajar to allow steam to escape. Carefully blend at low speed until the mixture is smooth. Return the puréed mixture to the pot, and stir to mix well.

4. Add the remaining carrots and celery to the pot, along with the undrained tomatoes, and bring to a boil over high heat. Reduce the heat to low, cover, and simmer for 10 minutes, or until the vegetables are barely tender.

5. Add the meatballs, green beans, and pasta to the pot, and bring to a boil over high heat. Reduce the heat to medium-low, cover, and simmer for about 8 minutes, or until the pasta is al dente. (Be careful not to overcook, as the pasta will continue to soften in the hot soup.)

6. Ladle the soup into individual serving bowls, and serve hot.

NUTRITIONAL FACTS (PER 1-CUP SERVING)
Calories: 142   Carbohydrates: 15.8 g   Cholesterol: 25 mg
Fat: 2.1 g   Fiber: 2.4 g   Protein: 15 g   Sodium: 356 mg

You Save: Calories: 86   Fat: 10.2 g

Savory Sausage Soup

1. Coat the bottom of a 4-quart pot with nonstick cooking spray, and place over medium heat. Add the sausage, and cook, stirring to crumble, until the meat is no longer pink. Drain off any excess fat. (If the meat is very lean, there will be no fat to drain off.)

2. Add the undrained tomatoes, carrots, celery, onion, stock, bouillon granules, basil, and pepper to the pot, and bring to a boil over high heat. Reduce the heat to low, cover, and simmer for 25 minutes, or until the vegetables are tender.

3. Add the cabbage and beans to the pot, and simmer for 10 additional minutes, or until the cabbage is tender and the flavors are well blended.

4. Ladle the soup into individual serving bowls, and serve hot.

NUTRITIONAL FACTS (PER 1-CUP SERVING)

Calories: 107   Carbohydrates: 9.6 g   Cholesterol: 21 mg
Fat: 1.4 g   Fiber: 3.5 g   Protein: 14 g   Sodium: 333 mg

You Save: Calories: 93   Fat: 10.5

Yield: 12 servings

1 pound Turkey Italian Sausage (page 182)

1 can (14½ ounces) unsalted tomatoes, crushed

3 medium carrots, peeled, halved lengthwise, and sliced

3 medium stalks celery, thinly sliced (include the leaves)

1 medium yellow onion, chopped

5 cups Savory Chicken or Turkey Stock (page 93)

2 teaspoons instant chicken bouillon granules

1½ teaspoons dried basil

¼ teaspoon ground black pepper

4 cups coarsely shredded cabbage

1 can (15 ounces) cannellini or kidney beans, rinsed and drained

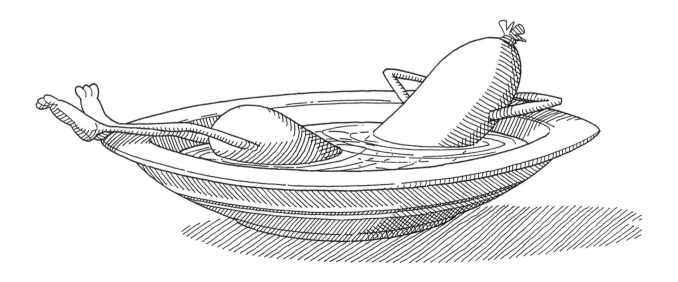

Hearty Minestrone

Yield: *14 servings*

6 cups Hearty Beef Stock (page 92) or water

1 tablespoon plus 1 teaspoon instant beef bouillon granules

2 teaspoons dried Italian seasoning

1/2 teaspoon ground black pepper

1 large Spanish onion, chopped, divided

4 medium carrots, peeled, halved lengthwise, and sliced, divided

4 medium stalks celery, sliced (include the leaves), divided

1 can (14 1/2 ounces) unsalted tomatoes, crushed

3 cups coarsely shredded cabbage

1 1/2 cups fresh or frozen (unthawed) whole kernel corn

1 1/2 cups sliced zucchini

1 can (15 ounces) cannellini, kidney, or garbanzo beans, rinsed and drained

3 ounces seashell pasta (about 1 1/4 cups)

1/2 cup plus 2 tablespoons grated nonfat or reduced-fat Parmesan cheese (garnish)

1. Place the stock or water, bouillon granules, Italian seasoning, pepper, half of the onion, half of the carrots, and half of the celery, in a 5-quart pot, and bring to a boil over high heat. Reduce the heat to low, cover, and simmer for 20 minutes, or until the vegetables are tender.

2. Using a slotted spoon, transfer the vegetables to a blender. Add 1 1/2 cups of the hot broth, and place the lid on the blender, leaving the top slightly ajar to allow steam to escape. Carefully blend at low speed until the mixture is smooth. Return the puréed mixture to the pot, and stir to mix well.

3. Add the remaining onion, carrots, and celery, along with the undrained tomatoes, to the pot, and bring to a boil over high heat. Reduce the heat to low, cover, and simmer for 10 minutes, or until the vegetables are barely tender.

4. Add the cabbage and corn to the pot, and simmer for 10 minutes, or until the cabbage is tender.

5. Add the zucchini, beans, and pasta to the pot, and bring to a boil over high heat. Reduce the heat to low, cover, and simmer for about 8 minutes, or until the pasta is al dente. (Be careful not to overcook, as the pasta will continue to soften in the hot soup.)

6. Ladle the soup into individual serving bowls, and serve hot, topping each serving with a rounded teaspoon of Parmesan.

NUTRITIONAL FACTS (PER 1-CUP SERVING)
Calories: 103   Carbohydrates: 18.6 g   Cholesterol: 2 mg
Fat: 0.4 g   Fiber: 3.8 g   Protein: 6.2 g   Sodium: 339 mg

You Save: Calories: 49   Fat: 6 g

White Bean and Pasta Soup

1. Place all of the ingredients except for the pasta in a 4-quart pot, and bring to a boil over high heat. Reduce the heat to low, cover, and simmer, stirring occasionally, for about 1 hour and 30 minutes, or until the beans are soft. Remove the bay leaf.

2. Transfer 3 cups of the soup—including beans, vegetables, and hot broth—to a blender. Place the lid on the blender, leaving the top slightly ajar to allow steam to escape, and carefully blend at low speed until the mixture is smooth. Return the puréed soup to the pot, and stir to mix well.

3. Add the pasta to the pot, and bring to a boil over medium-high heat. Reduce the heat to low, cover, and simmer for about 8 minutes, or until the pasta is al dente. (Be careful not to overcook, as the pasta will continue to soften in the hot soup.)

4. Ladle the soup into individual serving bowls, and serve hot.

NUTRITIONAL FACTS (PER 1-CUP SERVING)

Calories: 194 Carbohydrates: 32 g Cholesterol: 13 mg
Fat: 1.3 g Fiber: 7.1 g Protein: 13.5 g Sodium: 345 mg

You Save: Calories: 67 Fat: 7.5

Yield: 9 servings

1½ cups dried navy beans or Great Northern beans, cleaned and soaked (page 80)

8 cups water

8 ounces ham (at least 97% lean), diced

1 medium Spanish onion, chopped

2 medium carrots, peeled, halved lengthwise, and sliced

2 large stalks celery, thinly sliced (include the leaves)

2 teaspoons instant chicken bouillon granules

1 teaspoon crushed fresh garlic

1 teaspoon dried sage

1 bay leaf

½ teaspoon ground black pepper

4 ounces wagon wheel pasta (about 1½ cups)

Tuscan Tomato Soup

Yield: *5 servings*

1½ teaspoons crushed fresh garlic

½ cup chopped onion

2 cans (14½ ounces each) unsalted tomatoes, crushed

2 cups unsalted Savory Chicken or Turkey Stock (page 93) or Garden Vegetable Stock (page 94)

2 teaspoons instant chicken or vegetable bouillon granules

2 teaspoons dried Italian seasoning

¼ teaspoon coarsely ground black pepper

3 ounces orzo or other small pasta (about ½ cup)

2½ tablespoons grated nonfat or reduced-fat Parmesan cheese (garnish)

1. Coat a 2-quart pot with nonstick cooking spray, and preheat over medium heat. Add the garlic, and sauté for about 30 seconds, or until the garlic starts to turn color.

2. Add the onion, undrained tomatoes, stock, bouillon granules, Italian seasoning, and pepper to the pot, and bring to a boil over high heat. Reduce the heat to low, cover, and simmer for 20 minutes, or until the onions are soft.

3. Transfer 2 cups of the soup—including vegetables and hot broth—to a blender, and place the lid on the blender, leaving the top slightly ajar to allow steam to escape. Carefully blend the mixture at low speed until smooth. Repeat this procedure until all of the soup has been blended.

4. Return all of the puréed soup to the pot, and bring the mixture to a boil over medium-high heat. Add the orzo, and reduce the heat to medium-low. Cover and cook, stirring occasionally, for about 8 minutes, or until the orzo is al dente. (Be careful not to overcook, as the pasta will continue to soften in the hot soup.)

5. Ladle the soup into individual serving bowls, and serve hot, topping each serving with a rounded teaspoon of the Parmesan.

NUTRITIONAL FACTS (PER 1-CUP SERVING)

Calories: 113   Carbohydrates: 20 g   Cholesterol: 1 mg
Fat: 0.5 g   Fiber: 2.5 g   Protein: 7.1 g   Sodium: 362 mg

You Save: Calories: 74   Fat: 9.1

Top Left: Tuscan Tuna and Pasta Salad
(page 60)

Top Right: White Bean, Basil, and
Tomato Salad (page 51)

Bottom: Antipasto Pasta Salad (page 63)

Top: Spinach-Stuffed Tomatoes (page 75)

Center: Zucchini With Roasted Red Peppers and Onions (page 70)

Bottom: Carrots Marsala (page 72)

Top: Hearty Minestrone (page 84)

Center: Chicken Capellini Soup (page 78)

Bottom: Focaccia With Italian Vegetables (page 145)

Top and Bottom: Linguine With Ham and Artichoke Hearts (page 105)

Center: Italian Country Angel Hair Pasta (page 106)

Escarole and Orzo Soup

1. Place the water or stock, onion, carrot, celery, bouillon granules, garlic cloves, and pepper in a 4-quart pot, and bring to a boil over high heat. Reduce the heat to low, cover, and simmer for 20 minutes, or until the vegetables are tender.

2. Using a slotted spoon, transfer the vegetables and garlic cloves to a blender. Add 1 cup of the hot broth, and place the lid on the blender, leaving the top slightly ajar to allow steam to escape. Carefully blend the mixture at low speed until smooth. Return the puréed mixture to the pot, and stir to mix well.

3. Add the orzo to the pot, and bring to a boil over high heat. Reduce the heat to medium, cover, and cook for about 8 minutes, or until the orzo is almost al dente. Add the escarole, and cook, uncovered, for 2 additional minutes, or until the orzo is al dente and the escarole is wilted. (Be careful not to overcook, as the pasta will continue to soften in the hot soup.)

4. Ladle the soup into individual serving bowls, and serve hot, topping each serving with a heaping teaspoon of Parmesan.

Yield: 10 servings

8 cups water or Savory Chicken or Turkey Stock (page 93)

1 medium yellow onion, chopped

1 large carrot, peeled, halved lengthwise, and sliced

1 large stalk celery, thinly sliced (include the leaves)

1 tablespoon plus 1 teaspoon instant chicken bouillon granules

4 cloves garlic, peeled

$\frac{1}{8}$ teaspoon ground white pepper

3 ounces orzo (about $\frac{1}{2}$ cup)

1 head escarole (about 1 pound), rinsed well and torn into pieces

$\frac{1}{2}$ cup grated nonfat or reduced-fat Parmesan cheese (garnish)

NUTRITIONAL FACTS (PER 1-CUP SERVING)

Calories: 66   Carbohydrates: 11.5 g   Cholesterol: 2 mg
Fat: 0.3 g   Fiber: 1.3 g   Protein: 4.3 g   Sodium: 363 mg

You Save: Calories: 65   Fat: 8.2 g

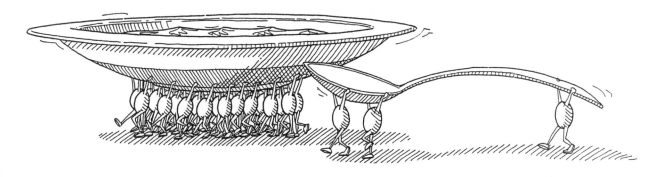

Lightening Up Your Soup Recipes

Like the soups of many other cuisines, Italian soups often rely on bacon fat, fatty ham, or other high-fat meats for flavor. Unhealthy amounts of butter and oil also add unwanted fat. But try and omit these ingredients and your soup is sure to taste flat—right? Not if you know a few tricks of the trade. Here are some ideas for getting the fat—as well as any excess salt—out of all your favorite soup recipes.

Reducing Fat

❑ When you omit the oil, butter, or high-fat meats from broths and soup stocks, enhance richness and flavor with puréed vegetables, as is done in Mama Mia Meatball Soup (page 82). In this recipe, onions, carrots, and celery are first cooked in the soup stock, and then puréed and returned to the pot. This results in a richer-tasting, more flavorful soup base.

❑ To add extra richness to low-fat bean soups, purée some of the broth and beans from the soup. Then return the mixture to the pot for added thickness.

❑ If your recipe contains beef, pork, or poultry, use the leanest cuts available, and trim off any visible fat. (See Chapter 1 for a discussion of lean meats and poultry.) If you have to brown the meat before adding it to the soup, use a nonstick cooking spray for browning, or—if you choose to brown in oil—be sure to drain off any excess fat before adding the meat to the soup pot. (See the inset on page 186 for tips on browning without fat.)

❑ After preparing a meat stock or soup, refrigerate it for a few hours or overnight to allow the fat to rise to the top and harden. Lift off the hardened fat for a fat-free broth that has almost no calories.

❑ When there's no time to refrigerate your stock or broth, defat it quickly by placing it in a fat separator cup. This specially designed cup has a spout that pours stock from the bottom of the cup. The fat, which floats to the top, stays in the cup.

❑ If you don't have a fat separator cup, quickly defat your stock with ice cubes. Just place a few cubes in a pot of warm—not hot—soup, and let the cubes remain in the stock for a few seconds. Then remove the cubes, as well as the fat that clings to them.

❑ If you choose to use a canned broth, keep in mind that most broths are quite low in fat, and that any fat present will have floated to the top. When you open the can, simply spoon out and discard the fat. Now you have fat-free broth!

❑ If your recipe contains milk, substitute 1-percent low-fat or skim milk for the whole milk. For a richer taste, add 1 to 2 tablespoons of instant nonfat dry milk powder to each cup of low-fat or skim milk.

❑ If your recipe contains cream, substitute evaporated skimmed milk—or 1 cup of low-fat or skim milk mixed with $\frac{1}{3}$ cup instant nonfat dry milk powder—for the high-fat cream.

❑ To add extra richness to low-fat cream soups, purée some of the broth and vegetables from the soup. Then return the mixture to the pot to thicken the soup.

❑ Another way to add richness to low-fat cream soups is to add a little grated nonfat Parmesan cheese to the soup. Let the soup simmer for a minute or two after adding the Parmesan. Since this product contains some added starches, it will both thicken and flavor the soup.

❑ If your recipe contains sour cream, substitute a reduced-fat or nonfat brand for the full-fat product.

❑ When you omit the fat from a soup recipe, increase the herbs and spices by about 25 percent. This will help compensate for the lost flavor, and at the same time reduce the need for salt.

Reducing Salt

❑ If your recipe has a stock or bouillon base, either use a commercial salt-free or low-salt stock, or make your own low- or no-salt stock. (See the inset on page 92 for salt-free soup stock recipes.)

□ To make your soup stock more flavorful without adding salt, reduce the stock by simmering it uncovered until some of the liquid evaporates. This will intensify the flavors.

□ To prevent your low-salt soup from tasting flat, add a little lemon juice or vinegar to the finished product. These ingredients give the impression of saltiness.

□ Add a pinch of white pepper to your pot of low-salt soup. The pungency of this spice will reduce the need for salt.

Cream of Cauliflower Soup

1. Remove and discard the cauliflower's outer leaves and core, and separate the cauliflower into small florets. Place the florets in a 2-quart pot and add the stock, onion, bouillon granules, and pepper. Bring to a boil over high heat. Reduce the heat to medium-low, cover, and cook, stirring occasionally, for about 10 minutes, or until the cauliflower is tender.

2. Using a slotted spoon, transfer half of the cauliflower to a blender. Add the milk, Parmesan, and nutmeg, and place the lid on the blender, leaving the top slightly ajar to allow steam to escape. Carefully blend at low speed until the mixture is smooth. Return the puréed mixture to the pot, and stir to mix well.

3. Place the pot over medium heat, and cook, stirring constantly, just until the soup begins to boil. Add a little more milk if the soup seems too thick.

4. Ladle the soup into individual serving bowls, and serve hot, topping each serving with a sprinkling of chives or dill.

Yield: 4 servings

1 large head cauliflower (about 2 pounds)

1 cup plus 2 tablespoons Savory Chicken or Turkey Stock (page 93)

½ cup chopped onion

1 teaspoon instant chicken bouillon granules

1 pinch ground white pepper

1 cup skim milk

¼ cup grated nonfat Parmesan cheese

1 pinch ground nutmeg

1 tablespoon finely chopped fresh chives or dill (garnish)

NUTRITIONAL FACTS (PER 1-CUP SERVING)

Calories: 89   Carbohydrates: 11.1 g   Cholesterol: 4 mg
Fat: 0.5 g   Fiber: 2.5 g   Protein: 10 g   Sodium: 335 mg

You Save: Calories: 189   Fat: 23.8 g

Potato and Leek Soup

Yield: *9 servings*

2 leeks

2½ pounds white potatoes, peeled and diced (about 6–7 medium)

2 medium stalks celery, thinly sliced (include the leaves)

4 cups Savory Chicken or Turkey Stock (page 93)

1 tablespoon instant chicken bouillon granules

¼ teaspoon ground white pepper

2 heads garlic, roasted (page 62)

¾ cup evaporated skimmed milk

1. Cut the leeks in half lengthwise and rinse well. Thinly slice the white and light green parts, and place in a 4-quart pot. Thinly slice the tender parts of the dark green shoots, and set aside as garnish.

2. Add the potatoes, celery, stock, bouillon granules, and white pepper to the pot, and bring to a boil over high heat. Reduce heat to low, cover, and simmer, stirring occasionally, for 15 to 20 minutes, or until the potatoes are tender.

3. Transfer half of the vegetables and 1½ cups of the hot broth to a blender. Squeeze the pulp from the roasted garlic heads, and add to the blender. Place the lid on the blender, leaving the top slightly ajar to allow steam to escape, and carefully blend the mixture at low speed until smooth. Return the puréed mixture to the pot, and stir to mix well.

4. Add the evaporated milk to the pot, and stir to mix. Cook, stirring frequently, for about 2 minutes, or until the mixture is heated through.

5. Ladle the soup into individual serving bowls, and serve hot, topping each serving with a sprinkling of the leek shoots.

NUTRITIONAL FACTS (PER 1-CUP SERVING)

Calories: 143   Carbohydrates: 30.8 g   Cholesterol: 1 mg
Fat: 0.3 g   Fiber: 2.8 g   Protein: 4.2 g   Sodium: 308 mg

You Save: Calories: 114   Fat: 15.9

Pasta Fagioli

1. Coat the bottom of a 4-quart pot with nonstick cooking spray, and preheat over medium heat. Add the ground beef and garlic, and cook, stirring to crumble, until the meat is no longer pink. Drain off any excess fat. (If the meat is 95% lean, there will be no fat to drain off.)

2. Add the onion, carrot, celery, undrained tomatoes, bouillon granules, Italian seasoning, pepper, and water to the pot, and bring to a boil over high heat. Reduce the heat to low, cover, and simmer for 15 minutes, or until the vegetables are tender.

3. Add the beans and pasta to the pot, and bring to a boil over high heat. Reduce the heat to medium-low, cover, and simmer for about 9 minutes, or until the pasta is al dente. (Be careful not to overcook, as the pasta will continue to soften in the hot soup.)

4. Ladle the soup into individual serving bowls, and serve hot.

Yield: *12 servings*

1 pound 95% lean ground beef

1 teaspoon crushed fresh garlic

1 medium Spanish onion, chopped

1 large carrot, peeled, halved lengthwise, and sliced

2 large stalks celery, thinly sliced (include the leaves)

2 cans (14½ ounces each) unsalted tomatoes, crushed

1 tablespoon instant beef bouillon granules

2½ teaspoons dried Italian seasoning

¼ teaspoon ground black pepper

4 cups water

1 can (1 pound) red kidney beans, rinsed and drained

6 ounces wagon wheel or ziti pasta (about 2¼ cups)

NUTRITIONAL FACTS (PER 1-CUP SERVING)

Calories: 179   Carbohydrates: 25.7 g   Cholesterol: 24 mg
Fat: 2.1 g   Fiber: 4.9 g   Protein: 14.3 g   Sodium: 287 mg

You Save: Calories: 61   Fat: 7 g

Flavorful Fat-Free Soup Stocks

Whether you're making Italian White Bean Soup or following your own treasured recipe, a rich-tasting, well-seasoned stock is sure to result in a more flavorful dish. And while many low- and no-fat stocks are now commercially available (see page 23 for details), the flavor of canned or made-from-mix brews simply can't compare with that of your own homemade stocks. Just as important, by making your stock from scratch, you can insure that your product is low in both fat and salt.

The following stocks are used throughout the recipes in this chapter, and will work beautifully in your own soup recipes, as well. These stocks are also a great way to enhance flavor when making rice or cooking vegetables. In fact, you can use these broths freely, as they are fat- and sodium-free, and contain only about 15 calories per cup!

Hearty Beef Stock

Yield: *about 2½ quarts*

4 pounds beef bones

3 medium yellow onions, quartered, or 2 leeks, washed, trimmed, and coarsely chopped

3 medium stalks celery, coarsely chopped (include the leaves)

6 garlic cloves, chopped

4 sprigs fresh parsley

1 teaspoon dried thyme

1 teaspoon dried marjoram

2 bay leaves

¼ teaspoon ground black pepper

4 quarts water

1. Coat a shallow roasting pan with nonstick cooking spray, and arrange the bones in a single layer in the pan. Roast the bones at 425°F for 45 minutes to 1 hour, or until they are browned, turning them after 25 minutes.

2. Place the bones in a 6-quart stock pot, and add the vegetables and seasonings. Pour ½ cup of the water into the roasting pan, and scrape up any crusty browned bits from the bottom of the pan. Add this mixture to the stock pot. Then add just enough of the water to cover the mixture by 1 inch.

3. Bring the mixture to a boil over high heat. Reduce the heat to low, and simmer uncovered for 5 minutes. Remove any froth that forms on surface of the stock.

4. Cover the pot, leaving the lid slightly ajar to allow steam to escape. Simmer the mixture slowly for at least 2 hours, and for up to 5 hours. The longer you simmer the stock, the more it will condense and intensify its flavors.

5. Cool the stock to room temperature, and pour it through a strainer lined with cheesecloth. Transfer the stock to a covered pot or other container, and refrigerate overnight.

6. The next day, remove and discard any fat that has risen to the surface of the stock. Use the stock immediately, or pour it into freezer containers and freeze for up to 6 months. (Note that when freezing stock, you should always leave a little room in the container for expansion.)

Savory Chicken or Turkey Stock

After slicing the meat off a roasted chicken or turkey, you are left with bones and, usually, small bits of meat. Instead of throwing out these leavings, use the carcass to make a rich, flavorful stock.

1. Break up the chicken or turkey carcass, and place in a 6-quart stock pot. (If using backs and wings, place them in the pot as is.) Add any defatted drippings left over from roasting the turkey or chicken. Add the vegetables, seasonings, and just enough of the water to cover the mixture by 1 inch.

2. Bring the mixture to a boil over high heat. Reduce the heat to low, and simmer uncovered for 5 minutes. Remove any froth that forms on the surface of the stock.

3. Cover the pot, leaving the lid slightly ajar to allow steam to escape. Simmer the mixture slowly for at least 2 hours, and for up to 5 hours. The longer you simmer the stock, the more it will condense and intensify its flavors.

4. Cool the stock to room temperature, and pour it through a strainer lined with cheesecloth. Transfer the stock to a covered pot or other container, and refrigerate overnight.

5. The next day, remove and discard any fat that has risen to the surface of the stock. Use the stock immediately, or pour it into freezer containers and freeze for up to 6 months. (Note that when freezing stock, you must always leave a little room in the container for expansion.)

Yield: *about 2½ quarts*

3 roast-chicken carcasses, 1 roast-turkey carcass, or 3 pounds chicken or turkey backs and wings

3 medium onions, quartered

2 medium carrots, peeled and sliced

2 medium stalks celery, sliced (include the leaves)

4 cloves garlic, chopped

2 bay leaves

1 teaspoon dried crushed thyme or savory

¼ teaspoon ground black pepper, or 6 whole peppercorns

4 quarts water

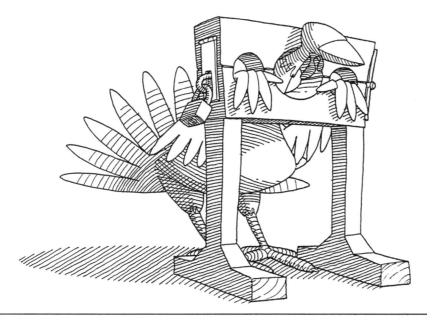

Garden Vegetable Stock

Yield: *about 2½ quarts*

3 medium yellow onions, thinly sliced

3 medium stalks celery, thinly sliced (include the leaves)

3 medium carrots, peeled, halved lengthwise, and thinly sliced

3 medium tomatoes, chopped

1½ cups thinly sliced fresh mushrooms

4 sprigs fresh parsley

4 cloves garlic, chopped

1 teaspoon dried marjoram

1 teaspoon dried thyme

1 bay leaf

¼ teaspoon ground white pepper

3 quarts water

You can vary this stock to make use of any leftover vegetables you have handy. Simply save up vegetable peelings (of organic produce only); bits of herbs; and leftover bits of onion, celery, carrots, potatoes, mushrooms, parsnips, turnips, rutabagas, and other vegetables. Toss all of these items into a freezer container until you're ready to make the stock. Avoid using any strong-flavored vegetables like cabbage; collard, mustard, and other greens; broccoli; and peppers, as they can overwhelm the flavors of the other ingredients.

1. Place all of the ingredients except for the water in a 6-quart stock pot. Add just enough of the water to start the vegetables cooking (about 1 cup). Bring the mixture to a boil over high heat. Reduce the heat to medium, cover, and cook for about 15 minutes, or until the vegetables are wilted and tender.

2. Add the remaining water to the pot, and bring the mixture to a boil over high heat. Reduce the heat to low and cover, leaving the lid slightly ajar to allow steam to escape. Simmer the mixture slowly for at least 1 hour, and for up to 2 hours. The longer you simmer the stock, the more it will condense and intensify its flavors.

3. Cool the stock to room temperature and pour it through a strainer lined with cheesecloth, pressing as much liquid as possible from the vegetables before discarding them. Use the stock immediately, or pour it into freezer containers and freeze for up to 6 months. (Note that when freezing stock, you must always leave a little room in the container for expansion.)

Golden Garbanzo Soup

1. Coat a 4-quart pot with nonstick olive oil cooking spray, and preheat over medium heat. Add the garlic, and sauté for about 30 seconds, or just until the garlic begins to turn color.

2. Add all of the remaining ingredients except for the pasta to the pot, and bring to a boil over high heat. Reduce the heat to low, cover, and simmer for 30 minutes, or until the vegetables are soft. Remove and discard the bay leaves.

3. Remove 4 cups of the soup—including vegetables and hot broth—from the pot. Place 2 cups of the removed soup in a blender, and place the lid on the blender, leaving the top slightly ajar to allow steam to escape. Carefully blend at low speed until the mixture is smooth. Return the puréed mixture to the pot, and stir to mix well. Repeat with the remaining 2 cups of removed soup.

4. Add the pasta to the pot, and bring to a boil over medium-high heat. Reduce the heat to medium-low, cover, and simmer for 10 minutes, or until the pasta is al dente. (Be careful not to overcook, as the pasta will continue to soften in the hot soup.)

5. Ladle the soup into individual serving bowls, and serve hot.

Yield: 9 servings

6 cloves fresh garlic, crushed

2 cans (1 pound each) garbanzo beans, rinsed and drained

1 large Spanish onion, chopped

2 medium carrots, peeled and diced

6 cups water or Savory Chicken or Turkey Stock (page 93)

2 tablespoons chopped fresh Italian parsley

2 teaspoons instant chicken bouillon granules

2 bay leaves

¼ teaspoon ground black pepper

4 ounces ziti or tube pasta (about 1½ cups)

NUTRITIONAL FACTS (PER 1-CUP SERVING)

Calories: 172   Carbohydrates: 30.8 g   Cholesterol: 0 mg
Fat: 1.9 g   Fiber: 4.4 g   Protein: 7.9 g   Sodium: 320 mg

You Save: Calories: 68   Fat: 7.5 g

Italian White Bean Soup

Yield: *11 servings*

2 cups dried navy beans or Great
   Northern beans, cleaned and
   soaked (page 80)

7 cups Savory Chicken or Turkey
   Stock (page 93) or water

1 large Spanish onion, chopped

6 medium plum tomatoes, peeled
   and diced

2 medium carrots, peeled, halved
   lengthwise, and sliced

2 large stalks celery, thinly sliced
   (include the leaves)

1 tablespoon plus 1½ teaspoons
   instant chicken bouillon
   granules

2½ teaspoons dried crushed
   oregano

¼ teaspoon ground black pepper

¼ teaspoon cayenne pepper

1 tablespoon white balsamic or
   white wine vinegar

1. Place all of the ingredients except for the vinegar in a 4-quart pot, and bring to a boil over high heat. Reduce the heat to low, cover, and simmer, stirring occasionally, for about 1 hour and 30 minutes, or until the beans are soft.

2. Transfer 4 cups of the soup—including vegetables, beans, and hot broth—to a blender. Place the lid on the blender, leaving the top slightly ajar to allow steam to escape, and carefully blend at low speed until the mixture is smooth. Return the puréed soup to the pot, and stir to mix well. Add the vinegar, and stir to mix well.

3. Ladle the soup into individual serving bowls, and serve hot.

NUTRITIONAL FACTS (PER 1-CUP SERVING)
Calories: 134   Carbohydrates: 24.2 g   Cholesterol: 0 mg
Fat: 0.5 g   Fiber: 7.5 g   Protein: 8.2 g   Sodium: 297 mg

You Save: Calories: 57   Fat: 6.5

Roasted Vegetable Soup

1. To make the roasted vegetables, combine all of the vegetables, including the garlic, in a large bowl, and toss to mix well. Add the vinegar, stock or water, rosemary, pepper, and, if desired, the olive oil, and stir to mix well.

2. Coat a nonstick 9-x-13-inch pan with the cooking spray, and spread the vegetables in an even layer in the pan. If you did not use the olive oil, spray the tops of the vegetables with the cooking spray.

3. Bake uncovered at 450°F for 15 minutes. Then turn the vegetables with a spatula, and bake for 15 additional minutes, or until the vegetables are tender and nicely browned.

4. Remove the vegetables from the oven, and pick out the roasted garlic cloves. Using the blade of a large knife, smash the cloves. Transfer the garlic and the other roasted vegetables to a 4-quart pot.

5. Use part of the stock or water to "rinse out" the pan used for roasting the vegetables. Add this liquid and the remainder of the stock or water to the pot, along with the bouillon granules and bay leaves. Bring the mixture to a boil over high heat. Reduce the heat to low, cover, and simmer for 15 minutes.

6. Add the barley to the pot, cover, and simmer for 15 additional minutes, or until the barley is tender and the flavors are well blended. Remove the bay leaves.

7. Ladle the soup into individual serving bowls, and serve hot.

NUTRITIONAL FACTS (PER 1-CUP SERVING)

Calories: 107   Carbohydrates: 22.3 g   Cholesterol: 0 mg
Fat: 0.7 g   Fiber: 2.7 g   Protein: 2.8 g   Sodium: 266 mg

You Save: Calories: 59   Fat: 6.8

Yield: *8 servings*

6 cups Hearty Beef Stock (page 92) or water

1 tablespoon beef bouillon granules

2 bay leaves

½ cup quick-cooking barley

ROASTED VEGETABLE MIXTURE

2 medium carrots, peeled and sliced ½-inch thick

2 medium yellow onions, cut into ½-inch-thick wedges

2 medium potatoes, unpeeled, cut into ¾-inch cubes

1½ cups thickly sliced fresh mushrooms

10 cloves garlic, peeled

1 tablespoon plus 1½ teaspoons balsamic vinegar

1 tablespoon Hearty Beef Stock (page 92) or water

1 tablespoon fresh rosemary or 1 teaspoon dried rosemary

¼ teaspoon coarsely ground black pepper

1 tablespoon extra virgin olive oil (optional)

Olive oil cooking spray (optional)

7

Pasta Perfection

Pasta is the very heart of Italian cooking. This is great news for people who live the low-fat lifestyle, since this popular food is practically fat-free. And pasta is also low in calories, with a modest 200 calories per cup. Just as important, if you choose whole grain products, your pasta dish will also provide you with much-needed B vitamins, minerals, and fiber, making it a real nutritional bargain.

But while pasta itself may be a fat-fighter's best friend, the same cannot always be said for the ingredients that top it. Take Fettuccine Alfredo, for example. Traditionally made with butter, cream, and Parmesan cheese, even a moderate portion of this dish delivers a whopping 600 calories and 40 grams of fat. For many people, this is almost half a day's calorie intake, and more than a full day's worth of fat!

Fortunately, there are many delicious alternatives to this and other fat-packed pasta dishes. In fact, with the multitude of low-fat and fat-free products now available, it is possible to transform *all* of your favorite pasta dishes into light and healthful meals. But can high-fat ingredients be eliminated without sacrificing flavor? Absolutely. This chapter will show you how.

The recipes in this chapter combine pasta with nonfat and low-fat cheeses and other dairy products, ultra-lean meats, poultry, seafood, vegetables, herbs and spices, and other wholesome ingredients. The result? Light and luscious pasta creations that even Mama would love. As a bonus, most of these dishes can be prepared in less than thirty minutes—a real benefit to the busy cook.

So if you've been afraid that adopting a low-fat lifestyle means giving up the irresistible flavors and aromas of your favorite pasta creations, put your fears aside. From Three-Cheese Manicotti to Fabulous Fettuccine Alfredo to Lemon Chicken Linguine, you'll find that pasta is the perfect answer whenever you want a dish that's light, healthy, and rich in the pleasures of Italian cuisine.

Fabulous Fettuccine Alfredo

Yield: *4 servings*

10 ounces fettuccine pasta

6 tablespoons grated nonfat Parmesan cheese

¼ cup thinly sliced scallions (garnish)

2 tablespoons chopped fresh parsley (garnish)

SAUCE

1 can (12 ounces) evaporated skimmed milk

2 tablespoons grated nonfat Parmesan cheese

2 teaspoons butter-flavored sprinkles

¼ teaspoon ground white pepper

1. Cook the pasta al dente according to package directions. Drain well, and return to the pot.

2. While the pasta is cooking, place all of the sauce ingredients in a small bowl. Stir to mix well.

3. Place the pot containing the pasta over medium heat, and pour the sauce over the pasta. Toss gently for a minute or 2, or until the sauce is heated through and just begins to boil. Add a little more milk if the sauce seems too dry.

4. Remove the pot from the heat, toss in the remaining 6 tablespoons of Parmesan, and serve immediately, topping each serving with some of the scallions and parsley.

NUTRITIONAL FACTS (PER 1½-CUP SERVING)

Calories: 390   Carbohydrates: 71 g   Cholesterol: 9 mg
Fat: 1.3 g   Fiber: 1.9 g   Protein: 22 g   Sodium: 352 mg

You Save: Calories: 355   Fat: 50 g

Variations

To make Fettuccine Alfredo With Sun-Dried Tomatoes, place ⅓ cup of sun-dried tomatoes and ⅓ cup of water in a small pot, and bring to a boil over high heat. Reduce the heat to low, cover, and simmer for 2 minutes, or until the tomatoes are plumped. Remove the pot from the heat and drain off any excess liquid. Add the plumped tomatoes to the pasta after tossing the pasta in the sauce in Step 3.

NUTRITIONAL FACTS (PER 1½-CUP SERVING)

Calories: 401   Carbohydrates: 74 g   Cholesterol: 9 mg
Fat: 1.5 g   Fiber: 2.5 g   Protein: 23 g   Sodium: 445 mg

You Save: Calories: 355   Fat: 50 g

To make Fettuccine Alfredo With Roasted Garlic, add 1 head of puréed roasted garlic (page 62) to the milk mixture in Step 2.

NUTRITIONAL FACTS (PER 1½-CUP SERVING)
Calories: 403   Carbohydrates: 74 g   Cholesterol: 9 mg
Fat: 1.4 g   Fiber: 2.1 g   Protein: 23 g   Sodium: 353 mg

You Save: Calories: 355   Fat: 50 g

FAT-FREE COOKING TIP

Reheating Pasta Without Fat

Try as you might, you can't always get pasta and its sauce ready at exactly the same time. When pasta is finished cooking before the sauce is done, the traditional method of holding the pasta is to drain it, toss it with butter or oil, return it to the pot, and cover to keep warm. The butter or oil keeps the pasta from forming a sticky mass. It also adds fat to an otherwise fat-free food.

The solution? Pour a little boiling water over the drained pasta—or simply use some of the pasta cooking water. Stir the pasta and hot water briefly, and drain again. Now you have fat-free pasta that is ready to be topped or tossed with your favorite sauce.

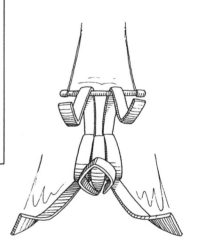

Getting the Fat Out of Your Pasta Recipes

It's a shame that most pasta recipes are so high in fat, as pasta is a natural for low-fat cooking. Happily, it's easy to do a healthy makeover of any pasta dish. Begin by taking the oil—and the salt, too—out of your cooking water. Then use the following table to replace high-fat foods like butter, cheese, and Italian sausage with low- and no-fat ingredients.

Substitutions That Save Fat

Instead of:	Substitute:	You Save:	Special Considerations:
1 cup butter or margarine.	1 cup Butter Buds liquid.	1,500 calories, 176 grams fat.	Butter Buds may be used in sauces, but not for sautéing.
	1 cup reduced-fat margarine or light butter.	800–1,200 calories, 88–112 grams fat.	*Nonfat* margarines generally do not melt well enough to be used for cooking or sautéing.
1 cup cream.	⅔ cup nonfat ricotta blended with ⅓ cup skim milk until smooth. (Add a little extra milk if the mixture is too thick.)	674 calories, 88 grams fat.	If using the ricotta mixture in a sauce that is to be heated, cook over low heat just until heated through. Some brands will separate if boiled.
	1 cup evaporated skimmed milk.	622 calories, 88 grams fat.	
	1 cup skim milk mixed with ⅓ cup nonfat dry milk powder.	622 calories, 88 grams fat.	
1 cup sour cream.	1 cup nonfat sour cream.	252 calories, 48 grams fat.	Some brands of nonfat sour cream will separate if heated. Choose a brand like Land O Lakes, which is heat-stable, if the sour cream will be used in a cooked sauce.
	1 cup plain nonfat yogurt.	355 calories, 48 grams fat.	All yogurts will separate if heated. To prevent this, stir 2 tablespoons of flour or 1 tablespoon of cornstarch into the yogurt before adding it to a cooked sauce.
1 cup whole ricotta.	1 cup nonfat ricotta.	248 calories, 32 grams fat.	This ingredient makes an excellent substitute in lasagna and other dishes.

Instead of:	Substitute:	You Save:	Special Considerations:
1 cup cream cheese.	1 cup nonfat cream cheese.	600 calories, 80 grams fat.	If using nonfat cream cheese in a sauce that is to be heated, cook over low heat just until heated through. Some brands will separate if boiled.
1 cup whole milk mozzarella.	1 cup nonfat mozzarella.	200 calories, 28 grams fat.	Both nonfat and reduced-fat mozzarella make an excellent substitute in lasagna and other dishes.
	1 cup reduced-fat mozzarella.	120 calories, 16 grams fat.	
1 cup whole milk provolone.	1 cup reduced-fat provolone.	120 calories, 12 grams fat.	This ingredient makes an excellent substitute in pizza and other dishes.
1 cup Parmesan.	1 cup nonfat Parmesan.	100 calories, 25 grams fat.	This ingredient makes an excellent substitute in lasagna and other dishes, and can be added to fat-free cream soups and sauces to add richness and thickness.
1 pound Italian sausage.	1 pound turkey Italian sausage.	936 calories, 114 grams fat.	This ingredient makes an excellent substitute in lasagna and other dishes.

Pesto Pasta With Sun-Dried Tomatoes

Yield: *4 servings*

½ cup chopped sun-dried
  tomatoes (not packed in oil)

½ cup unsalted chicken broth

8 ounces fettuccine or linguine
  pasta

¼ cup pine nuts (optional)

PESTO SAUCE

½ cup unsalted chicken broth

¾ cup (packed) chopped fresh
  spinach

½ cup (packed) chopped fresh
  basil

½ cup plus 2 tablespoons grated
  nonfat or reduced-fat
  Parmesan cheese

1 tablespoon plus 1 teaspoon
  extra virgin olive oil

4 cloves garlic

¼ teaspoon ground black pepper

1. Place the sun-dried tomatoes and the broth in a small pot, and bring to a boil over high heat. Reduce the heat to low, cover, and simmer for 2 minutes, or until the tomatoes have plumped. Remove the pot from the heat and drain off any excess liquid. Cover the pot and set aside.

2. Cook the pasta al dente according to package directions. Drain well, return to the pot, and cover to keep warm.

3. While the pasta is cooking, place all of the pesto ingredients in a blender or food processor, and blend until smooth.

4. Pour the pesto over the pasta, and toss to mix well. Add the tomatoes and, if desired, the pine nuts, and toss to mix well. Add a little more broth if the sauce seems too dry. Serve immediately.

NUTRITIONAL FACTS (PER 1⅓-CUP SERVING)

Calories: 334   Carbohydrates: 54 g   Cholesterol: 7 mg
Fat: 5.6 g   Fiber: 2.7 g   Protein: 17 g   Sodium: 419 mg

You Save: Calories: 213   Fat: 27.2 g

Capellini Carbonara

Yield: *4 servings*

8 ounces capellini (angel hair)
  pasta or thin spaghetti

1½ teaspoons crushed fresh garlic

3 ounces Canadian bacon, thinly
  sliced and cut into thin strips

¼ cup thinly sliced scallions

1. Cook the pasta al dente according to package directions. Drain well, return to the pot, and cover to keep warm.

2. While the pasta is cooking, place all of the sauce ingredients in a small bowl. Stir to mix well, and set aside.

3. Coat a large nonstick skillet with butter-flavored cooking spray, and place the skillet over medium-high heat. Add the garlic and Canadian bacon, and stir-fry for about 2 minutes, or until the bacon just begins to brown.

4. Reduce the heat under the skillet to medium-low, and add the pasta. Slowly pour the sauce mixture over the pasta mixture, tossing gently for a minute or 2, or until the sauce just begins to boil, and thickens slightly. Add a little more evaporated milk if the sauce seems too dry.

5. Add the scallions to the pasta mixture, and toss to mix well. Remove the skillet from the heat, and serve immediately.

SAUCE

1¼ cups evaporated skimmed milk

¼ cup plus 2 tablespoons fat-free egg substitute

⅓ cup grated nonfat Parmesan cheese

¼ teaspoon coarsely ground black pepper

NUTRITIONAL FACTS (PER 1⅓-CUP SERVING)

Calories: 345   Carbohydrates: 56 g   Cholesterol: 56 mg
Fat: 2.3 g   Fiber: 1.5 g   Protein: 24 g   Sodium: 455 mg

You Save: Calories: 298 Fat: 37 g

Angel Hair With Ham and Artichoke Hearts

1. To make the sauce, place all of the sauce ingredients in a blender or food processor, and blend until smooth. Set aside.

2. Cook the pasta until al dente according to package directions. Drain well, return to the pot, and cover to keep warm.

3. While the pasta is cooking, coat a large nonstick skillet with nonstick cooking spray, and preheat over medium-high heat. Add the ham and garlic, and stir-fry for about 2 minutes, or until the ham is lightly browned.

4. Add the artichoke hearts, Italian seasoning, and broth or wine to the skillet, and sauté for about 2 minutes, or until the artichoke hearts are heated through and the liquid is reduced by half.

5. Reduce the heat to medium, add the pasta to the skillet, and toss to mix well. Pour the sauce over the pasta mixture, and toss gently for a minute or 2, or until the sauce is heated through. (Do not let the sauce boil.) Add a little more milk if the sauce seems too dry. Serve immediately.

Yield: 4 servings

8 ounces capellini (angel hair) pasta

5 ounces ham (at least 97% lean), thinly sliced and cut into thin strips

1 teaspoon crushed fresh garlic

1 cup coarsely chopped frozen (thawed) or canned (drained) artichoke hearts

¾ teaspoon dried Italian seasoning

¼ cup chicken broth or dry white wine

SAUCE

1 cup nonfat ricotta cheese

1 cup skim milk

2 tablespoons grated nonfat Parmesan cheese

¼ teaspoon ground white pepper

NUTRITIONAL FACTS (PER 1½-CUP SERVING)

Calories: 352   Carbohydrates: 55 g   Cholesterol: 24 mg
Fat: 2.2 g   Fiber: 3.6 g   Protein: 27.6 g   Sodium: 463 mg

You Save: Calories: 328 Fat: 42.8 g

Italian Country Linguine

Yield: *4 servings*

8 ounces linguine pasta

4 ounces ham (at least 97% lean), thinly sliced and cut into thin strips

1 teaspoon crushed fresh garlic

2 cups thinly sliced fresh mushrooms

3 tablespoons dry white wine or chicken broth

2 cups coarsely chopped fresh plum tomatoes (about 4 medium)

1 teaspoon dried oregano

$\frac{1}{4}$ cup sliced scallions

$\frac{1}{4}$ cup grated nonfat or reduced-fat Parmesan cheese

1. Cook the pasta al dente according to package directions. Drain well, return to the pot, and cover to keep warm.

2. While the pasta is cooking, coat a large nonstick skillet with nonstick cooking spray, and preheat over medium-high heat. Add the ham and garlic, and stir-fry for about 2 minutes, or until the ham begins to brown.

3. Add the mushrooms and wine or broth to the skillet, and stir-fry for about 2 minutes, or until the mushrooms begin to release their juices. Add a little more broth or wine if the skillet becomes too dry.

4. Add the tomatoes and oregano to the skillet, and reduce the heat to medium. Cover and cook for about 3 minutes, or just until the tomatoes are heated through and begin to soften.

5. Add the pasta and scallions to the skillet, and toss to mix well. Serve immediately, topping each serving with a tablespoon of Parmesan.

NUTRITIONAL FACTS (PER 1$\frac{2}{3}$-CUP SERVING)

Calories: 290 Carbohydrates: 51 g Cholesterol: 18 mg
Fat: 2 g Fiber: 2.6 g Protein: 17 g Sodium: 307 mg

You Save: Calories: 134 Fat: 16 g

COOKING TIP

Cooking With Fresh Pasta

A variety of fresh pastas is now available in the refrigerated section of most grocery stores, and in many specialty shops, as well. Like their dried counterparts, most fresh pastas contain no added fats.

To substitute fresh pasta for dried pasta in any of the recipes in this book, replace the required amount of dried pasta with 1$\frac{1}{4}$ times as much fresh. For example, if a recipe calls for 8 ounces of dried linguine, use 10 ounces of fresh linguine. Fresh pasta cooks much faster than dried, so be sure to check the label for the recommended cooking time. Then enjoy the incomparable tenderness and delicacy of fresh pasta in a delicious low-fat dish.

Rigatoni With Spicy Olive Sauce

1. Cook the pasta al dente according to package directions. Drain well, return to the pot, and cover to keep warm.

2. While the pasta is cooking, coat a large nonstick skillet with nonstick cooking spray, and preheat over medium-high heat. Add the garlic, and stir-fry for about 30 seconds, or just until the garlic begins to turn color.

3. Add the tomatoes, olives, brine, Italian seasoning, and red pepper to the skillet, and stir to mix. Reduce the heat to medium, cover, and cook, stirring constantly, for 8 to 10 minutes, or until the tomatoes are soft.

4. Add the cooked pasta to the skillet, and toss to mix well. Remove the skillet from the heat, and toss in first the Parmesan and then the mozzarella. Serve immediately.

Yield: 4 servings

8 ounces rigatoni pasta

2 teaspoons crushed fresh garlic

1 ¼ pounds fresh plum tomatoes (about 8 medium), chopped

⅓ cup sliced black olives

¼ cup olive brine (from the can of olives)

2 teaspoons dried Italian seasoning

½ teaspoon crushed red pepper

¼ cup grated nonfat or reduced-fat Parmesan cheese

1 cup diced nonfat or reduced-fat mozzarella cheese

NUTRITIONAL FACTS (PER 1½-CUP SERVING)

Calories: 321 Carbohydrates: 54 g Cholesterol: 8 mg
Fat: 2.7 g Fiber: 3.4 g Protein: 20 g Sodium: 523 mg

You Save: Calories: 144 Fat: 19 g

Penne With Spinach Cream Sauce

1. Cook the pasta al dente according to package directions. Drain well, return to the pot, and cover to keep warm.

2. While the pasta is cooking, place all of the sauce ingredients in a blender or food processor, and blend until smooth. Set aside.

3. Coat a large nonstick skillet with butter-flavored cooking spray, and preheat over medium heat. Add the garlic, and stir-fry for about 30 seconds, or just until the garlic begins to turn color. Add the spinach and Italian seasoning, and stir-fry for about 1 minute, or just until the spinach is wilted.

4. Add the pasta to the skillet. Reduce the heat to low, and pour the sauce over the pasta mixture. Toss gently over low heat for a minute or 2, or just until the sauce is heated through. (Do not let the sauce boil.) Add a little more milk if the sauce seems too dry.

Yield: 5 servings

12 ounces penne or tube pasta

1 ½ teaspoons crushed fresh garlic

4 cups (packed) chopped fresh spinach

½ teaspoon dried Italian seasoning

¼ cup plus 2 tablespoons grated nonfat or reduced-fat Parmesan cheese

SAUCE

1 cup nonfat ricotta cheese

1 cup skim milk

1 tablespoon butter-flavored
sprinkles

$\frac{1}{8}$ teaspoon ground white pepper

5. Remove the skillet from the heat, and toss in the Parmesan. Serve immediately.

NUTRITIONAL FACTS (PER 1$\frac{1}{2}$-CUP SERVING)
Calories: 346   Carbohydrates: 62 g   Cholesterol: 6 mg
Fat: 1.2 g   Fiber: 2.2 g   Protein: 22 g   Sodium: 245 mg

You Save: Calories: 315   Fat: 41.8 g

Fettuccine With Fresh Tomatoes

Yield: *4 servings*

10 ounces fettuccine or linguine
pasta

1 tablespoon extra virgin olive oil
(optional)

$\frac{1}{4}$ cup grated nonfat or
reduced-fat Parmesan cheese

SAUCE

4 cups chopped fresh tomatoes
(about 4 medium)

$\frac{1}{4}$ cup plus 2 tablespoons thinly
sliced scallions

$\frac{1}{4}$ cup sliced black olives

$\frac{1}{4}$ cup bottled fat-free Italian
salad dressing

1 tablespoon chopped fresh basil,
or 1 teaspoon dried

1 tablespoon chopped fresh
oregano, or 1 teaspoon dried

1 teaspoon crushed fresh garlic

$\frac{1}{4}$ teaspoon ground black pepper

1. To make the sauce, place all of the sauce ingredients in a medium-sized bowl, and toss to mix well. Set the mixture aside for 30 minutes at room temperature.

2. Cook the pasta al dente according to package directions. Drain well, and return to the pot. Add the olive oil if desired, and toss to mix well. Add the sauce, and toss to mix well.

3. Serve immediately, topping each serving with a tablespoon of Parmesan.

NUTRITIONAL FACTS (PER 2-CUP SERVING)
Calories: 346   Carbohydrates: 67 g   Cholesterol: 3 mg
Fat: 2.7 g   Fiber: 4.1 g   Protein: 14 g   Sodium: 375 mg

You Save: Calories: 115   Fat: 15.4 g

Bow Ties With Broccoli and Tomatoes

1. Cook the pasta almost al dente according to package directions. Two minutes before the pasta is done, add the broccoli to the pot. Cook until the broccoli turns bright green and is crisp-tender, and the pasta is al dente. Drain well, return to the pot, and cover to keep warm.

2. While the pasta is cooking, coat a large nonstick skillet with olive oil cooking spray, and preheat over medium-high heat. Add the garlic, and stir-fry for about 30 seconds, or just until the garlic begins to turn color.

3. Add the tomatoes, broth, Italian seasoning, and red pepper to the skillet, and reduce the heat to medium-low. Cover and cook, stirring occasionally, for 4 to 5 minutes, or just until the tomatoes are heated through and just beginning to soften.

4. Add the pasta and broccoli to the skillet, and toss to mix well. Remove the skillet from the heat, and toss in the Parmesan. Serve immediately, topping each serving with $\frac{1}{4}$ cup of the ricotta.

Yield: 4 servings

8 ounces bow tie pasta

3 cups fresh broccoli florets

2 teaspoons crushed fresh garlic

1 pound fresh plum tomatoes (6–7 medium), diced

$\frac{1}{4}$ cup chicken or vegetable broth

$1\frac{1}{2}$ teaspoons dried Italian seasoning

$\frac{1}{2}$ teaspoon crushed red pepper

$\frac{1}{4}$ cup grated nonfat or reduced-fat Parmesan cheese

1 cup nonfat ricotta cheese

NUTRITIONAL FACTS (PER 2-CUP SERVING)

Calories: 326   Carbohydrates: 56 g   Cholesterol: 5 mg
Fat: 1.5 g   Fiber: 4.5 g   Protein: 22 g   Sodium: 264 mg

You Save: Calories: 123   Fat: 16.7 g

Lemon Chicken Linguine

Yield: *4 servings*

For variety, substitute scallops or shrimp for the chicken.

8 ounces linguine pasta

¾ pound boneless skinless chicken breasts

¼ teaspoon salt

⅛ teaspoon ground black pepper

¼ cup chicken broth

3 tablespoons lemon juice

1 tablespoon freshly grated lemon rind

1 cup evaporated skimmed milk

3 tablespoons grated nonfat Parmesan cheese

2 teaspoons crushed fresh garlic

¼ cup sliced scallions

¼ cup finely chopped fresh parsley

1. Cook the pasta al dente according to package directions. Drain well, return to the pot, and cover to keep warm.

2. While the pasta is cooking, rinse the chicken with cool water, and pat dry with paper towels. Cut the chicken into ¾-inch cubes, sprinkle with the salt and pepper, and set aside.

3. Combine the broth, lemon juice, and lemon rind in a small bowl, and set aside. Combine the evaporated milk and Parmesan in another bowl, and set aside.

4. Coat a large nonstick skillet with olive oil cooking spray, and preheat over medium-high heat. Add the garlic and chicken, and stir-fry for about 4 minutes, or until the chicken is nicely browned and no longer pink inside.

5. Reduce the heat to medium, and add the pasta to the skillet. Pour the broth mixture over the pasta and chicken, and toss to mix well. Slowly pour the milk mixture over the pasta, tossing gently for a minute or 2, or until the sauce just begins to boil, and thickens slightly. Add a little more evaporated milk if the sauce seems too dry.

6. Add the scallions and parsley to the skillet, and toss to mix well. Serve immediately.

NUTRITIONAL FACTS (PER 1⅔-CUP SERVING)

Calories: 378   Carbohydrates: 55 g   Cholesterol: 54 mg
Fat: 2.2 g   Fiber: 1.7 g   Protein: 34 g   Sodium: 392 mg

You Save: Calories: 211   Fat: 29 g

Spaghetti and Shrimp Florentine

1. Rinse the shrimp with cool water, and pat dry with paper towels. Sprinkle with the salt and pepper, and set aside.

2. Cook the pasta al dente according to package directions. Drain well, return to the pot, and toss with the olive oil if desired. Cover to keep warm.

3. While the pasta is cooking, coat a large nonstick skillet with olive oil cooking spray, and preheat over medium-high heat. Add the garlic, and stir-fry for 30 seconds, or until the garlic just begins to turn color. Add the shrimp, and stir-fry for about 4 minutes, or until the shrimp turn opaque, and any liquid that is released from the shrimp during cooking has evaporated.

4. Add the wine, lemon juice, and oregano to the skillet, and cook for about 2 minutes, or until the volume is reduced by half. Reduce the heat to medium, add the spinach, and stir-fry for a minute or 2, or just until the spinach is wilted. Stir in the roasted red peppers.

5. Add the pasta to the skillet. Place the chicken broth in a small bowl, and stir in the cornstarch. Pour the mixture over the pasta and toss gently for about 1 minute, or until the sauce thickens slightly. Add a little more broth if the mixture seems too dry.

6. Remove the skillet from the heat, and serve hot, topping each serving with a tablespoon of Parmesan.

Yield: *4 servings*

¾ pound cleaned raw shrimp

¼ teaspoon salt

¼ teaspoon ground black pepper

8 ounces thin spaghetti

1 tablespoon extra virgin olive oil (optional)

1½ teaspoons crushed fresh garlic

½ cup dry white wine

1 tablespoon lemon juice

¾ teaspoon dried oregano

4 cups (packed) chopped fresh spinach

⅓ cup roasted red pepper strips (page 57)

¾ cup reduced-sodium chicken broth

1 teaspoon cornstarch

¼ cup grated nonfat or reduced-fat Parmesan cheese

NUTRITIONAL FACTS (PER 1½-CUP SERVING)

Calories: 320   Carbohydrates: 50 g   Cholesterol: 141 mg
Fat: 1.8 g   Fiber: 2.1 g   Protein: 26 g   Sodium: 476 mg

You Save: Calories: 136   Fat: 16.3 g

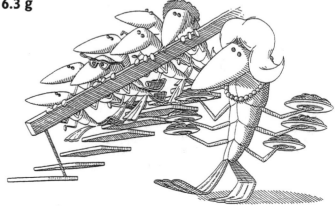

Linguine With Roasted Vegetables

Yield: *4 servings*

1 cup fresh mushrooms, cut in half

1 cup ³⁄₄-inch cubes of eggplant

1 medium zucchini, halved lengthwise and sliced ¹⁄₂-inch thick

1 medium yellow onion, cut into thin wedges

¹⁄₄ teaspoon salt

1 tablespoon balsamic vinegar

Olive oil cooking spray

8 ounces linguine pasta

1 tablespoon extra virgin olive oil (optional)

2 teaspoons crushed fresh garlic

1 pound fresh plum tomatoes (6–7 medium), chopped

¹⁄₄ cup chicken or vegetable broth

1¹⁄₂ teaspoons dried oregano, or 1¹⁄₂ tablespoons fresh

¹⁄₂ teaspoon crushed red pepper

¹⁄₄ cup plus 2 tablespoons nonfat or reduced-fat Parmesan cheese or crumbled feta cheese

1. Place the mushrooms, eggplant, zucchini, and onion in a large bowl. Sprinkle with the salt and vinegar, and toss to mix well.

2. Coat a large baking sheet with olive oil cooking spray, and arrange the vegetables on the sheet in a single layer. Spray the vegetables lightly with the cooking spray, and bake at 475°F for 10 minutes. Turn the vegetables with a spatula, and bake for 10 additional minutes, or until nicely browned. Remove the vegetables from the oven, and set aside.

3. Cook the pasta al dente according to package directions. Drain well, and return to the pot. Toss with the olive oil if desired, and cover to keep warm.

4. Coat a large nonstick skillet with olive oil cooking spray, and preheat over medium-high heat. Add the garlic, and stir-fry for about 30 seconds, or just until the garlic begins to turn color.

5. Reduce the heat to medium, and add the tomatoes, broth, oregano, and red pepper to the skillet. Cover and cook for about 8 minutes, or until the tomatoes soften and begin to break down.

6. Add the vegetables and pasta to the skillet, and toss to mix well. Add a little more broth if the sauce seems too dry. Serve hot, topping each serving with a rounded tablespoon of the Parmesan or feta cheese.

NUTRITIONAL FACTS (PER 1¹⁄₂-CUP SERVING)

Calories: 297   Carbohydrates: 55 g   Cholesterol: 5 mg
Fat: 1.9 g   Fiber: 4 g   Protein: 16 g   Sodium: 339 mg

You Save: Calories: 131   Fat: 17.3 g

Three-Cheese Manicotti

1. Cook the manicotti al dente according to package directions. Drain well, and set aside.

2. To make the filling, place all of the filling ingredients in a large bowl, and stir to mix well. Using a small spoon, stuff about $\frac{1}{3}$ cup of the filling mixture into each tube.

3. Spoon a thin layer of sauce over the bottom of a large baking pan, and arrange the filled pasta in the pan. Pour the remaining sauce evenly over the manicotti.

4. Bake uncovered at 350°F for about 40 minutes, or until hot and bubbly. Sprinkle the cup of mozzarella cheese over the top and bake for 10 additional minutes, or until the cheese has melted. Remove the dish from the oven, and let sit for 10 minutes before serving.

Yield: *7 servings*

14 manicotti tubes (about 8 ounces)

1 recipe Basic Marinara Sauce (page 166), 1 recipe Arrabbiata Sauce (page 171), or 3$\frac{1}{2}$ cups Savory Meat Sauce (page 173)

1 cup shredded nonfat or reduced-fat mozzarella cheese

CHEESE FILLING

3 cups nonfat ricotta cheese

1$\frac{1}{2}$ cups shredded nonfat or reduced-fat mozzarella cheese

$\frac{1}{4}$ cup fat-free egg substitute

$\frac{1}{3}$ cup grated nonfat Parmesan cheese

3 tablespoons finely chopped fresh parsley

NUTRITIONAL FACTS (PER SERVING)

Calories: 343 Carbohydrates: 46 g Cholesterol: 12 mg
Fat: 0.7 g Fiber: 4.4 g Protein: 38 g Sodium: 539 mg

You Save: Calories: 228 Fat: 31.5 g

FAT-FREE COOKING TIP

Cooking with Nonfat Cheeses

If you have been cooking with nonfat cheeses for a while, you have probably noticed that they do not melt as well as their full-fat counterparts. However, if you know a few tricks of the trade, you can use these products to create guilt-free cheese-filled lasagna, casseroles, and other dishes that are just as delicious as their full-fat versions.

First, when using fat-free cheeses like mozzarella, look for a finely shredded brand, which is often labelled "fancy shredded." These finely shredded cheeses will melt better than coarsely shredded brands. Then, when topping a casserole dish like lasagna or manicotti, sprinkle the cheese on top, cover with aluminum foil, and bake, removing the foil only for the last 10 minutes of baking. Or add the cheese 5 to 10 minutes before the casserole is done. This will ensure that the cheese melts nicely and the casserole remains moist and delicious.

Fettuccine al Forno

Yield: *8 servings*

8 ounces fettuccine pasta

¼ cup grated nonfat or
   reduced-fat Parmesan cheese

2 cups grated nonfat or
   reduced-fat mozzarella cheese

SAUCE

¾ pound 95% lean ground beef
   or Turkey Italian Sausage
   (page 182)

2 teaspoons crushed fresh garlic

1 can (28 ounces) crushed
   unsalted tomatoes

2 cups sliced fresh mushrooms

1 cup chopped onion

½ cup unsalted beef broth

2 teaspoons dried Italian
   seasoning

½ teaspoon ground black pepper

1. To make the sauce, coat a 3-quart pot with nonstick cooking spray, and preheat over medium heat. Add the ground beef or sausage and the garlic, and cook, stirring to crumble, until the meat is no longer pink.

2. Add the tomatoes, mushrooms, onions, broth, Italian seasoning, and pepper to the skillet, and bring to a boil over medium-high heat. Reduce the heat to low, cover, and simmer, stirring occasionally, for 15 minutes, or until the vegetables are tender.

3. While the sauce is cooking, cook the pasta according to package directions for about 7 minutes, or until not quite al dente. Drain well, return to the pot, and cover to keep warm.

4. Remove the sauce from the heat, add the pasta, and stir to mix well. Stir in the Parmesan.

5. Coat a 9-x-13-inch pan with nonstick cooking spray, and spread the pasta mixture in the pan. Cover the pan with aluminum foil, and bake at 350°F for 30 minutes, or until hot and bubbly. Sprinkle the mozzarella over the top, and bake uncovered for 5 to 10 additional minutes, or until the cheese is melted. Cut into squares and serve hot.

NUTRITIONAL FACTS (PER SERVING)

Calories: 282   Carbohydrates: 37.6 g   Cholesterol: 34 mg
Fat: 2.6 g   Fiber: 4.4 g   Protein: 27 g   Sodium: 364 mg

You Save: Calories: 141 Fat: 18.4 g

Lasagna Classico

1. Cook the noodles al dente according to package directions. Drain well, rinse with cool water, and drain again. Set aside.

2. To make the filling, place all of the filling ingredients in a medium-sized bowl, and stir to mix well. Set aside.

3. To assemble the lasagna, spread 1 cup of the sauce over the bottom of a 9-x-13-inch pan. Arrange 4 of the noodles over the bottom of the pan, slightly overlapping them to fit. Spread $1\frac{1}{2}$ cups of the sauce over the noodles, and top with half of the cheese filling and $\frac{2}{3}$ cup of the mozzarella. Repeat the noodles, sauce, and cheese layers. Arrange the remaining 4 noodles over the top, and spread the remaining sauce over the noodles.

4. Cover the pan with aluminum foil, and bake at 350°F for 30 minutes. Remove the foil, spread the remaining $\frac{2}{3}$ cup of mozzarella over the top, and bake uncovered for 10 additional minutes, or until the dish is bubbly and the cheese is melted.

5. Remove the dish from the oven, and let sit for 10 minutes before cutting into squares and serving.

Yield: *10 servings*

12 lasagna noodles (about 9 ounces)

6 cups Italian Sausage Sauce (page 174) or Savory Meat Sauce (page 173)

2 cups shredded nonfat or reduced-fat mozzarella cheese

CHEESE FILLING

3 cups nonfat ricotta cheese

½ cup grated nonfat Parmesan cheese

2 tablespoons finely chopped fresh parsley

NUTRITIONAL FACTS (PER SERVING)

Calories: 275   Carbohydrates: 35 g   Cholesterol: 25 mg
Fat: 1.3 g   Fiber: 2.7 g   Protein: 31 g   Sodium: 483 mg

You Save: Calories: 193   Fat: 26.1 g

Tempting Turkey Tetrazzini

Yield: *6 servings*

8 ounces spaghetti

¼ cup dry white wine or chicken broth

¼ cup unbleached flour

1½ cups sliced fresh mushrooms

2 cups chicken broth

1 can (12 ounces) evaporated skimmed milk

½ teaspoon dried thyme

⅛ teaspoon ground nutmeg

⅛ teaspoon ground white pepper

2 cups diced cooked turkey or chicken breast

¼ cup grated Parmesan cheese

When preparing this dish, be sure to use regular Parmesan cheese, rather than the fat-free product.

1. Cook the pasta al dente according to package directions. Drain well, return to the pot, and cover to keep warm.

2. While the pasta is cooking, place the wine or broth and the flour in a jar with a tight-fitting lid, and shake until smooth. Set aside.

3. Coat a large deep skillet with nonstick cooking spray, and preheat over medium-high heat. Add the mushrooms, and sauté for several minutes, or until the mushrooms begin to soften and release their juices.

4. Add the broth, evaporated milk, thyme, nutmeg, and pepper to the skillet. Reduce the heat to medium, and cook, stirring frequently, until the mixture begins to boil. Add the flour mixture, and cook, stirring constantly, for about 2 minutes, or until the mixture is bubbly and slightly thickened.

5. Remove the skillet from the heat, add the pasta and turkey, and toss to mix well. Coat an 8-x-12-inch baking pan with nonstick cooking spray, and spread the mixture evenly in the dish. Sprinkle with the Parmesan.

6. Bake uncovered at 350°F for 35 minutes, or until the casserole is hot and bubbly. Remove the dish from the oven, and let sit for 5 to 10 minutes before serving.

NUTRITIONAL FACTS (PER 1½-CUP SERVING)

Calories: 297   Carbohydrates: 40 g   Cholesterol: 45 mg
Fat: 2.6 g   Fiber: 1.3 g   Protein: 26 g   Sodium: 399 mg

You Save: Calories: 185   Fat: 24.8 g

Spinach Pasta Primavera

1. Cook the pasta al dente according to package directions. Drain well, return to the pot, and cover to keep warm.

2. While the pasta is cooking, coat a large nonstick skillet with olive oil cooking spray, and preheat over medium-high heat. Add the garlic, and stir-fry for about 30 seconds, or just until the garlic begins to turn color.

3. Add the broccoli, squash, mushrooms, carrots, broth, basil, and pepper to the skillet. Cover the skillet, and cook, stirring occasionally, for about 2 minutes, or just until the vegetables are almost crisp-tender. Add the tomatoes, cover, and cook for 2 additional minutes, or until the tomatoes are heated through and just beginning to soften.

4. Add the cooked pasta to the skillet, and toss to mix well. Add more broth if the mixture seems too dry, and serve immediately, topping each serving with 1 tablespoon of the Parmesan.

Yield: 4 servings

8 ounces spinach linguine pasta

1½ teaspoons crushed fresh garlic

1½ cups fresh broccoli florets

¾ cup sliced yellow squash or zucchini

¾ cup sliced fresh mushrooms

½ cup thinly sliced carrots

½ cup vegetable or chicken broth

1 teaspoon dried basil

¼ teaspoon ground black pepper

1½ cups chopped fresh plum tomatoes (about 5 medium)

¼ cup grated nonfat or reduced-fat Parmesan cheese

NUTRITIONAL FACTS (PER 2-CUP SERVING)

Calories: 267 Carbohydrates: 53 g Cholesterol: 3 mg
Fat: 1.2 g Fiber: 3.5 g Protein: 12.3 g Sodium: 196 mg

You Save: Calories: 125 Fat: 15.4 g

Seafood Lasagna Roll-Ups

1. To make the filling, combine the ricotta, Parmesan, egg substitute, and parsley in a medium-sized bowl, and stir to mix well. Add the crab meat or shrimp and the mozzarella, and stir to mix. Set aside.

2. Cook the noodles al dente according to package directions. Drain well, rinse with cool water, and drain again.

3. Coat a 2½-quart casserole dish with nonstick cooking spray. To assemble the roll-ups, arrange the noodles on a flat surface and spread ⅛ of the filling mixture along the length of each noodle. Roll each noodle up jelly-roll style and place in the prepared dish, seam side down. Pour the sauce over the roll-ups.

Yield: 4 servings

8 lasagna noodles (about 6½ ounces)

1 recipe Almost Alfredo Sauce (page 178)

½ cup shredded nonfat or reduced-fat mozzarella cheese

FILLING

15 ounces nonfat ricotta cheese

1/4 cup grated nonfat Parmesan cheese

3 tablespoons fat-free egg substitute

2 tablespoons finely chopped fresh parsley

1 cup cooked crab meat or diced cooked shrimp (or 1/2 cup each)

1 cup shredded nonfat or reduced-fat mozzarella cheese

4. Cover the dish with aluminum foil, and bake at 350°F for 30 minutes. Remove the foil, spread the mozzarella over the top, and bake uncovered for 10 additional minutes, or until the cheese is melted. Serve hot.

NUTRITIONAL FACTS (PER SERVING)

Calories: 412 Carbohydrates: 55 g Cholesterol: 92 mg
Fat: 1.4 g Fiber: 1.1 g Protein: 44 g Sodium: 851 mg

You Save: Calories: 296 Fat: 42.5 g

Savory Baked Ziti

Yield: 10 servings

1 pound ziti pasta

5 cups Savory Meat Sauce (page 173) or Italian Sausage Sauce (page 174)

1/4 cup grated nonfat Parmesan cheese

1 cup shredded nonfat or reduced-fat mozzarella cheese

CHEESE FILLING

3 cups nonfat ricotta cheese

1/4 cup plus 2 tablespoons fat-free egg substitute

1/2 cup grated nonfat Parmesan cheese

3 tablespoons finely chopped fresh parsley

1. Cook the ziti according to package directions until barely al dente. Drain well, and return to the pot. Add 3 cups of the sauce, and toss to mix well. Set aside.

2. To make the cheese filling, place all of the filling ingredients in a medium-sized bowl, and stir to mix well. Set aside.

3. To assemble the casserole, coat a 9-x-13-inch pan with nonstick cooking spray, and spread half of the ziti in the pan. Spread all of the filling over the ziti. Then cover the filling with the remaining ziti. Spread the remaining 2 cups of sauce over the top, and sprinkle with the 1/4 cup of Parmesan.

4. Cover the pan with aluminum foil, and bake at 350°F for 40 minutes, or until hot and bubbly. Remove the foil, spread the mozzarella over the top, and bake for 10 additional minutes, or until the cheese is melted.

5. Remove the dish from the oven, and let sit for 10 minutes before cutting into squares and serving.

NUTRITIONAL FACTS (PER SERVING)

Calories: 344 Carbohydrates: 51 g Cholesterol: 24 mg
Fat: 2.1 g Fiber: 2.9 g Protein: 32 g Sodium: 466 mg

You Save: Calories: 174 Fat: 23.7 g

A Pasta Primer

Pasta comes in a wide variety of shapes and sizes. Here is a guide to some of the pasta shapes you may find in your local store. Most of these pastas are traditionally made from semolina—refined durum wheat. Many, though, are available in whole wheat versions, as well. And some pastas also contain spinach, beets, tomatoes, or garlic and parsley. These ingredients add flavor and variety, and, if present in large enough amounts, can boost the nutritional value of your dish. Feel free to experiment with different pastas and to interchange similar pasta shapes in your favorite recipes.

Acini de Pepe. A small peppercorn-shaped pasta, acini de pepe is often used in soups.

Alphabets. These tiny pasta letters are often used in soups.

Capellini. Also known as angel hair pasta, this is the thinnest of the spaghetti shapes. It may be topped with sauce, or broken and cooked in soups.

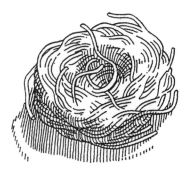

Cavatelli. This short, curled pasta shell is usually topped with sauce.

Conchiglie. These medium-sized pasta shells are usually topped with sauce.

Conchigliette. Small pasta shells, conchigliette are often used in soups.

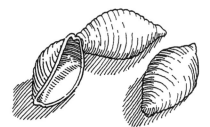

Conchiglioni. These large pasta shells are often stuffed with meat, vegetables, and/or cheese.

Ditali. Short ridged tubes or "thimbles," about ½-inch long, this pasta is used in casseroles, soups, or salads, or topped with sauce.

Ditalini. A shorter version of ditali, ditalini pasta is often used in soups.

Egg Noodles. These short flat pasta ribbons are often used in casseroles and side dishes.

Elbow Macaroni. Short, curved pasta tubes, elbow macaroni is often used in soups and salads.

Farfalle. This bow tie-shaped pasta is usually topped with sauce.

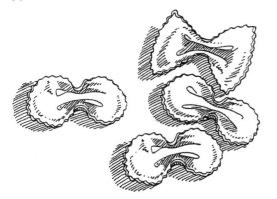

Fettuccine. These long flat ribbons—about ¼-inch wide—are often tossed with Alfredo Sauce.

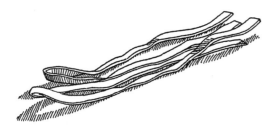

Fusilli. This twisted spaghetti is usually topped with a sauce.

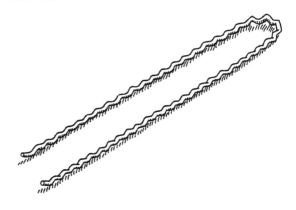

Lasagna Noodles. These broad pasta ribbons are layered in baked dishes.

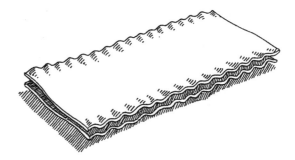

Linguine. Long thin flat pasta strands, linguine is usually topped with a sauce.

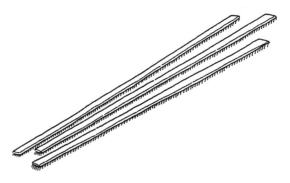

Manicotti. These large hollow tubes are usually stuffed with cheese or meat and baked.

Mostaccioli. Diagonally cut pasta tubes of about 2 inches length, mostaccioli may be either smooth or ridged (rigati). This pasta is used in casseroles or topped with a sauce.

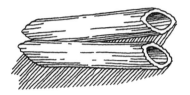

Orzo. This pasta, which resembles rice, is often used in soups and side dishes.

Penne. Diagonally cut pasta tubes of about $1\frac{1}{4}$ inches length, penne is also known as quills. Either smooth or ridged, this pasta can be used in soups and casseroles, or topped with a sauce.

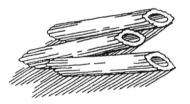

Radiatori. A "radiator"-shaped pasta, this is good with chunky sauces.

Ravioli. Pasta squares filled with vegetables, meat, or cheese, ravioli is served with a sauce.

Rigatoni. Moderately-sized ridged pasta tubes, rigatoni is often used in casseroles or topped with a hearty sauce.

Rotelle. Corkscrew pasta, rotelle is good with chunky sauces.

Ruote. This wagon wheel pasta is often served in soups or with chunky sauces.

Spaghetti. Long, round, thin ribbons, spaghetti is usually topped with a sauce.

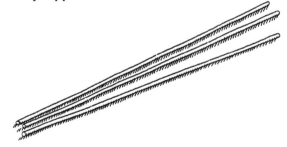

Spaghettini. Thin spaghetti, spaghettini is usually topped with a sauce.

Stellini. These little stars are often used in soups.

Tagliatelle. These long egg noodles, approximately $\frac{3}{4}$-inch wide, are often used in casseroles or served with a creamy sauce.

Tortellini. These small stuffed pasta twists may be served in soups or with a sauce.

Tripolini. These tiny bows are often used in soups.

Tubetti. Tiny pasta tubes, tubetti is often used in soups.

Vermicelli. This very thin spaghetti is served with sauces.

Ziti. A tubular pasta, ziti is often tossed with sauce and baked.

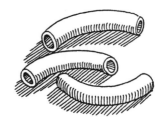

8

Crusty Pizzas, Calzones, and Breads

Elementally satisfying and delicious, bread is loved the world over. And in Italy, as in many other countries, both yeast bread itself and a number of bread-based foods form an important and delectable part of the cuisine.

One bread-based dish with which virtually every American is familiar is the pizza. Yet for many years, pizza was almost always a fat-fighter's nightmare, blanketed in high-fat cheeses and glistening with oil. Now that so many low- and no-fat ingredients are available, though, it has become possible to enjoy low-fat versions of even the cheese-and-sauce pie. And a variety of new pizza creations—sparked with ingredients like sun-dried tomatoes and roasted eggplant—dazzle the pizza lover with greater choices than ever existed before.

Although perhaps not as well known as the pizza, the calzone—a turnover filled with cheese and other ingredients—is a popular food that can be easily adapted for different tastes. And like the pizza, the calzone can now be made low in fat while retaining the delightful chewiness of its crust and the satisfying savor of its filling.

Of all the foods presented in this chapter, the least well known may be focaccia—the flat, wonderfully versatile bread that is enjoyed throughout Italy, as well as in many parts of this country. Whether focaccia is new to you or is an old friend, you're sure to be delighted by a food that can accompany a range of entrées or can stand on its own as a flavorful and satisfying treat.

If the thought of making yeast dough from scratch scares you, relax and get ready for a fuss-free baking experience. The dough recipes in this chapter are streamlined versions of traditional recipes, and can be easily made either by hand or in a bread machine. After that, no- and low-fat ingredients ranging from nonfat cheeses to ultra-lean meats will give your creations plenty of flavor and nutritional value, but little or no fat. The result? An amazing assortment of easy-to-make, great-tasting, *guilt-free* pizzas, calzones, and breads that you will be proud to serve, and that family and friends will ask for time and time again.

PIZZA CRUSTS

Parmesan-Polenta Pizza Dough

Yield: About ¾ pound dough, enough for a 14-inch thin crust or a 12-inch thick crust

1¼ cups plus 2 tablespoons bread flour or unbleached flour

⅓ cup whole grain medium or finely ground cornmeal

¼ cup grated nonfat or reduced-fat Parmesan cheese

1½ teaspoons Rapid Rise yeast

1 teaspoon sugar

¼ teaspoon salt

½ cup plus 2 tablespoons water or skim milk

1. Place ¾ cup of the flour and all of the cornmeal, Parmesan, yeast, sugar, and salt in a large bowl, and stir to mix well. Place the water or milk in a small saucepan, and heat until very warm (125°F to 130°F). Add the water to the flour mixture, and stir for 1 minute. Stir in enough of the remaining flour, 2 tablespoons at a time, to form a soft dough.

2. Sprinkle 2 tablespoons of the remaining flour over a flat surface, and turn the dough onto the surface. Knead the dough for 5 minutes, gradually adding just enough of the remaining flour to form a smooth, satiny ball. (Be careful not to make the dough too stiff, or it will be hard to roll out.)

3. Coat a large bowl with nonstick cooking spray, and place the ball of dough in the bowl. Cover the bowl with a clean kitchen towel, and let rise in a warm place for about 35 minutes, or until doubled in size.

4. When the dough has risen, punch it down, shape it into a ball, and turn it onto a lightly floured surface. The dough is now ready for shaping, topping, and baking.

Getting a Rise Out of Your Pizza Dough

Like all breads, pizza crusts, calzone crusts, and focaccia rounds must rise and stretch to have a pleasing texture. While a number of factors can affect the rising of your dough, the following perhaps deserve the most consideration.

❏ **Yeast.** You will notice that all of the crust recipes in this chapter call for Rapid Rise yeast. This finely granulated, fast-acting product is much simpler to use than regular active dry yeast. Unlike active dry yeast, Rapid Rise yeast can be mixed directly with a recipe's dry ingredients, rather than first being dissolved in a liquid. Fleischmann's Rapid Rise yeast is widely available in supermarkets, and will help you achieve delicious results when making your Italian yeast breads.

❏ **Flour.** Either bread flour or unbleached flour can be used to make your pizza doughs, although the results will differ according to the product used. Bread flour, with its high protein content, will make a very stretchy, elastic dough that bakes into a delightfully chewy crust. Unbleached dough will make a dough that has less stretch, and a crust that is more tender. Both of these products are available in your supermarket. Experiment to see which you prefer.

Multigrain Pizza Dough

1. Place ¾ cup of the flour and all of the cornmeal, wheat bran, oats, yeast, and salt in a large bowl, and stir to mix well. Place the water or milk and the honey in a small saucepan, and heat until very warm (125°F to 130°F). Add the water mixture to the flour mixture, and stir for 1 minute. Stir in enough of the remaining flour, 2 tablespoons at a time, to form a soft dough.

2. Sprinkle 2 tablespoons of the remaining flour over a flat surface, and turn the dough onto the surface. Knead the dough for 5 minutes, gradually adding just enough of the remaining flour to form a smooth, satiny ball. (Be careful not to make the dough too stiff, or it will be hard to roll out.)

3. Coat a large bowl with nonstick cooking spray, and place the ball of dough in the bowl. Cover the bowl with a clean kitchen towel, and let rise in a warm place for about 35 minutes, or until doubled in size.

4. When the dough has risen, punch it down, shape it into a ball, and turn it onto a lightly floured surface. The dough is now ready for shaping, topping, and baking.

Yield: *About ¾ pound dough, enough for a 14-inch thin crust or a 12-inch thick crust*

1¼ cups plus 2 tablespoons bread flour or unbleached flour

2 tablespoons whole grain cornmeal

2 tablespoons wheat bran

2 tablespoons quick-cooking oats

1½ teaspoons Rapid Rise yeast

¼ teaspoon salt

½ cup plus 2 tablespoons water or skim milk

1 teaspoon honey

❑ **Liquid.** When making yeast doughs, it is critical that the liquid be the right temperature—125°F to 130°F for the recipes in this chapter. If the liquid is too cool, the yeast may not be properly activated. If the liquid is too hot, the yeast may be inactivated. An instant-read thermometer—available in most grocery stores—is a simple way to test the liquid's temperature. Use either water or skim milk in these recipes. Milk will produce a slightly richer, more tender dough than will water.

❑ **Rising Time.** The pizza, calzone, focaccia, and other yeast doughs in this chapter must rise for about 35 minutes before being shaped and baked. Since yeast multiplies best at 80°F to 90°F, you must find a warm spot in which the dough can rise. Your oven is an ideal place for this. Simply turn the oven on for a minute or 2, or until the temperature reaches 80°F to 90°F. Then turn the oven off. Place the dough in a large cooking spray-coated bowl, and cover with a towel. Then place the bowl in the oven and close the door. Check the dough near the end of the recommended cooking time.

How can you tell when the dough has fully risen? It is done when it has doubled in size. For another test of readiness, press the dough with your fingertips. The dough should feel light and spongy, and the indentation left by your finger should fill in slowly. If the space fills in quickly, it is not ready. If it does not fill in at all, it was allowed to rise too long. But don't worry if you let your pizza dough rise a little longer than necessary! This won't affect the quality of the finished product. Simply punch it down and proceed with the recipe. When making bread sticks, focaccia, and other breads that are placed in the oven fully risen, however, it is more important to let the dough rise to the proper degree.

Oatmeal Pizza Dough

Yield: *About ³⁄₄ pound dough, enough for a 14-inch thin crust or a 12-inch thick crust*

1¼ cups plus 2 tablespoons bread flour or unbleached flour

⅓ cup quick-cooking oats or oat bran

1½ teaspoons Rapid Rise yeast

1 teaspoon sugar

¼ teaspoon salt

½ cup plus 2 tablespoons skim milk or water

1. Place ³⁄₄ cup of the flour and all of the oats or oat bran, yeast, sugar, and salt in a large bowl, and stir to mix well. Place the milk or water in a small saucepan, and heat until very warm (125°F to 130°F). Add the milk to the flour mixture, and stir for 1 minute. Stir in enough of the remaining flour, 2 tablespoons at a time, to form a soft dough.

2. Sprinkle 2 tablespoons of the remaining flour over a flat surface, and turn the dough onto the surface. Knead the dough for 5 minutes, gradually adding just enough of the remaining flour to form a smooth, satiny ball. (Be careful not to make the dough too stiff, or it will be hard to roll out.)

3. Coat a large bowl with nonstick cooking spray, and place the ball of dough in the bowl. Cover the bowl with a clean kitchen towel, and let rise in a warm place for about 35 minutes, or until doubled in size.

4. When the dough has risen, punch it down, shape it into a ball, and turn it onto a lightly floured surface. The dough is now ready for shaping, topping, and baking.

Hearty Wheat Pizza Dough

Yield: *About ³⁄₄ pound dough, enough for a 14-inch thin crust or a 12-inch thick crust*

1¼ cups plus 2 tablespoons bread flour or unbleached flour

⅓ cup toasted wheat germ

1½ teaspoons Rapid Rise yeast

¼ teaspoon salt

½ cup plus 2 tablespoons water or skim milk

1 teaspoon honey

1. Place ³⁄₄ cup of the flour and all of the wheat germ, yeast, and salt in a large bowl, and stir to mix well. Place the water or milk and the honey in a small saucepan, and heat until very warm (125°F to 130°F). Add the water mixture to the flour mixture, and stir for 1 minute. Stir in enough of the remaining flour, 2 tablespoons at a time, to form a soft dough.

2. Sprinkle 2 tablespoons of the remaining flour over a flat surface, and turn the dough onto the surface. Knead the dough for 5 minutes, gradually adding just enough of the remaining flour to form a smooth, satiny ball. (Be careful not to make the dough too stiff, or it will be hard to roll out.)

3. Coat a large bowl with nonstick cooking spray, and place the ball of dough in the bowl. Cover the bowl with a clean kitchen towel, and let rise in a warm place for about 35 minutes, or until doubled in size.

4. When the dough has risen, punch it down, shape it into a ball, and turn it onto a lightly floured surface. The dough is now ready for shaping, topping, and baking.

PIZZAS

Margherita Pizza

Yield: 8 slices

1. Place the drained tomatoes in a small bowl, and mash with a fork until coarsely crushed. Drain off any liquid that has accumulated, stir in the garlic, and set aside.

2. Turn the dough onto a lightly floured surface. Using a rolling pin, roll the dough into a 14-inch circle. (For a thick crust, roll the dough into a 12-inch circle.) Coat a 14-inch (or 12-inch) pizza pan with nonstick cooking spray. Place the dough on the pan, forming a slight rim around the edges.

3. Spread the tomato mixture over the crust to within $\frac{1}{2}$ inch of the edges. Sprinkle first the mozzarella and then the provolone over the tomatoes. Sprinkle with the basil.

4. Bake at 450°F for about 10 minutes, or until the cheese is melted and the crust is lightly browned. Slice and serve immediately.

1 can (14$\frac{1}{2}$ ounces) unsalted whole tomatoes, drained

$\frac{1}{2}$ teaspoon crushed fresh garlic

1 recipe Oatmeal Pizza Dough (page 126) or Multigrain Pizza Dough (page 125)

$\frac{1}{2}$ cup shredded nonfat mozzarella cheese

$\frac{1}{2}$ cup shredded reduced-fat provolone cheese

1 tablespoon chopped fresh basil, or 1 teaspoon dried

NUTRITIONAL FACTS (PER SLICE)
Calories: 125   Carbohydrates: 19.4 g   Cholesterol: 5 mg
Fat: 1.7 g   Fiber: 1.2 g   Protein: 8 g   Sodium: 147 mg

You Save: Calories: 66   Fat: 7.6 g

Savory Sausage, Pepper, and Onion Pizza

Yield: *8 slices*

1 recipe Multigrain Pizza Dough (page 125) or Parmesan-Polenta Pizza Dough (page 124)

¾ cup canned tomato purée or Arrabbiata Sauce (page 171)

1 cup shredded nonfat or reduced-fat mozzarella cheese

6 ounces Turkey Italian Sausage (page 182), cooked, drained, and crumbled

8 thin rings green bell pepper

3–4 thin slices onion, separated into rings

½ teaspoon dried Italian seasoning

1. Turn the dough onto a lightly floured surface. Using a rolling pin, roll the dough into a 14-inch circle. (For a thick crust, roll the dough into a 12-inch circle.) Coat a 14-inch (or 12-inch) pizza pan with nonstick cooking spray. Place the dough on the pan, forming a slight rim around the edges.

2. Spread the sauce over the crust to within ½ inch of the edges. Sprinkle the mozzarella over the sauce, and top with the sausage, peppers, and onions. Sprinkle with the Italian seasoning.

3. Bake at 450°F for about 12 minutes, or until the cheese is melted and the crust is lightly browned. Slice and serve immediately.

NUTRITIONAL FACTS (PER SLICE)

Calories: 145 Carbohydrates: 23.8 g Cholesterol: 13 mg
Fat: 0.9 g Fiber: 2.1 g Protein: 11.5 g Sodium: 198 mg

You Save: Calories: 99 Fat: 12 g

Making Pizza on the Run

Even when time is in short supply, you can enjoy the incomparable flavor and nutrition of a delicious homemade pizza. Here are some ideas that will allow you to whip up a mouth-watering low-fat pizza on any night of the week.

❑ To make pizza dough in a bread machine, place all

of the dough ingredients except for 2 tablespoons of the bread flour in the machine's bread pan. (Do not heat the water or milk.) Turn the machine on to the "rise," "dough," "manual," or equivalent setting so that the machine will mix, knead, and let the dough rise once. Check the dough about 5 minutes after the machine has started. If the dough seems

White Pizza

1. Turn the dough onto a lightly floured surface. Using a rolling pin, roll the dough into a 14-inch circle. (For a thick crust, roll the dough into a 12-inch circle.) Coat a 14-inch (or 12-inch) pizza pan with nonstick cooking spray. Place the dough on the pan, forming a slight rim around the edges.

2. Place the ricotta and Parmesan in a small bowl, and stir to mix well. Spread the cheese mixture over the crust to within $\frac{1}{2}$ inch of the edges. Sprinkle the mozzarella and provolone over the ricotta. Sprinkle the cheeses with the scallions, olives, Italian seasoning, and fennel seeds.

3. Bake at 450°F for about 12 minutes, or until the cheese is melted and the crust is lightly browned. Slice and serve immediately.

Yield: *8 slices*

1 recipe Oatmeal Pizza Dough (page 126) or Parmesan-Polenta Pizza Dough (page 124)

$\frac{3}{4}$ cup nonfat ricotta cheese

2 tablespoons grated nonfat Parmesan cheese

$\frac{1}{2}$ cup shredded nonfat or reduced-fat mozzarella cheese

$\frac{1}{2}$ cup shredded reduced-fat provolone cheese

$\frac{1}{4}$ cup thinly sliced scallions

3 tablespoons sliced black olives (optional)

$\frac{3}{4}$ teaspoon dried Italian seasoning

$\frac{1}{2}$ teaspoon whole fennel seeds

NUTRITIONAL FACTS (PER SLICE)

Calories: 149 Carbohydrates: 21.4 g Cholesterol: 7 mg
Fat: 1.7 g Fiber: 1.2 g Protein: 12 g Sodium: 229 mg

You Save: Calories: 84 Fat: 10.7 g

---

too sticky, add more of the remaining flour, a tablespoon at a time. When the dough is ready, remove it from the machine and proceed to shape, top, and bake it as directed in the recipe.

❏ One excellent quick-crust option is frozen bread dough. Simply thaw the dough (you'll need about $\frac{3}{4}$ pound), roll it out, add your favorite toppings, and bake. Or try refrigerated pizza doughs and pizza dough mixes. All of these products are low in fat and easy to use.

❏ If you don't mind your pizzas being a bit unconventional, you'll find a range of ready-made low-fat crusts at your supermarket. To make individual pizzas, try rounds of pita bread (choose oat bran or whole wheat), English muffin and bagel halves, and fat-free flour tortillas. For larger pizzas, horizontally sliced French or Italian breads make a great base.

Primavera Pan Pizza

Yield: 8 servings

1 recipe Hearty Wheat Pizza Dough (page 126) or Multigrain Pizza Dough (page 125)

1 teaspoon crushed fresh garlic

3 cups (moderately packed) chopped fresh spinach

$\frac{1}{2}$ cup Arrabbiata Sauce (page 171), Basic Marinara Sauce (page 166), or bottled fat-free marinara sauce

1 tablespoon grated nonfat or reduced-fat Parmesan cheese

1 cup shredded nonfat or reduced-fat mozzarella cheese

$\frac{1}{2}$ cup fresh or frozen (thawed) cut broccoli florets

$\frac{1}{4}$ cup diced red bell pepper

$\frac{1}{4}$ cup thinly sliced fresh mushrooms

$\frac{1}{2}$ teaspoon dried Italian seasoning

1. Turn the dough onto a lightly floured surface. Using a rolling pin, roll the dough into a 10-x-14-inch rectangle. Coat a 9-x-13-inch pan with nonstick cooking spray, and press the dough over the bottom and $\frac{1}{2}$-inch up the sides of the pan. Let the crust sit for 10 to 15 minutes, or until it rises slightly.

2. While the crust is rising, coat a large nonstick skillet with nonstick cooking spray, and preheat over medium heat. Add the garlic, and stir-fry for about 30 seconds, or until the garlic just begins to turn color. Add the spinach, and stir-fry for another minute, or just until the spinach is wilted. Remove the skillet from the heat, and set aside.

3. Spread the sauce over the bottom of the crust. Sprinkle the Parmesan over the sauce, and top with the spinach. Follow with layers of the mozzarella, broccoli, peppers, and mushrooms, and sprinkle with the Italian seasoning.

4. Bake at 450°F for about 12 minutes, or until the cheese is melted and the crust is lightly browned. Slice and serve immediately.

NUTRITIONAL FACTS (PER SLICE)

Calories: 129　Carbohydrates: 21.4 g　Cholesterol: 3 mg
Fat: 0.8 g　Fiber: 3 g　Protein: 9 g　Sodium: 230 mg

You Save:　Calories: 64　Fat: 8.3 g

Ham and Mushroom Pizza

1. Turn the dough onto a lightly floured surface. Using a rolling pin, roll the dough into a 14-inch circle. (For a thick crust, roll the dough into a 12-inch circle.) Coat a 14-inch (or 12-inch) pizza pan with nonstick cooking spray. Place the dough on the pan, forming a slight rim around the edges.

2. Spread the sauce over the crust to within $\frac{1}{2}$ inch of the edges. Sprinkle the mozzarella over the sauce. Arrange the ham strips in concentric circles over the sauce. Top with the mushrooms, and sprinkle with the Italian seasoning.

3. Bake at 450°F for about 12 minutes, or until the cheese is melted and the crust is lightly browned. Slice and serve immediately.

NUTRITIONAL FACTS (PER SLICE)
Calories: 134   Carbohydrates: 21.5 g   Cholesterol: 7 mg
Fat: 1 g   Fiber: 0.9 g   Protein: 9.7 g   Sodium: 248 mg

You Save: Calories: 73   Fat: 9.1 g

Yield: *8 slices*

1 recipe Hearty Wheat Pizza Dough (page 126) or Multigrain Pizza Dough (page 125)

$\frac{3}{4}$ cup Arrabbiata Sauce (page 171) or bottled fat-free marinara sauce

1 cup shredded nonfat or reduced-fat mozzarella cheese

3 oz. ham (at least 97% lean), thinly sliced and cut into thin strips

$\frac{3}{4}$ cup thinly sliced fresh mushrooms

$\frac{1}{2}$ teaspoon dried Italian seasoning

Zucchini and Tomato Pizza

Yield: *8 slices*

1 recipe Multigrain Pizza Dough (page 125) or Parmesan-Polenta Pizza Dough (page 124)

¾ cup diced plum tomatoes (about 2 medium)

1 teaspoon crushed fresh garlic

2 tablespoons grated nonfat or reduced-fat Parmesan cheese

¾ cup shredded nonfat or reduced-fat mozzarella cheese

½ medium zucchini, quartered lengthwise and thinly sliced (about ½ cup)

1 small yellow onion, quartered and thinly sliced (about ½ cup)

1 teaspoon dried basil, or 1 tablespoon minced fresh basil

1. Turn the dough onto a lightly floured surface. Using a rolling pin, roll the dough into a 14-inch circle. (For a thick crust, roll the dough into a 12-inch circle.) Coat a 14-inch (or 12-inch) pizza pan with nonstick cooking spray. Place the dough on the pan, forming a slight rim around the edges.

2. Place the tomatoes and garlic in a small bowl, and toss to mix well. Spread the mixture over the crust to within ½ inch of the edges. Sprinkle the tomato mixture first with the Parmesan, and then with the mozzarella. Top with the zucchini and onions, and sprinkle with the basil.

3. Bake at 450°F for about 12 minutes, or until the cheese is melted and the crust is lightly browned. Slice and serve immediately.

NUTRITIONAL FACTS (PER SLICE)

Calories: 114   Carbohydrates: 20.5 g   Cholesterol: 4 mg
Fat: 0.5 g   Fiber: 1.7 g   Protein: 6.8 g   Sodium: 181 mg

You Save: Calories: 60   Fat: 7.8 g

Puttanesca Pizza

1. Place the drained tomatoes in a small bowl, and mash with a fork until coarsely crushed. Drain off any liquid that has accumulated, and set aside.

2. Turn the dough onto a lightly floured surface. Using a rolling pin, roll the dough into a 14-inch circle. (For a thick crust, roll the dough into a 12-inch circle.) Coat a 14-inch (or 12-inch) pizza pan with nonstick cooking spray. Place the dough on the pan, forming a slight rim around the edges.

3. Spread the tomatoes over the crust to within $1/2$ inch of the edges. Sprinkle first the Parmesan and then the mozzarella over the tomatoes. Top with the olives and capers, and sprinkle with the Italian seasoning and red pepper.

4. Bake at 450°F for about 10 minutes, or until the cheese is melted and the crust is lightly browned. Slice and serve immediately.

Yield: 8 slices

1 can (14$1/2$ ounces) unsalted whole tomatoes, drained

1 recipe Parmesan-Polenta Pizza Dough (page 124) or Oatmeal Pizza Dough (page 126)

1 tablespoon plus 1$1/2$ teaspoons grated nonfat or reduced-fat Parmesan cheese

1 cup shredded nonfat or reduced-fat mozzarella cheese

$1/4$ cup sliced black olives

1 tablespoon capers

$3/4$ teaspoon dried Italian seasoning

$1/2$ teaspoon crushed red pepper

NUTRITIONAL FACTS (PER SLICE)

Calories: 139 Carbohydrates: 24.5 g Cholesterol: 5 mg
Fat: 0.9 g Fiber: 1.7 g Protein: 9 g Sodium: 352 mg

You Save: Calories: 68 Fat: 9.5 g

Neapolitan Pizza

Yield: 8 slices

1 can (14½ ounces) unsalted whole tomatoes, drained

1 teaspoon crushed fresh garlic

¼ teaspoon coarsely ground black pepper

1 recipe Oatmeal Pizza Dough (page 126) or Parmesan-Polenta Pizza Dough (page 124)

1 tablespoon plus 1½ teaspoons grated nonfat or reduced-fat Parmesan cheese

1 cup shredded nonfat mozzarella cheese

4 anchovy fillets, drained and coarsely chopped

1 tablespoon finely chopped fresh oregano, or 1 teaspoon dried

1. Place the drained tomatoes in a small bowl, and mash with a fork until coarsely crushed. Drain off any liquid that has accumulated, stir in the garlic and pepper, and set aside.

2. Turn the dough onto a lightly floured surface. Using a rolling pin, roll the dough into a 14-inch circle. (For a thick crust, roll the dough into a 12-inch circle.) Coat a 14-inch (or 12-inch) pizza pan with nonstick cooking spray. Place the dough on the pan, forming a slight rim around the edges.

3. Spread the tomato mixture over the crust to within ½ inch of the edges. Sprinkle first the Parmesan and then the mozzarella over the tomatoes. Top with the anchovies, and sprinkle with the oregano.

4. Bake at 450°F for about 10 minutes, or until the cheese is melted and the crust is lightly browned. Slice and serve immediately.

NUTRITIONAL FACTS (PER SLICE)

Calories: 132   Carbohydrates: 22.4 g   Cholesterol: 5 mg
Fat: 0.7 g   Fiber: 1.5 g   Protein: 9 g   Sodium: 265 mg

You Save: Calories: 65   Fat: 8.5 g

Top: Three-Cheese Manicotti (page 113)
Center: Capellini Carbonara (page 104)
Bottom: Spinach Pasta Primavera (page 117)

Top Left: Sausage and
Ricotta Pan Pizza (page 140)

Top Right: Spinach and
Mushroom Calzones (page 142)

Bottom: Margherita Pizza (page 127)

Top: Spinach and Potato Gnocchi (page 163) with Basic Marinara Sauce (page 166)

Center: Risotto With Shrimp and Asparagus (page 159)

Bottom: Creamy Firm Polenta, sliced and broiled (page 152), with Bolognese Mushroom Sauce (page 175)

Top: Chicken Rollatini (page 190)

Center: Eggplant Parmesan (page 193)

Bottom: Braised Beef With Hearty Mushroom Sauce (page 180)

Pesto Pizza

1. To make the pesto, place all of the pesto sauce ingredients in a blender or food processor, and process into a paste. Add a little water if the mixture seems too dry, and set aside.

2. Turn the dough onto a lightly floured surface. Using a rolling pin, roll the dough into a 14-inch circle. (For a thick crust, roll the dough into a 12-inch circle.) Coat a 14-inch (or 12-inch) pizza pan with nonstick cooking spray. Place the dough on the pan, forming a slight rim around the edges.

3. Spread the pesto over the crust, extending the sauce to within $\frac{1}{2}$ inch of the edges. Arrange the tomatoes over the pesto, and top with the mozzarella.

4. Bake at 450°F for about 12 minutes, or until the cheese is melted and the crust is lightly browned. Slice and serve immediately.

NUTRITIONAL FACTS (PER SLICE)
Calories: 130 Carbohydrates: 22.3 g Cholesterol: 4 mg
Fat: 0.5 g Fiber: 1.3 g Protein: 9 g Sodium: 225 mg

You Save: Calories: 82 Fat: 10.8 g

Yield: *8 slices*

1 recipe Oatmeal Pizza Dough (page 126) or Multigrain Pizza Dough (page 125)

2 medium plum tomatoes, thinly sliced

1 cup shredded nonfat or reduced-fat mozzarella cheese

PESTO SAUCE

$\frac{1}{2}$ cup (packed) chopped fresh spinach

$\frac{1}{4}$ cup (packed) chopped fresh basil

$\frac{1}{4}$ cup grated nonfat or reduced-fat Parmesan cheese

1 teaspoon crushed fresh garlic

2 tablespoons bottled fat-free Italian salad dressing

2 teaspoons extra virgin olive oil (optional)

Ground Beef and Onion Pizza

Yield: *8 servings*

1 teaspoon crushed fresh garlic

8 ounces 95% lean ground beef

$\frac{1}{8}$ teaspoon salt

$\frac{1}{4}$ teaspoon ground black pepper

1 recipe Parmesan-Polenta Pizza Dough (page 124) or Hearty Wheat Pizza Dough (page 126)

$\frac{3}{4}$ cup canned tomato purée or Arrabbiata Sauce (page 171)

1 cup shredded nonfat or reduced-fat mozzarella cheese

1 medium yellow onion, cut into thin wedges and separated into pieces

1 teaspoon dried oregano

1. Coat a medium nonstick skillet with nonstick cooking spray, and place over medium heat. Add the garlic, ground beef, salt, and pepper, and cook, stirring to crumble, until the meat is no longer pink. Drain off and discard any fat, and set aside. (If the meat is 95% lean, there will be no fat to drain off.)

2. Turn the dough onto a lightly floured surface. Using a rolling pin, roll the dough into a 14-inch circle. (For a thick crust, roll the dough into a 12-inch circle). Coat a 14-inch (or 12-inch) pizza pan with nonstick cooking spray. Place the dough on the pan, forming a slight rim around the edges.

3. Spread the tomato purée or sauce over the crust to within $\frac{1}{2}$ inch of the edges. Top with the ground beef, followed by the mozzarella and onions. Sprinkle with the oregano.

4. Bake at 450°F for about 12 minutes, or until the cheese is melted and the crust is lightly browned. Slice and serve immediately.

NUTRITIONAL FACTS (PER SLICE)

Calories: 158 Carbohydrates: 22.6 g Cholesterol: 20 mg
Fat: 1.7 g Fiber: 2 g Protein: 13 g Sodium: 218 mg

You Save: Calories: 78 Fat: 9.9 g

Change-of-Pace Pizza Shapes

Although most of the pizzas in this chapter are baked as flat 12- or 14-inch circular pies, any of these Italian classics can alternatively be made in a 12-inch ovenproof skillet, in a 9-x-13-inch baking pan, or as individual mini pizzas. Just follow the directions below, and delight family and friends with truly designer creations.

Pan Pizzas

To make a rectangular pan pizza, prepare any of

Roasted Red Pepper Pizza

1. Turn the dough onto a lightly floured surface. Using a rolling pin, roll the dough into a 14-inch circle. (For a thick crust, roll the dough into a 12-inch circle.) Coat a 14-inch (or 12-inch) pizza pan with nonstick cooking spray. Place the dough on the pan, forming a slight rim around the edges.

2. Spread the sauce over the crust to within $\frac{1}{2}$ inch of the edges. Sprinkle with the Parmesan, and arrange the roasted pepper strips in concentric circles over the sauce and cheese. Top first with the mozzarella, and then with the onions and, if desired, the olives. Sprinkle with the basil and oregano.

3. Bake at 450°F for about 12 minutes, or until the cheese is melted and the crust is lightly browned. Slice and serve immediately.

NUTRITIONAL FACTS (PER SLICE)

Calories: 126   Carbohydrates: 22.6 g   Cholesterol: 2 mg
Fat: 0.6 g   Fiber: 2 g   Protein: 7.5 g   Sodium: 238 mg

You Save: Calories: 67   Fat: 8.3 g

Yield: *8 slices*

1 recipe Multigrain Pizza Dough (page 125) or Parmesan-Polenta Pizza Dough (page 124)

$\frac{1}{2}$ cup bottled fat-free marinara sauce, Basic Marinara Sauce (page 166), or Arrabbiata Sauce (page 171)

2 tablespoons grated nonfat or reduced-fat Parmesan cheese

2 medium red bell peppers, roasted and cut into thin strips (page 57)

1 cup shredded nonfat or reduced-fat mozzarella cheese

1 small yellow onion, quartered and thinly sliced

$\frac{1}{4}$ cup sliced black olives (optional)

$\frac{1}{2}$ teaspoon dried basil

$\frac{1}{2}$ teaspoon dried oregano

---

the pizza doughs on pages 124 to 126 as directed, but roll the dough into a 10-x-14-inch rectangle. Coat a 9-x-13-inch pan with nonstick cooking spray, and press the dough over the bottom and $\frac{1}{2}$ inch up the sides of the pan. Let the crust sit for 10 to 15 minutes, or until it rises slightly. Then add the toppings, and bake as directed.

To make a round skillet pizza, first coat the bottom and sides of a 12-inch ovenproof skillet with nonstick cooking spray. (Note that the bottom of a 12-inch skillet is only 10 inches wide.) Then roll the prepared dough into an 11-inch circle, and press it over the bottom and $\frac{1}{2}$ inch up the sides of the prepared skillet.

Let the crust sit for 10 to 15 minutes, or until it rises slightly. Then add your favorite toppings, and bake as directed.

Mini Pizzas

To make individual pizzas, prepare the pizza dough as directed, but divide it into 4 equal portions. To make thin-crusted pizzas, roll each piece into an 8-inch circle. For thicker crusts, roll out $6\frac{1}{2}$-inch circles. Immediately add the toppings and bake for about 10 minutes, or until the cheese is melted and the crust is lightly browned.

Artichoke and Sun-Dried Tomato Pizza

Yield: *8 slices*

¼ cup plus 2 tablespoons diced sun-dried tomatoes (not packed in oil)

¼ cup plus 2 tablespoons water

1 package (9 ounces) frozen (thawed) artichoke hearts, or 1 can (14 ounces) artichoke hearts, drained

1 recipe Oatmeal Pizza Dough (page 126) or Parmesan-Polenta Pizza Dough (page 124)

½ cup shredded nonfat or reduced-fat mozzarella cheese

½ cup shredded reduced-fat provolone cheese

1 teaspoon dried Italian seasoning

1. Place the sun-dried tomatoes and water in a small saucepan, and bring to a boil over high heat. Reduce the heat to low, cover, and simmer for 2 minutes, or just until the tomatoes have plumped. Remove the pot from the heat, and set aside.

2. Cut the artichoke hearts into quarters, and set aside.

3. Turn the dough onto a lightly floured surface. Using a rolling pin, roll the dough into a 14-inch circle. (For a thick crust, roll the dough into a 12-inch circle.) Coat a 14-inch (or 12-inch) pizza pan with nonstick cooking spray. Place the dough on the pan, forming a slight rim around the edges.

4. Sprinkle first the mozzarella and then the provolone over the crust to within ½ inch of the edges. Top with the artichoke hearts and tomatoes, and sprinkle with the Italian seasoning.

5. Bake at 450°F for about 12 minutes, or until the cheese is melted and the crust is lightly browned. Slice and serve immediately.

NUTRITIONAL FACTS (PER SLICE)

Calories: 141   Carbohydrates: 23.4 g   Cholesterol: 5 mg
Fat: 1.9 g   Fiber: 3 g   Protein: 9 g   Sodium: 215 mg

You Save: Calories: 89   Fat: 11.6 g

Roasted Eggplant Pizza

1. Place the eggplant in a medium-sized bowl. Add the vinegar, garlic, salt, and pepper, and toss to mix well.

2. Coat a medium-sized baking sheet with olive oil cooking spray, and spread the eggplant in a single layer on the sheet. Spray the cubes lightly with the cooking spray, and bake at 450°F for about 10 minutes. Turn with a spatula, and bake for 10 additional minutes, or until the eggplant is soft and nicely browned. Remove from the oven, and set aside.

3. Turn the dough onto a lightly floured surface. Using a rolling pin, roll the dough into a 14-inch circle. (For a thick crust, roll the dough into a 12-inch circle). Coat a 14-inch (or 12-inch) pizza pan with nonstick cooking spray. Place the dough on the pan, forming a slight rim around the edges.

4. Spread the sauce over the crust to within $\frac{1}{2}$ inch of the edges. Top with first the eggplant, and then the mozzarella. Sprinkle with the oregano.

5. Bake at 450°F for about 12 minutes, or until the cheese is melted and the crust is lightly browned. Slice and serve immediately.

Yield: 8 slices

4 cups diced peeled eggplant (about 1 medium)

1 tablespoon balsamic vinegar

1 teaspoon crushed fresh garlic

$\frac{1}{4}$ teaspoon salt

$\frac{1}{4}$ teaspoon ground black pepper

Olive oil cooking spray

1 recipe Oatmeal Pizza Dough (page 126) or Multigrain Pizza Dough (page 125)

$\frac{3}{4}$ cup Arrabbiata Sauce (page 171), Basic Marinara Sauce (page 166), or bottled fat-free marinara sauce

1 cup shredded nonfat or reduced-fat mozzarella cheese

$\frac{3}{4}$ teaspoon dried oregano

NUTRITIONAL FACTS (PER SLICE)

Calories: 135 Carbohydrates: 24 g Cholesterol: 3 mg
Fat: 0.7 g Fiber: 2.5 g Protein: 8 g Sodium: 271 mg

You Save: Calories: 63 Fat: 8.5 g

Sausage and Ricotta Pan Pizza

Yield: *8 slices*

1 recipe Oatmeal Pizza Dough
(page 126) or
Parmesan-Polenta Pizza Dough
(page 124)

3 tablespoons chopped sun-dried
tomatoes (not packed in oil)

3 tablespoons water

$\frac{3}{4}$ cup nonfat ricotta cheese

2 tablespoons grated nonfat
Parmesan cheese

8 ounces Turkey Italian Sausage
(page 182), cooked, drained,
and crumbled

1 cup shredded nonfat or
reduced-fat mozzarella cheese

1. Turn the dough onto a lightly floured surface. Using a rolling pin, roll the dough into an 11-inch circle. Coat a 12-inch ovenproof skillet with nonstick cooking spray, and press the dough over the bottom and $\frac{1}{2}$ inch up the sides of the skillet. (Note that the bottom of a 12-inch skillet is only 10 inches wide.) Let the crust sit for 10 to 15 minutes, or until it rises slightly.

2. While the crust is rising, place the sun-dried tomatoes and water in a small saucepan, and bring to a boil over high heat. Reduce the heat to low, cover, and simmer for 2 minutes, or until the tomatoes have plumped. Remove the pot from the heat, and set aside.

3. Place the ricotta and Parmesan in a small bowl, and stir to mix well. Spread the mixture over the bottom of the crust, and top with the sausage. Drain any excess liquid from the tomatoes, and scatter the tomatoes over the sausage. Top with the mozzarella.

4. Bake at 450°F for about 15 minutes, or until the cheese is melted and the crust is lightly browned. Slice and serve immediately.

NUTRITIONAL FACTS (PER SLICE)

Calories: 174   Carbohydrates: 22.5 g   Cholesterol: 22 mg
Fat: 1.2 g   Fiber: 1.1 g   Protein: 18.3 g   Sodium: 337 mg

You Save: Calories: 132   Fat: 16.7 g

Fresh Tomato and Herb Pizza

1. Place the tomatoes, garlic, and pepper in a medium-sized bowl, and stir to mix well. Set aside.

2. Turn the dough onto a lightly floured surface. Using a rolling pin, roll the dough into a 14-inch circle. (For a thick crust, roll the dough into a 12-inch circle.) Coat a 14-inch (or 12-inch) pizza pan with nonstick cooking spray. Place the dough on the pan, forming a slight rim around the edges.

3. Spread the tomato mixture over the crust, extending it to within $1/2$ inch of the edges. Sprinkle first with the Parmesan and then with the mozzarella. Sprinkle with the herbs.

4. Bake at 450°F for about 12 minutes, or until the cheese is melted and the crust is lightly browned. Slice and serve immediately.

Yield: *8 slices*

$1\frac{1}{4}$ cups chopped plum tomatoes (about 4 medium)

1 teaspoon crushed fresh garlic

$\frac{1}{4}$ teaspoon ground black pepper

1 recipe Oatmeal Pizza Dough (page 126) or Parmesan-Polenta Pizza Dough (page 124)

2 tablespoons grated nonfat or reduced-fat Parmesan cheese

1 cup shredded nonfat or reduced-fat mozzarella cheese

$1\frac{1}{2}$ teaspoons finely chopped fresh basil, or $\frac{1}{2}$ teaspoon dried

$1\frac{1}{2}$ teaspoons finely chopped fresh oregano, or $\frac{1}{2}$ teaspoon dried

$1\frac{1}{2}$ teaspoons finely chopped fresh rosemary, or $\frac{1}{2}$ teaspoon dried

---

NUTRITIONAL FACTS (PER SLICE)
Calories: 128 Carbohydrates: 21.5 g Cholesterol: 4 mg
Fat: 0.6 g Fiber: 1.4 g Protein: 9 g Sodium: 198 mg

You Save: Calories: 66 Fat: 8.8 g

CALZONES

Spinach and Mushroom Calzones

Yield: *4 calzones*

1 recipe Oatmeal Pizza Dough (page 126) or Parmesan Polenta Pizza Dough (page 124)

3 tablespoons beaten egg white or fat-free egg substitute

1⅓ cups bottled fat-free marinara sauce or Basic Marinara Sauce (page 166)

FILLING

1 teaspoon crushed fresh garlic

1½ cups sliced fresh mushrooms

5 cups (packed) coarsely chopped fresh spinach leaves (about 5 ounces)

¼ teaspoon dried thyme

¼ teaspoon coarsely ground black pepper

2 tablespoon grated nonfat or reduced-fat Parmesan cheese

¾ cup shredded nonfat or reduced-fat mozzarella cheese

1. To make the filling, coat a large nonstick skillet with olive oil cooking spray, and preheat over medium-high heat. Add the garlic and mushrooms, and stir-fry for about 3 minutes, or until the mushrooms are tender and most of the liquid has evaporated. Add the spinach, thyme, and pepper, and stir-fry for 2 additional minutes, or until the spinach is wilted and any excess liquid has evaporated. Remove the skillet from the heat, and stir in the Parmesan. Set aside.

2. Divide the dough into 4 portions, and shape each portion into a ball. Working on a lightly floured surface, roll each ball into a 7-inch circle.

3. Spread a quarter of the spinach mixture over half of each crust to within ½ inch of the edges, and top with 3 tablespoons of mozzarella. Moisten the edges of the dough with water, and fold the circle in half to enclose the filling. Seal the edges by pressing with the tines of a fork.

4. Coat a baking sheet with nonstick cooking spray, and transfer the calzones to the sheet. Brush the tops lightly with the beaten egg white, and prick the tops in a couple of places with a fork. Bake at 450°F for about 10 minutes, or until the crust is golden brown.

5. While the calzones are baking, place the sauce in a small saucepan, and cook over medium heat until warmed through. Serve the calzones hot with a side dish of the warm dipping sauce.

NUTRITIONAL FACTS (PER CALZONE)

Calories: 284 Carbohydrates: 50.3 g Cholesterol: 6 mg
Fat: 1.2 g Fiber: 5.2 g Protein: 18 g Sodium: 288 mg

You Save: Calories: 120 Fat: 15.7 g

Roasted Vegetable Calzones

1. To make the filling, place the sun-dried tomatoes and the water in a small saucepan, and bring to a boil over high heat. Reduce the heat to low, cover, and simmer for 2 minutes, or until the tomatoes have plumped. Remove the pot from the heat, and set aside.

2. Place the mushrooms, eggplant, zucchini, and onion in a large bowl. Add the vinegar, garlic, salt, and pepper, and toss to mix well.

3. Coat a medium-sized baking sheet with olive oil cooking spray, and arrange the vegetables in a single layer on the sheet. Spray the vegetables lightly with the cooking spray, and bake at 475°F for 10 minutes. Turn the vegetables with a spatula, and bake for 10 additional minutes, or until tender and nicely browned. Remove the vegetables from the oven.

4. Drain any excess water from the tomatoes. Add the tomatoes to the roasted vegetables, and toss to mix well. Set aside.

5. Divide the dough into 4 portions, and shape each portion into a ball. Working on a lightly floured surface, roll each ball into a 7-inch circle.

6. Spread a quarter of the vegetable mixture over half of each crust to within $\frac{1}{2}$ inch of the edges, and top with 3 tablespoons of mozzarella or provolone. Moisten the edges of the dough with water, and fold the circle in half to enclose the filling. Seal the edges by pressing with the tines of a fork.

7. Coat a baking sheet with nonstick cooking spray, and transfer the calzones to the sheet. Brush the tops lightly with the beaten egg white, and prick the tops in a couple of places with a fork. Bake at 450°F for about 10 minutes, or until the crust is golden brown. Serve hot.

Yield: 4 calzones

1 recipe Hearty Wheat Pizza Dough (page 126) or Multigrain Pizza Dough (page 125)

3 tablespoons beaten egg white or fat-free egg substitute

FILLING

$\frac{1}{4}$ cup diced sun-dried tomatoes (not packed in oil)

$\frac{1}{4}$ cup water

$\frac{3}{4}$ cup halved fresh mushrooms

$\frac{3}{4}$ cup $\frac{3}{4}$-inch cubes eggplant (about $\frac{1}{4}$ medium)

$\frac{3}{4}$ cup sliced zucchini (about $\frac{3}{4}$ medium)

$\frac{1}{2}$ medium yellow onion, cut into thin wedges

1 tablespoon balsamic vinegar

1 teaspoon crushed fresh garlic

$\frac{1}{8}$ teaspoon salt

$\frac{1}{8}$ teaspoon ground black pepper

Olive oil cooking spray

$\frac{3}{4}$ cup shredded nonfat or reduced-fat mozzarella cheese or reduced-fat provolone cheese

---

NUTRITIONAL FACTS (PER CALZONE)
Calories: 241 Carbohydrates: 42 g Cholesterol: 3 mg
Fat: 1.6 g Fiber: 4.2 g Protein: 14.6 g Sodium: 413 mg

You Save: Calories: 147 Fat: 18.1 g

Ham and Cheese Calzones

Yield: *4 servings*

1 recipe Multigrain Pizza Dough
   (page 125) or
   Parmesan-Polenta Pizza Dough
   (page 124)

3 tablespoons beaten egg white
   or fat-free egg substitute

FILLING

3 ounces ham (at least 97% lean),
   finely chopped ($\frac{2}{3}$ cup)

$\frac{2}{3}$ cup nonfat ricotta cheese

$\frac{2}{3}$ cup shredded nonfat or
   reduced-fat mozzarella cheese

$\frac{1}{2}$ teaspoon dried Italian
   seasoning

1. To make the filling, place all of the filling ingredients in a medium-sized bowl, and stir to mix well. Set aside.

2. Divide the dough into 4 portions, and shape each portion into a ball. Working on a lightly floured surface, roll each ball into a 7-inch circle.

3. Spread a quarter of the ham mixture over half of each crust to within $\frac{1}{2}$ inch of the edges. Moisten the edges of the dough with water, and fold the circle in half to enclose the filling. Seal the edges by pressing with the tines of a fork.

4. Coat a baking sheet with nonstick cooking spray, and transfer the calzones to the sheet. Brush the tops lightly with the beaten egg white, and prick the tops in a couple of places with a fork. Bake at 450°F for about 10 minutes, or until the crust is golden brown. Serve hot.

NUTRITIONAL FACTS (PER SERVING)

Calories: 258 Carbohydrates: 41.5 g Cholesterol: 16 mg
Fat: 1.3 g Fiber: 2.6 g Protein: 20 g Sodium: 465 mg

You Save: Calories: 150 Fat: 19.1 g

FOCACCIA AND OTHER BREADS

Focaccia With Italian Vegetables

When making this delectable bread, be sure to use regular Parmesan cheese—not a no- or low-fat brand.

Yield: *8 slices*

1. Turn the dough onto a lightly floured surface. Using a rolling pin, roll the dough into a 12-inch circle. Coat a 12-inch pizza pan with nonstick cooking spray, and place the dough in the pan. Cover with a clean kitchen towel, and let rise in a warm place for about 25 minutes, or until doubled in size.

2. Brush the top of the dough lightly with the skim milk. Arrange the vegetables over the crust, extending it to within $\frac{1}{2}$ inch of the edges. Sprinkle with the Parmesan.

3. Bake at 450°F for about 12 minutes, or until lightly browned. Slice and serve immediately.

1 recipe Oatmeal Pizza Dough (page 126) or Parmesan-Polenta Pizza Dough (page 124)

1 tablespoon skim milk

$\frac{1}{2}$ red pepper, roasted and cut into thin strips (page 57), or $\frac{1}{2}$ fresh red bell pepper, cut into thin strips

$\frac{1}{2}$ cup thinly sliced mushrooms, thinly sliced zucchini, or chopped frozen (thawed) or canned (drained) artichoke hearts

3 tablespoons grated Parmesan cheese

NUTRITIONAL FACTS (PER SLICE)

Calories: 106   Carbohydrates: 19.7 g   Cholesterol: 2 mg
Fat: 1.1 g   Fiber: 1.2 g   Protein: 4.3 g   Sodium: 122 mg

You Save: Calories: 45   Fat: 5 g

Onion-Herb Focaccia

Yield: *8 slices*

1 recipe Oatmeal Pizza Dough
   (page 126) or
   Parmesan-Polenta Pizza Dough
   (page 124)

2 teaspoons extra virgin olive oil

2 teaspoons Dijon mustard

1 teaspoon crushed fresh garlic

1 medium yellow onion,
   quartered and thinly sliced

1 teaspoon dried rosemary, or 1
   tablespoon fresh

1. Turn the dough onto a lightly floured surface. Using a rolling pin, roll the dough into a 12-inch circle. Coat a 12-inch pizza pan with cooking spray, and place the dough on the pan. Cover with a clean kitchen towel, and let rise in a warm place for about 25 minutes, or until doubled in size.

2. Place the olive oil, mustard, and garlic in a small bowl, and stir to mix well. Spread the mixture over the crust, extending it to within $\frac{1}{2}$ inch of the edges. Scatter the onions over the mustard mixture and sprinkle with the rosemary.

3. Bake at 450°F for about 12 minutes, or until lightly browned. Slice and serve immediately.

NUTRITIONAL FACTS (PER SLICE)

Calories: 105   Carbohydrates: 20 g   Cholesterol: 0 mg
Fat: 1.6 g   Fiber: 1.2 g   Protein: 2.7 g   Sodium: 84 mg

You Save: Calories: 34 Fat: 3.9 g

Glazed Onion Focaccia

Yield: *12 slices*

1 recipe Multigrain Pizza Dough
   (page 124) or Hearty Wheat
   Pizza Dough (page 126)

1 medium Spanish onion, thinly
   sliced

1 teaspoon dried thyme

$\frac{1}{4}$ teaspoon salt

1 teaspoon sugar

2 teaspoons balsamic vinegar

1. Turn the dough onto a lightly floured surface. Using a rolling pin, roll the dough into a 12-inch circle. Coat a 12-inch pizza pan with cooking spray, and place the dough on the pan. Cover with a clean kitchen towel, and let rise in a warm place for about 25 minutes, or until doubled in size.

2. Coat a large nonstick skillet with olive oil cooking spray, and preheat over medium heat. Add the onion, thyme, and salt, and sauté for about 7 minutes, or until the onions are wilted and just starting to brown. (If the skillet becomes too dry, add a few teaspoons of chicken broth, white wine, or water as needed.) Add the sugar, and sauté for another minute. Add the vinegar, and stir to mix well. Remove the skillet from the heat.

3. Spread the onion mixture over the crust, extending it to within $\frac{1}{2}$ inch of the edges. Bake at 450°F for about 12 minutes, or until lightly browned. Slice and serve immediately.

NUTRITIONAL FACTS (PER SLICE)

Calories: 95   Carbohydrates: 19.7 g   Cholesterol: 0 mg
Fat: 0.5 g   Fiber: 1.5 g   Protein: 2.9 g   Sodium: 135 mg

You Save: Calories: 45 Fat: 5 g

Sun-Dried Tomato and Herb Focaccia

Make this sensational bread with regular Parmesan cheese, rather than a nonfat brand.

Yield: *8 slices*

1. Prepare the dough as directed, but combine the Italian seasoning with the flour when mixing up the dough.

2. While the dough is rising, place the sun-dried tomatoes in a small bowl, and pour the hot tap water over the tomatoes. Set aside.

3. Turn the dough onto a lightly floured surface. Drain the tomatoes, and knead them into the dough. Using a rolling pin, roll the dough into a 12-inch circle. Coat a 12-inch pizza pan with nonstick cooking spray, and place the dough on the pan. Cover with a clean kitchen towel, and let rise in a warm place for about 25 minutes, or until doubled in size.

4. Place the milk and garlic in a small bowl, and stir to mix well. Spread the mixture over the crust, extending it to within $\frac{1}{2}$ inch of the edges. Sprinkle the Parmesan over the garlic, and spray the top lightly with the cooking spray.

5. Bake at 450°F for 9 minutes, or until lightly browned. Slice and serve immediately.

1 recipe Oatmeal Pizza Dough (page 126) or Parmesan-Polenta Pizza Dough (page 124)

$\frac{1}{2}$ teaspoon dried Italian seasoning

2 tablespoons finely chopped sun-dried tomatoes (not packed in oil)

3 tablespoons hot tap water

2 teaspoons skim milk

1 teaspoon crushed fresh garlic

2 tablespoons Parmesan cheese

Olive oil cooking spray

NUTRITIONAL FACTS (PER SLICE)

Calories: 102   Carbohydrates: 19 g   Cholesterol: 2 mg
Fat: 1 g   Fiber: 1 g   Protein: 4 g   Sodium: 124 mg

You Save: Calories: 45   Fat: 5 g

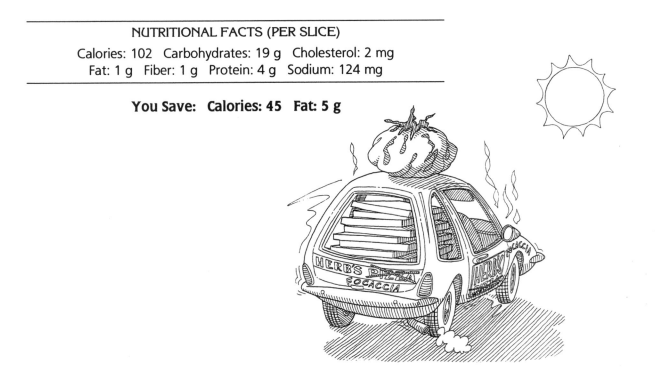

Italian Chop Bread

Yield: *12 servings*

2 tablespoons chopped sun-dried tomatoes (not packed in oil)

2 tablespoons water

¾ cup shredded nonfat or reduced-fat mozzarella cheese or reduced-fat provolone cheese

1 teaspoon dried Italian seasoning, or 1 tablespoon finely chopped fresh basil

3 tablespoons chopped black olives

2 tablespoons pine nuts (optional)

1 recipe Oatmeal Pizza Dough (page 126) or Parmesan-Polenta Pizza Dough (page 124)

1 tablespoon fat-free egg substitute or beaten egg white

1. Place the sun-dried tomatoes and water in a small saucepan, and bring to a boil over high heat. Reduce the heat to low, cover, and simmer for 2 minutes, or until the tomatoes have plumped. Remove the pot from the heat, drain off any excess liquid, and set aside.

2. Place the cheese, Italian seasoning or basil, olives, plumped tomatoes, and, if desired, the pine nuts in a small bowl, and toss to mix well.

3. Place the dough on a large lightly floured cutting board, and pat into a 10-inch circle. Pile the cheese mixture on top of the dough, and draw the dough up and around the cheese mixture so that the edges of the dough meet in the middle, completely covering the filling. Flatten the dough into an 8-inch circle.

4. Using a large sharp knife, slice the dough-wrapped mound 5 times in one direction, cutting all the way through to the board. Then slice 5 times in the other direction to form pieces of dough that are about 2 inches square. Use the knife to gently mix the dough and cheese mixture by lifting the dough and cheese from the bottom and piling it back on the top.

5. Coat a baking sheet with nonstick cooking spray, and gently mound the mixture onto the sheet. Using your hands, gently shape the mixture into an 8-inch circle, making sure that most of the cheese mixture is touching pieces of dough. (This will insure that the bread sticks together as it bakes.)

6. Cover the loaf with a clean kitchen towel, and let rise in a warm place for about 25 minutes, or until nearly doubled in size. Brush the top with the egg substitute, and bake at 350°F for about 23 minutes, or until the bread is golden brown and puffy.

7. Let the bread sit for 5 minutes before removing from the sheet. Cut the bread into wedges or simply pull off chunks, and serve warm.

NUTRITIONAL FACTS (PER SERVING)

Calories: 113 Carbohydrates: 20 g Cholesterol: 2 mg
Fat: 0.7 g Fiber: 1.2 g Protein: 6.5 g Sodium: 185 mg

You Save: Calories: 79 Fat: 8.4 g

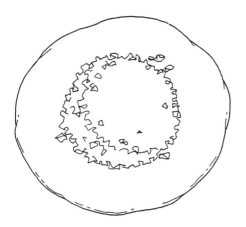

a. Pile the filling on the circle of dough.

b. Draw the dough up and around the filling.

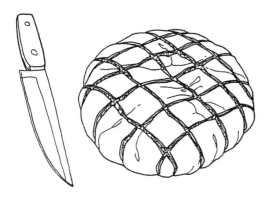

c. Slice the dough-wrapped mound 5 times in each direction.

d. Use a knife to gently mix the dough and the filling.

Making Italian Chop Bread.

Garlic and Herb Bread Sticks

Yield: *8 bread sticks*

1 recipe Oatmeal Pizza Dough
  (page 126) or
  Parmesan-Polenta Pizza Dough
  (page 124)

1 tablespoon fat-free egg
  substitute

1 teaspoon crushed fresh garlic

¾ teaspoon dried rosemary or
  Italian seasoning

¼ teaspoon coarse salt

1. Divide the dough into 8 pieces, and shape each piece into a 15-inch rope. Fold each rope in half and twist several times. Pinch the ends to seal.

2. Coat a medium-sized baking sheet with nonstick cooking spray, and arrange bread sticks on the pan. Cover with a clean kitchen towel, and let rise in a warm place for about 25 minutes, or until nearly doubled in size.

3. Place the egg substitute and garlic in a small dish, and stir to mix. Brush some of this mixture over the top of each bread stick, and top with a pinch of herbs and a few grains of salt.

4. Bake at 400°F for 8 minutes, or until lightly browned. Serve hot.

NUTRITIONAL FACTS (PER BREAD STICK)

Calories: 93   Carbohydrates: 18.9 g   Cholesterol: 0 mg
Fat: 0.4 g   Fiber: 1 g   Protein: 3.4 g   Sodium: 147 mg

You Save: Calories: 45   Fat: 5 g

Variations

To make Two-Seed Bread Sticks, shape the sticks and allow them to rise as directed above. Brush the tops lightly with 1 tablespoon of fat-free egg substitute. Then combine 1 teaspoon of poppy seeds and 1 teaspoon of sesame seeds, and sprinkle ¼ teaspoon of this mixture over each bread stick. Bake as directed.

NUTRITIONAL FACTS (PER BREAD STICK)

Calories: 97   Carbohydrates: 19 g   Cholesterol: 0 mg
Fat: 0.8 g   Fiber: 1.1 g   Protein: 3.6 g   Sodium: 80 mg

You Save: Calories: 45   Fat: 5 g

To make Parmesan Bread Sticks, shape the sticks and allow them to rise as directed above. Then sprinkle ½ teaspoon of grated Parmesan cheese—use regular Parmesan, not fat-free—over each bread stick. Bake as directed.

NUTRITIONAL FACTS (PER BREAD STICK)

Calories: 98   Carbohydrates: 19 g   Cholesterol: 1 mg
Fat: 0.8 g   Fiber: 1 g   Protein: 3.7 g   Sodium: 97 mg

You Save: Calories: 45   Fat: 5 g

9

Pasta Alternatives– Polenta, Risotto, and Gnocchi

Most of us could eat pasta nearly every day of the week and never tire of it. However, Italian cuisine offers three delicious alternatives for those times when you want a change of pace. Polenta, made from cornmeal; risotto, made from rice; and gnocchi, made from potatoes, each present a wide variety of exciting new possibilities.

The first of these pasta alternatives, polenta, is simply a thick mush made from coarsely ground yellow cornmeal. Polenta can be served as a simple but satisfying side dish, or can be topped with a thick tomato sauce and used as an entrée. This versatile food may even be chilled until firm, and then sliced and used as a pasta substitute in dishes like lasagna.

Risotto is a creamy dish made from a short grain rice known as arborio rice. Served plain, risotto makes a wonderful side dish. Or add seafood or chicken and vegetables, and enjoy an elegant yet substantial main dish.

Gnocchi (pronounced *nyó-kee*) are small, delicious potato dumplings. Topped with your favorite sauce and some grated cheese, gnocchi make a comforting, stick-to-your-ribs main dish.

Polenta, risotto, and gnocchi are naturally low in fat. However, like pasta, these foods are often cooked with butter, cream, egg yolks, and high-fat cheeses—ingredients that can boost calorie and fat counts to astronomic heights. But as you will see, there are plenty of other ways to prepare creamy polentas and risottos and delicious gnocchi. Ingredients like evaporated skimmed milk, nonfat milk, fat-free egg substitute, fat-free broth, and nonfat and reduced-fat cheeses can replace the usual high-fat ingredients to produce flavorful dishes that are filling but not fattening.

So get ready for some new taste treats. From Polenta Lasagna, to Risotto with Sun-Dried Tomatoes, to Cheese and Potato Gnocchi, the recipes that follow will show you just how exciting, flavorful, and fun, fat-free Italian cooking can be.

Creamy Firm Polenta

Yield: *6 servings*

3 cups water

3 cups skim milk

½ teaspoon salt

2 cups polenta

Make firm polenta when you want to mold and broil the polenta, or when you want to use it as a pasta substitute in lasagna or other dishes. For some delicious variations, see page 154.

1. Place the water and milk in a 4-quart pot, and bring to a boil over high heat, stirring frequently.

2. Add the salt, and, using a wire whisk, slowly whisk in the polenta. Change to a wooden spoon, and stir the mixture until it begins to thicken.

3. Reduce the heat to medium, and cook, stirring constantly, until the mixture begins to bubble and pop. Reduce the heat to low, and continue to cook, stirring constantly, for about 20 minutes, or until the polenta becomes very thick and pulls completely away from the sides of the pot as you stir. (Note that some brands of polenta will take longer to cook than others.) Use the polenta as your recipe directs, or mold and broil it by following the directions below.

4. To mold the polenta, coat a 9-x-5-inch loaf pan with nonstick cooking spray, and spread the hot polenta in the pan. Allow the polenta to cool to room temperature. Then refrigerate for several hours or overnight, or until the mixture is firm enough to slice.

5. To broil the polenta, cut the chilled mixture into eighteen ½-inch slices. Coat a large baking sheet with nonstick cooking spray, arrange the pieces on the sheet, and spray the tops lightly with olive oil or butter-flavored cooking spray. Broil the polenta 6 inches under a preheated broiler for 4 minutes. Turn, and broil for 4 additional minutes, or until browned on both sides. Serve hot, topped or plain.

NUTRITIONAL FACTS (PER 3-SLICE SERVING)

Calories: 211   Carbohydrates: 41 g   Cholesterol: 2 mg

Fat: 0.9 g   Fiber: 3.4 g   Protein: 8 g   Sodium: 242 mg

You Save: Calories: 32   Fat: 4 g

Creamy Soft Polenta

Plain soft polenta can be served as a side dish instead of rice or potatoes, or topped with your choice of pasta sauce and served as an entrée. At breakfast time, try stirring in raisins and maple syrup or honey for a change-of-pace breakfast cereal. For other delicious variations, see page 154.

Yield: *6 servings*

5 cups water

3 cups skim milk

½ teaspoon salt

2 cups polenta

1. Place the water and milk in a 4-quart pot, and bring to a boil over high heat, stirring frequently.

2. Add the salt, and, using a wire whisk, slowly whisk in the polenta. Change to a wooden spoon, and stir the mixture until it begins to thicken.

3. Reduce the heat to medium, and cook, stirring constantly, until the mixture begins to bubble and pop. Reduce the heat to low, and continue to cook, stirring constantly, for about 20 minutes, or until the polenta becomes creamy and just starts to pull away from the sides of the pot as you stir. (Note that some brands of polenta will take longer to cook than others.) Serve hot, topped or plain.

NUTRITIONAL FACTS (PER 1-CUP SERVING)

Calories: 211 Carbohydrates: 41 g Cholesterol: 2 mg
Fat: 0.9 g Fiber: 3.4 g Protein: 8 g Sodium: 242 mg

You Save: Calories: 32 Fat: 4 g

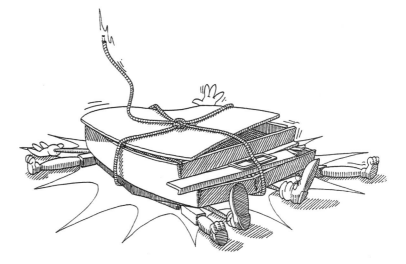

Variations

To make Polenta Parmesan, eliminate the salt from either Creamy Soft Polenta or Creamy Firm Polenta. About 5 minutes before the polenta is finished cooking, stir in $\frac{1}{4}$ cup plus 2 tablespoons of grated nonfat or reduced-fat Parmesan cheese. Serve hot.

NUTRITIONAL FACTS (PER SERVING)

Calories: 234 Carbohydrates: 44 g Cholesterol: 3 mg
Fat: 0.9 g Fiber: 3.4 g Protein: 11 g Sodium: 162 mg

You Save: Calories: 38 Fat: 5.8 g

To make Polenta With Olives and Sun-Dried Tomatoes, cover $\frac{1}{4}$ cup of finely chopped sun-dried tomatoes with boiling water, and set aside for 10 minutes, or until plumped. Drain the tomatoes, and set aside. Prepare either Creamy Soft Polenta or Creamy Firm Polenta, reducing the salt to $\frac{1}{4}$ teaspoon. As soon as the polenta is finished cooking, stir in the tomatoes and $\frac{1}{2}$ cup of coarsely chopped black olives. Serve hot.

NUTRITIONAL FACTS (PER SERVING)

Calories: 233 Carbohydrates: 44 g Cholesterol: 2 mg
Fat: 2.4 g Fiber: 4.2 g Protein: 8.6 g Sodium: 382 mg

You Save: Calories: 32 Fat: 4 g

To make Saucy Polenta, cook Polenta Parmesan (above) using Creamy Firm Polenta. When the polenta is thick and pulls away from the sides of the pan, spoon it onto a large round serving platter or a large shallow serving bowl. Using a large spoon, make a well in the center of the polenta. Then spoon some sauce—either Bolognese Mushroom Sauce (page 175) or your choice of sauce—into the well. Serve the remaining sauce separately. Makes 6 servings.

NUTRITIONAL FACTS (PER SERVING)

Calories: 306 Carbohydrates: 51 g Cholesterol: 21 mg
Fat: 1.7 g Fiber: 5.1 g Protein: 19.3 g Sodium: 376 mg

You Save: Calories: 204 Fat: 23.7 g

Polenta Lasagna

1. Prepare the polenta as directed through Step 3. Coat a $4\frac{1}{2}$-x-$8\frac{1}{2}$-inch loaf pan with nonstick cooking spray, and spread the hot polenta in the pan. Allow the polenta to cool to room temperature. Then cover and chill for several hours, or until firm. (This step can be done the day before.)

2. Coat a large nonstick skillet with nonstick cooking spray, and preheat over medium heat. Add the ground beef, and cook, stirring to crumble, until the meat is no longer pink. Add the peppers and onion, cover, and cook for 4 additional minutes, or until the vegetables are tender, stirring occasionally. (Add a little water or broth if the skillet becomes too dry.) Remove the skillet from the heat, and set aside.

3. To assemble the lasagna, unmold the polenta from the loaf pan, and slice into sixteen $\frac{1}{2}$-inch-thick slices. Coat a 9-x-13-inch pan with nonstick cooking spray, and arrange half of the polenta slices in a single layer over the bottom of the pan. Cover the polenta with half of the beef mixture, half of the sauce, and 1 cup of the mozzarella. Repeat the polenta, beef, and sauce layers, and top with the Parmesan.

4. Bake uncovered at 350°F for 40 minutes, or until hot and bubbly. Sprinkle the remaining mozzarella over the top, and bake for 10 additional minutes, or until the cheese is melted. Remove the dish from the oven, and let sit for 15 minutes before cutting into squares and serving.

Yield: 8 servings

1 recipe Creamy Firm Polenta (page 152)

$\frac{1}{2}$ pound 95% lean ground beef

1 medium green bell pepper, cut into thin strips

1 medium red bell pepper, cut into thin strips

1 medium yellow onion, cut into thin wedges

1 recipe Basic Marinara Sauce (page 166) or $3\frac{1}{2}$ cups bottled fat-free marinara sauce

$1\frac{1}{2}$ cups shredded nonfat or reduced-fat mozzarella cheese

3 tablespoons grated nonfat or reduced-fat Parmesan cheese

NUTRITIONAL FACTS (PER SERVING)

Calories: 291   Carbohydrates: 45 g   Cholesterol: 26 mg
Fat: 2.2 g   Fiber: 6.2 g   Protein: 22.7 g   Sodium: 587 mg

You Save: Calories: 154   Fat: 18.8 g

Risotto With Scallops and Spinach

Yield: *4 servings*

1 teaspoon crushed fresh garlic

8 ounces cleaned raw scallops

1¾ cups arborio rice

4⅓ cups unsalted chicken broth

⅛ teaspoon ground black pepper

⅛ teaspoon ground white pepper

Pinch ground nutmeg

½ cup evaporated skimmed milk

3 tablespoons grated nonfat or reduced-fat Parmesan cheese

1½ cups (packed) chopped fresh spinach

1. Coat a large nonstick skillet with butter-flavored cooking spray, and preheat over medium-high heat. Add the garlic and scallops, and stir-fry for about 3 minutes, or until the scallops turn opaque.

2. Stir the rice, broth, black pepper, white pepper, and nutmeg into the skillet mixture, and bring to a boil. Reduce the heat to low, cover, and simmer without stirring for about 15 minutes, or until most of the liquid has been absorbed.

3. Add the evaporated milk to the skillet, and, if necessary, increase the heat slightly to return the mixture to a simmer. Cook uncovered, stirring frequently, for about 5 minutes, or until the rice is tender but still a little firm to the bite, and most of the liquid has been absorbed. Add a little more broth during cooking if needed, leaving just enough liquid to make the mixture moist and creamy.

4. Stir in the Parmesan. If the risotto seems too dry at this point, add a little more evaporated milk or broth. Stir in the spinach, cover, and cook over low heat without stirring for about 2 minutes, or until the spinach is wilted. Serve hot, topping each serving with a rounded teaspoon of additional Parmesan if desired.

NUTRITIONAL FACTS (PER 1½-CUP SERVING)

Calories: 424   Carbohydrates: 72 g   Cholesterol: 22 mg
Fat: 1.4 g   Fiber: 1.6 g   Protein: 30.8 g   Sodium: 291 mg

You Save: Calories: 184   Fat: 23.9 g

FAT-FIGHTING TIP

Making Creamy Fat-Free Risotto

Risotto is a true comfort food—hot, creamy, and utterly delicious. But made the traditional way, this dish can contain an uncomfortable amount of fat. In fact, the first step in making a traditional risotto is to coat the rice with a liberal amount of butter or oil. Then other fatty ingredients like cream and cheese are often added. Another problem that risotto presents is the need for constant attention, with at least 25 minutes of continual stirring.

But if you've ever tried to make your favorite risotto without the fat, you may have ended up with a pasty, mushy dish instead of one that's creamy and nicely textured. The reason? Coating the rice kernels

Mushroom Risotto Milanese

1. Coat a 3-quart pot with butter-flavored cooking spray, and preheat over medium-high heat. Add the garlic and mushrooms, and sauté for about 3 minutes, or just until the mushrooms begin to brown and start to release their juices. (Add a little white wine or stock if the pot becomes too dry.)

2. Stir the rice, broth, pepper, and, if desired, the saffron into the mushrooms, and bring to a boil. Reduce the heat to low, cover, and simmer without stirring for about 15 minutes, or until most of the liquid has been absorbed.

3. Add the evaporated milk to the pot, and, if necessary, increase the heat slightly to return the mixture to a simmer. Cook uncovered, stirring frequently, for about 5 minutes, or until the rice is tender but still a little firm to the bite, and most of the liquid has been absorbed. During cooking, add a little more broth if needed, leaving just enough liquid to make the mixture moist and creamy.

4. Stir in the Parmesan. If the risotto seems too dry at this point, add a little more evaporated milk or broth. Serve hot, topping each serving with a rounded teaspoon of additional Parmesan if desired.

Yield: 5 servings

1 teaspoon crushed fresh garlic

2 cups sliced fresh mushrooms

2 cups arborio rice

5 cups unsalted beef, chicken, or vegetable broth

⅛ teaspoon ground black pepper

¼ teaspoon saffron (optional)

½ cup plus 2 tablespoons evaporated skimmed milk

¼ cup grated nonfat or reduced-fat Parmesan cheese

NUTRITIONAL FACTS (PER 1⅓-CUP SERVING)

Calories: 340   Carbohydrates: 67 g   Cholesterol: 2 mg
Fat: 0.6 g   Fiber: 1.3 g   Protein: 15.7 g   Sodium: 189 mg

You Save: Calories: 184   Fat: 24 g

with fat keeps them separate and firm, preventing the overdevelopment of starch during stirring. But take heart. Rich-tasting, creamy, firm-textured risotto can be made without any added fat simply by eliminating most of the stirring.

To make your own favorite risotto recipe without the fat, simply combine the required amount of rice with two and a half times as much broth. Bring the mixture to a boil, reduce the heat to low, and cover. Simmer without stirring for 15 minutes, or until most of the liquid has been absorbed. (If you are going to add ingredients like thawed frozen vegetables or fresh asparagus, stir them into the pot after about 12 minutes of cooking.)

After the 15 minutes, add ½ cup of additional broth or—for an ultra-creamy texture—add the same amount of evaporated skimmed milk. Simmer the risotto uncovered, stirring frequently, for an additional 5 minutes, adding more broth if necessary. Cook until the risotto is creamy and the rice is tender, yet still al dente in the center. Now you have a creamy guilt-free risotto that is simple enough to make any night of the week!

Risotto With Sun-Dried Tomatoes

Yield: *5 servings*

¼ cup plus 1 tablespoon chopped sun-dried tomatoes (not packed in oil)

¼ cup plus 1 tablespoon boiling water

1 teaspoon crushed fresh garlic

⅓ cup finely chopped shallots or onions

2 cups arborio rice

4½ cups unsalted chicken broth

½ cup dry white wine

⅛ teaspoon ground black pepper

⅛ teaspoon ground white pepper

½ cup plus 2 tablespoons evaporated skimmed milk

¼ cup grated nonfat or reduced-fat Parmesan cheese

2 tablespoons finely chopped Italian parsley

1. Place the sun-dried tomatoes in a small bowl, and pour the boiling water over the tomatoes. Let sit for about 10 minutes, or until the tomatoes have plumped.

2. Coat a 3-quart pot with butter-flavored cooking spray, and preheat over medium heat. Add the garlic and the shallots or onion, and sauté for about 1 minute, or until the garlic begins to turn color and the shallots or onions start to soften. (Add a little white wine or chicken broth if the pot becomes too dry.)

3. Stir the rice, broth, wine, black pepper, and white pepper into the garlic mixture, and bring to a boil over medium-high heat. Reduce the heat to low, cover, and simmer without stirring for about 15 minutes, or until the most of the liquid has been absorbed.

4. Add the evaporated milk to the pot, and, if necessary, increase the heat slightly to return the mixture to a simmer. Cook uncovered, stirring frequently, for about 5 minutes, or until the rice is tender but still a little firm to the bite, and most of the liquid has been absorbed. During cooking, add a little more broth if needed, leaving just enough liquid to make the mixture moist and creamy.

5. Drain any excess liquid from the tomatoes, and add them to the risotto. Stir in the Parmesan and parsley. If the risotto seems too dry at this point, add a little more evaporated milk or broth. Serve hot, topping each serving with a rounded teaspoon of additional Parmesan if desired.

NUTRITIONAL FACTS (PER 1⅓-CUP SERVING)

Calories: 377   Carbohydrates: 69 g   Cholesterol: 3 mg
Fat: 1 g   Fiber: 1.5 g   Protein: 18.1 g   Sodium: 260 mg

You Save: Calories: 164   Fat: 21.1 g

Risotto With Shrimp and Asparagus

1. Coat a large nonstick skillet with butter-flavored cooking spray, and preheat over medium-high heat. Add the garlic and shrimp, and stir-fry for about 3 minutes, or until the shrimp turn opaque.

2. Stir the rice, broth, wine, and pepper into the skillet mixture, and bring to a boil. Reduce the heat to low, cover, and simmer without stirring for about 12 minutes, or until about three-fourths of the liquid has been absorbed.

3. Add the asparagus to the skillet, and stir to mix well. Increase the heat to medium-high, and return the mixture to a boil. Reduce the heat to low, cover, and simmer without stirring for about 3 minutes, or until most of the liquid has been absorbed.

4. Add the evaporated milk to the skillet, and, if necessary, increase the heat slightly to return the mixture to a simmer. Cook uncovered, stirring frequently, for about 5 minutes, or until the rice is tender but still a little firm to the bite, and most of the liquid has been absorbed. Add a little more broth during cooking if needed, leaving just enough liquid to make the mixture moist and creamy.

5. Stir in the Parmesan. If the risotto seems too dry at this point, add a little more evaporated milk or broth. Serve hot, topping each serving with a rounded teaspoon of additional Parmesan if desired.

Yield: *4 servings*

1 teaspoon crushed fresh garlic

½ pound cleaned raw shrimp

1½ cups arborio rice

3¼ cups unsalted chicken broth

½ cup dry white wine

⅛ teaspoon ground black pepper

¾ cup 1-inch pieces fresh asparagus, or ¾ cup frozen (thawed) 1-inch pieces asparagus

½ cup evaporated skimmed milk

3 tablespoons grated nonfat or reduced-fat Parmesan cheese

NUTRITIONAL FACTS (PER 1½-CUP SERVING)

Calories: 402   Carbohydrates: 63 g   Cholesterol: 89 mg
Fat: 1.9 g   Fiber: 1.4 g   Protein: 28 g   Sodium: 259 mg

You Save: Calories: 187   Fat: 23.5 g

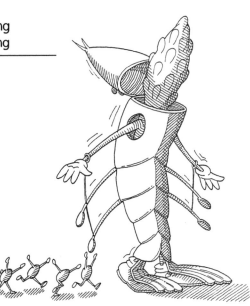

Chicken and Mushroom Risotto

Yield: *4 servings*

8 ounces boneless skinless chicken breast

$\frac{1}{8}$ teaspoon salt

$\frac{1}{8}$ teaspoon ground black pepper

$\frac{3}{4}$ cup sliced fresh mushrooms

1 teaspoon crushed fresh garlic

$1\frac{1}{2}$ cups arborio rice

$3\frac{3}{4}$ cups unsalted chicken broth

$\frac{3}{4}$ cup frozen (thawed) green peas

$\frac{1}{4}$ cup plus 2 tablespoons evaporated skimmed milk

3 tablespoons grated nonfat or reduced-fat Parmesan cheese

1. Rinse the chicken and pat it dry with paper towels. Cut the chicken into $\frac{1}{2}$-inch pieces, and sprinkle with the salt and pepper.

2. Coat a large nonstick skillet with butter-flavored cooking spray, and preheat over medium-high heat. Add the chicken, and stir-fry for 3 to 4 minutes, or until nicely browned. Add the mushrooms and garlic, and stir-fry for another minute or 2, or until the mushrooms begin to brown and start to release their juices. (Add a little white wine or chicken broth if the pot becomes too dry.)

3. Stir the rice and broth into the skillet mixture, and bring to a boil. Reduce the heat to low, cover, and simmer without stirring for about 12 minutes, or until about three-fourths of the liquid has been absorbed. Stir in the peas, and cook covered for another 3 minutes, or until most of the liquid has been absorbed.

4. Add the evaporated milk to the pot, and, if necessary, increase the heat slightly to return the mixture to a simmer. Cook uncovered, stirring frequently, for about 5 minutes, or until the rice is tender but still a little firm to the bite, and most of the liquid has been absorbed. During cooking, add a little more broth if needed, leaving just enough liquid to make the mixture moist and creamy.

5. Stir in the Parmesan. If the risotto seems too dry at this point, add a little more evaporated milk or broth. Serve hot, topping each serving with a rounded teaspoon of additional Parmesan if desired.

NUTRITIONAL FACTS (PER $1\frac{1}{2}$-CUP SERVING)

Calories: 411   Carbohydrates: 65 g   Cholesterol: 36 mg
Fat: 1.7 g   Fiber: 2.7 g   Protein: 31.5 g   Sodium: 302 mg

You Save: Calories: 164   Fat: 21.1 g

Perfect Potato Gnocchi

Yield: *4 servings*

1. Peel the potatoes, and cut them into chunks. Place in a 3-quart pot, cover with water, and bring to a boil over high heat. Reduce the heat to medium-high and cook for about 12 minutes, or until the potatoes are easily pierced with a fork.

2. Drain the potatoes and return them to the pot. Place the pot over low heat (to evaporate some of the moisture), and, using a potato masher, mash the potatoes well.

3. Remove the pot from the heat, and stir in the salt, pepper, and nutmeg. Add the flour and egg substitute, and stir just until the dough holds together.

4. Turn the dough onto a lightly floured surface, and knead in a little additional flour if necessary. (The dough should be soft and pliable, but not moist or sticky.) Divide the dough into 8 equal pieces, and shape each piece into a 10-inch-long, ³⁄₄-inch-wide rope. Using a sharp knife, cut each rope into 1-inch pieces; then press each piece lightly with the tines of a fork to create some ridges on the surface of each gnocchi. (This helps the sauce stick to the dumplings.)

5. Fill a 4-quart pot with water, and bring to a boil over high heat. Drop half of the dough pieces into the water, 1 piece at a time. (They will sink to the bottom of the pan.) Boil for about 3 minutes, or until the dumplings rise to the surface and float. During cooking, reduce the heat slightly if the water starts to boil too rapidly.

6. Remove the gnocchi with a slotted spoon, drain well, and cover to keep warm. Repeat with the remaining dough, and serve hot with your choice of sauce.

1 pound baking potatoes (about 3 medium)

½ teaspoon salt

⅛ teaspoon ground white pepper

Pinch ground nutmeg

1¼ cups unbleached flour

3 tablespoons fat-free egg substitute

NUTRITIONAL FACTS (PER 1-CUP SERVING)

Calories: 237   Carbohydrates: 51 g   Cholesterol: 0 mg
Fat: 0.4 g   Fiber: 2.7 g   Protein: 7 g   Sodium: 24 mg

You Save: Calories: 39   Fat: 3.9 g

Cheese and Potato Gnocchi

Yield: *4 servings*

1 pound baking potatoes (about 3 medium)

⅛ teaspoon ground white pepper

Pinch ground nutmeg

1 cup unbleached flour

¼ cup grated nonfat or reduced-fat Parmesan cheese

¼ cup nonfat ricotta cheese

1. Peel the potatoes, and cut them into chunks. Place in a 3-quart pot, cover with water, and bring to a boil over high heat. Reduce the heat to medium-high and cook for about 12 minutes, or until the potatoes are easily pierced with a fork.

2. Drain the potatoes and return them to the pot. Place the pot over low heat (to evaporate some of the moisture), and, using a potato masher, mash the potatoes well.

3. Remove the pot from the heat, and stir in the pepper and nutmeg. Add the flour, Parmesan, and ricotta, and stir just until the dough holds together.

4. Turn the dough onto a lightly floured surface, and knead in a little additional flour if necessary. (The dough should be soft and pliable, but not moist or sticky.) Divide the dough into 8 equal pieces, and shape each piece into a 10-inch-long, ¾-inch-wide rope. Using a sharp knife, cut each rope into 1-inch pieces; then press each piece lightly with the tines of a fork to create ridges on the surface of each gnocchi. (This helps the sauce stick to the dumplings.)

5. Fill a 4-quart pot with water, and bring to a boil over high heat. Drop half of the dough pieces into the water, 1 piece at a time. (They will sink to the bottom of the pan.) Boil for about 3 minutes, or until the dumplings rise to the surface and float. During cooking, reduce the heat slightly if the water starts to boil too rapidly.

6. Remove the gnocchi with a slotted spoon, drain well, and cover to keep warm. Repeat with the remaining dough, and serve hot with your choice of sauce.

NUTRITIONAL FACTS (PER 1-CUP SERVING)
Calories: 237   Carbohydrates: 48 g   Cholesterol: 3 mg
Fat: 0.4 g   Fiber: 2.7 g   Protein: 10.4 g   Sodium: 124 mg

You Save: Calories: 48   Fat: 5.9 g

Spinach and Potato Gnocchi

1. Coat a medium-sized nonstick skillet with nonstick cooking spray, and preheat over medium heat. Add the spinach, and stir-fry for about 2 minutes, or until the spinach is wilted. Place the spinach on a cutting board and chop it very fine, or place it in a food processor and purée it into a paste. Set aside.

2. Peel the potatoes, and cut them into chunks. Place in a 3-quart pot, cover with water, and bring to a boil over high heat. Reduce the heat to medium-high and cook for about 12 minutes, or until the potatoes are easily pierced with a fork.

3. Drain the potatoes and return them to the pot. Place the pot over low heat (to evaporate some of the moisture), and, using a potato masher, mash the potatoes well.

4. Remove the pot from the heat, and stir in the spinach, salt, pepper, and nutmeg. Add the flour, and stir just until the dough holds together.

5. Turn the dough onto a lightly floured surface, and knead in a little additional flour if necessary. (The dough should be soft and pliable, but not moist or sticky.) Divide the dough into 8 equal pieces, and shape each piece into a 10-inch long, $\frac{3}{4}$-inch-wide rope. Using a sharp knife, cut each rope into 1-inch pieces. Then press each piece lightly with the tines of a fork to create ridges on the surface of each gnocchi. (This helps the sauce stick to the dumplings.)

6. Fill a 4-quart pot with water, and bring to a boil over high heat. Drop half of the dough pieces into the water, 1 piece at a time. (They will sink to the bottom of the pan.) Boil for about 3 minutes, or until the dumplings rise to the surface and float. During cooking, reduce the heat slightly if the water starts to boil too rapidly.

7. Remove the gnocchi with a slotted spoon, drain well, and cover to keep warm. Repeat with the remaining dough, and serve hot with your choice of sauce.

Yield: 4 servings

1½ cups (packed) fresh spinach leaves

1 pound baking potatoes (about 3 medium)

½ teaspoon salt

⅛ teaspoon ground white pepper

Pinch ground nutmeg

1¼ cups unbleached flour

NUTRITIONAL FACTS (PER 1-CUP SERVING)
Calories: 238 Carbohydrates: 51 g Cholesterol: 0 mg
Fat: 0.6 g Fiber: 3.5 g Protein: 6.7 g Sodium: 294 mg

You Save: Calories: 44 Fat: 3.9 g

10

Savory Sauces

For most people, the mention of Italian cooking conjures up the image of a pot of savory tomato sauce simmering on the back of the stove for hours and hours. Indeed, sauces play a vital role in Italian cuisine, and are considered every bit as important as the pastas they top.

Unfortunately, sauces are also what so often turns a lean plate of pasta into a fat-fighter's nightmare. Tomato sauces such as marinara and arrabbiata tend to be lowest in fat, although even these sauces can be slimmed down by omitting or reducing the oil in the recipe. But meat sauces, Alfredo sauce, and many others are typically loaded with fatty ingredients like greasy sausage, oil, and heavy cream. If you know the secrets of fat-free Italian cooking, though, you can create fat-free and very low-fat versions of even these culinary treats. The recipes in this chapter start out with wholesome ingredients like fresh plum tomatoes, unsalted canned tomatoes, fat-free broths, and plenty of fresh vegetables, garlic, and herbs. Ultra-lean meats replace their fatty counterparts in savory meat sauces, and evaporated skimmed milk replaces cream in white sauces.

Salt, too, is kept to a minimum in these recipes. In fact, these sauces have less than half the sodium of most commercial bottled brands, which typically deliver close to 400 milligrams per half cup of sauce! The skillful use of herbs and spices, fresh or roasted garlic, plenty of garden vegetables, and a splash of wine add so much robust flavor that you will never miss the salt—or the fat.

Think you're too busy to make homemade sauce? Think again. Contrary to popular belief, tomato sauces do not have to simmer all day on the stove. In fact, the longer a tomato sauce cooks, the more bitter and acidic it will become—which increases the need for added sugar and oil. Most of the sauces in this chapter, including the tomato sauces, cook in twenty minutes or less.

So whether you like your sauces savory or spicy, smooth or chunky, red or white, you need look no further. In the following pages, you will find sauces that are surprisingly fast and easy to make, yet so delectably rich and flavorful that no one but you will guess just how fuss-free—and *fat*-free—they are!

Basic Marinara Sauce

Yield: *3½ cups*

1 tablespoon extra virgin olive oil (optional)

2 teaspoons crushed fresh garlic

1 medium yellow onion, finely chopped

1 can (28 ounces) unsalted crushed tomatoes

½ cup beef, chicken, or vegetable broth

1½ teaspoons dried basil, oregano, or Italian seasoning

¼ teaspoon salt

¼ teaspoon crushed red pepper

1. Coat a 2-quart pot with olive oil cooking spray or with the olive oil, and preheat over medium heat. Add the garlic, and stir-fry for about 30 seconds, or just until the garlic begins to turn color. Add the remaining ingredients, increase the heat to medium-high, and bring the mixture to a boil.

2. Reduce the heat to low, cover, and simmer, stirring occasionally, for 20 minutes, or until the onions are soft, the sauce is thick, and the flavors are well blended. Serve hot over your choice of pasta.

NUTRITIONAL FACTS (PER ½-CUP SERVING)

Calories: 47   Carbohydrates: 10 g   Cholesterol: 0 mg
Fat: 0.1 g   Fiber: 3.1 g   Protein: 2 g   Sodium: 161 mg

You Save: Calories: 54   Fat: 6 g

Variations

To make Mushroom Marinara Sauce, add 2 cups of sliced fresh mushrooms along with the other ingredients. Makes about 4 cups.

NUTRITIONAL FACTS (PER ½-CUP SERVING)

Calories: 47   Carbohydrates: 10 g   Cholesterol: 0 mg
Fat: 0.1 g   Fiber: 3.6 g   Protein: 2 g   Sodium: 148 mg

You Save: Calories: 54   Fat: 6 g

To make Marinara With Roasted Garlic, add 30 to 40 cloves (about 2 heads) of coarsely chopped roasted garlic (page 62) along with the other ingredients. Makes about 4 cups.

NUTRITIONAL FACTS (PER ½-CUP SERVING)

Calories: 54   Carbohydrates: 13 g   Cholesterol: 0 mg
Fat: 0.1 g   Fiber: 3.6 g   Protein: 2.4 g   Sodium: 149 mg

You Save: Calories: 54   Fat: 6 g

To make Marinara With Roasted Red Peppers, add 1 cup of diced roasted red peppers (page 57) along with the other ingredients. Makes about 4 cups.

NUTRITIONAL FACTS (PER $\frac{1}{2}$-CUP SERVING)

Calories: 47 Carbohydrates: 10 g Cholesterol: 0 mg
Fat: 0.1 g Fiber: 3.6 g Protein: 2 g Sodium: 141 mg

You Save: Calories: 54 Fat: 6 g

To make Marinara With Shrimp, cook Basic Marinara Sauce as directed. When the sauce has finished simmering, add 8 ounces of fresh cleaned raw shrimp or frozen cooked shrimp. Return the mixture to a boil, reduce the heat to low, and simmer, stirring frequently, for 10 minutes, or until the shrimp are cooked and the sauce is thick. Makes about $4\frac{1}{2}$ cups.

NUTRITIONAL FACTS (PER $\frac{1}{2}$-CUP SERVING)

Calories: 63 Carbohydrates: 8 g Cholesterol: 38 mg
Fat: 0.5 g Fiber: 2.2 g Protein: 6.6 g Sodium: 163 mg

You Save: Calories: 54 Fat: 6 g

Fresh Tomato Sauce

***Yield:** 4 cups*

Use only good-quality vine-ripened tomatoes for best results.

2 teaspoons crushed fresh garlic

1 medium yellow onion, finely chopped

3 pounds fresh plum tomatoes (about 14 to 18 medium), peeled and finely chopped

¼ cup dry red wine or broth

1 teaspoon dried basil, or 1 tablespoon fresh

1 teaspoon dried oregano, or 1 tablespoon fresh

½ teaspoon salt

¼ teaspoon ground black pepper

1. Coat a large nonstick skillet with nonstick cooking spray, and preheat over medium heat. Add the garlic, and stir-fry for about 30 seconds, or just until the garlic begins to turn color. Add the remaining ingredients, increase the heat to medium-high, and bring the mixture to a boil.

2. Reduce the heat to low, cover, and simmer, stirring occasionally, for 30 minutes, or until the tomatoes have cooked down and the sauce is thick. If you prefer a chunky sauce, serve the sauce as is. For a smooth sauce, place half of the sauce in a blender, and blend until smooth. Repeat with the remaining sauce, and serve hot over your choice of pasta.

NUTRITIONAL FACTS (PER ½-CUP SERVING)

Calories: 42   Carbohydrates: 8.5 g   Cholesterol: 0 mg
Fat: 0.5 g   Fiber: 1.8 g   Protein: 1.5 g   Sodium: 148 mg

You Save: Calories: 60   Fat: 6.7 g

Peeling Fresh Tomatoes

Fresh tomatoes add that special touch to a variety of Italian dishes, including sauces. In many cases, the tomatoes must be skinned before they can be added to the dish. This task is easily accomplished by following these simple steps:

1. Bring a pot of water to a boil over high heat.

Carefully drop the tomatoes into the water, and boil for 1 minute.

2. Drain the tomatoes in a colander, and rinse under cool tap water.

3. Using your fingers, slip the skins off the tomatoes—they should come off easily—and use the tomatoes in your recipe as directed.

Roasted Tomato Sauce

1. Place the vegetables and garlic cloves in a large bowl, and toss to mix well. Add the vinegar, oregano, salt, pepper, and, if desired, the olive oil, and stir to mix well.

2. Coat a 9-x-13-inch nonstick pan with olive oil cooking spray, and spread the vegetables in a single layer in the pan. If you did not use the olive oil, spray the tops of the vegetables with the cooking spray.

3. Cover the pan with aluminum foil, and bake at 450°F for 20 minutes. Remove the foil, and bake for 30 additional minutes, or until the vegetables are tender and nicely browned. Serve hot over your choice of pasta.

Yield: 3 cups

1¾ pounds fresh plum tomatoes (about 8 medium-large), quartered lengthwise

1 medium-large yellow onion, cut into thin wedges

2 cups sliced fresh mushrooms

1 large red bell pepper, cut into ¼-inch-thick strips

10 cloves garlic, peeled

1 tablespoon balsamic vinegar

1 teaspoon dried oregano

¼ teaspoon salt

¼ teaspoon coarsely ground black pepper

1 tablespoon extra virgin olive oil (optional)

Olive oil cooking spray

NUTRITIONAL FACTS (PER ¾-CUP SERVING)

Calories: 57 Carbohydrates: 12.8 g Cholesterol: 0 mg
Fat: 0.6 g Fiber: 3 g Protein: 2.4 g Sodium: 145 mg

You Save: Calories: 120 Fat: 13.5 g

Broiled Tomato-Basil Sauce

1. Place the tomatoes, onion, basil, garlic, salt, pepper, and, if desired, the olive oil in a large bowl, and toss to mix well.

2. Coat a large baking sheet with olive oil cooking spray, and spread the mixture in a single layer over the sheet. If you did not use the olive oil, spray the top of the tomato mixture lightly with the cooking spray.

3. Place the tomato mixture 6 inches below a preheated broiler, and broil for about 5 minutes, or until the tomatoes are soft and the onions begin to brown. Serve hot over your choice of pasta.

Yield: 4 servings

1 pound fresh plum tomatoes, coarsely chopped (about 6 medium)

1 medium-large yellow onion, cut into very thin wedges

½ cup coarsely chopped fresh basil

2 teaspoons crushed fresh garlic

¼ teaspoon salt

¼ teaspoon ground black pepper

1 tablespoon extra virgin olive oil (optional)

NUTRITIONAL FACTS (PER ⅔-CUP SERVING)

Calories: 35 Carbohydrates: 8 g Cholesterol: 0 mg
Fat: 0.4 g Fiber: 1.8 g Protein: 1.4 g Sodium: 144 mg

You Save: Calories: 150 Fat: 18.1 g

Puttanesca Sauce

Yield: *4 cups*

2 teaspoons crushed fresh garlic

½ cup chopped onion

⅓ cup sliced black olives

¼ cup finely chopped fresh parsley

1 can (28 ounces) unsalted crushed tomatoes

½ cup chicken broth

3 tablespoons chopped capers

1 tablespoon mashed anchovy fillets (optional)

1 tablespoon dark brown sugar

¼ teaspoon crushed red pepper

1. Coat a 2-quart pot with nonstick cooking spray, and preheat over medium heat. Add the garlic, and stir-fry for about 30 seconds, or just until the garlic begins to turn color. Add the remaining ingredients, increase the heat to medium-high, and bring the mixture to a boil.

2. Reduce the heat to low, cover, and simmer, stirring occasionally, for 20 minutes, or until the onions are soft, the sauce is thick, and the flavors are well blended. Serve hot over your choice of pasta.

NUTRITIONAL FACTS (PER ½-CUP SERVING)

Calories: 65   Carbohydrates: 13 g   Cholesterol: 0 mg
Fat: 0.7 g   Fiber: 3.7 g   Protein: 3.5 g   Sodium: 296 mg

You Save: Calories: 59   Fat: 6.7 g

Broiled Portabella and Plum Tomato Sauce

Yield: *4 servings*

2 cups ½-inch chunks Portabella mushrooms (about 4 ounces)

2 cups chopped seeded fresh plum tomatoes (about 6 medium)

2 teaspoons crushed fresh garlic

1 teaspoon dried oregano

¼ teaspoon salt

¼ teaspoon coarsely ground black pepper

1 tablespoon extra virgin olive oil (optional)

1. Place the mushrooms, tomatoes, garlic, oregano, salt, pepper, and, if desired, the olive oil in a large bowl, and toss to mix well.

2. Coat a large baking sheet with the cooking spray, and spread the mixture in a single layer over the sheet. If you did not use the olive oil, spray the top of the tomato mixture lightly with the cooking spray.

3. Place the tomato mixture 6 inches below a preheated broiler, and broil for about 5 minutes, or until the tomatoes are soft and the mushrooms begin to brown. Serve hot over your choice of pasta.

NUTRITIONAL FACTS (PER ⅔-CUP SERVING)

Calories: 31   Carbohydrates: 5.3 g   Cholesterol: 0 mg
Fat: 0.8 g   Fiber: 1.8 g   Protein: 1.3 g   Sodium: 142 mg

You Save: Calories: 118   Fat: 13.6 g

Garden Marinara Sauce

1. Coat a 2-quart pot with nonstick cooking spray, and preheat over medium heat. Add the garlic, and stir-fry for about 30 seconds, or just until the garlic begins to turn color. Add the remaining ingredients, increase the heat to medium-high, and bring the mixture to a boil.

2. Reduce the heat to low, cover, and simmer, stirring occasionally, for 20 to 25 minutes, or until the vegetables are soft and the flavors are well blended. Remove the bay leaves. If you prefer a chunky sauce, serve the sauce as is. For a smooth sauce, place half of the sauce in a blender, and blend until smooth. Repeat with the remaining sauce, and serve hot over your choice of pasta.

1 teaspoon crushed fresh garlic

2 medium carrots, peeled and grated

2 stalks celery, finely chopped (include the leaves)

1 medium onion, finely chopped

1 can (28 ounces) unsalted crushed tomatoes

¼ cup chicken, beef, or vegetable broth

2 bay leaves

2 teaspoons dried oregano

1 teaspoon sugar

½ teaspoon salt

¼ teaspoon ground black pepper

NUTRITIONAL FACTS (PER ½-CUP SERVING)

Calories: 47 Carbohydrates: 10 g Cholesterol: 0 mg
Fat: 0.1 g Fiber: 3.6 g Protein: 2 g Sodium: 179 mg

You Save: Calories: 36 Fat: 4 g

Arrabbiata Sauce

A simple spicy sauce.

1. Coat a 2-quart pot with nonstick cooking spray, and preheat over medium heat. Add the garlic, and stir-fry for about 30 seconds, or just until the garlic begins to turn color. Add the remaining ingredients, increase the heat to medium-high, and bring the mixture to a boil.

2. Reduce the heat to low, cover, and simmer, stirring occasionally, for 20 minutes, or until the sauce is thick and the flavors are well blended. Serve hot over your choice of pasta.

1½ teaspoons crushed fresh garlic

1 can (28 ounces) unsalted crushed tomatoes

½ cup chicken, beef, or vegetable broth

3 tablespoons finely chopped fresh parsley

1 teaspoon crushed red pepper

½ teaspoon salt

NUTRITIONAL FACTS (PER ½-CUP SERVING)

Calories: 47 Carbohydrates: 10 g Cholesterol: 0 mg
Fat: 0.1 g Fiber: 3.6 g Protein: 2 g Sodium: 213 mg

You Save: Calories: 54 Fat: 6 g

Porcini Mushroom Sauce

Yield: *4 cups*

½ ounce dried porcini
  mushrooms (about ½ cup)

1 cup warm tap water

1 tablespoon extra virgin olive oil
  (optional)

¼ cup plus 2 tablespoons finely
  chopped shallots

2 cups sliced fresh mushrooms

1 can (28 ounces) unsalted
  crushed tomatoes

1 teaspoon dried oregano

1 bay leaf

½ teaspoon salt

¼ teaspoon ground black pepper

1. Place the mushrooms in a small bowl, and add the warm water. Let the mixture sit for about 20 minutes, or until the mushrooms are rehydrated.

2. Remove the mushrooms with a slotted spoon and rinse them well with cool running water. Set aside. Place a paper towel in a strainer, and pour the soaking liquid through the strainer. Reserve the strained liquid.

3. Coat a large nonstick skillet with olive oil cooking spray or with the olive oil, and preheat over medium-high heat. Add the shallots and the fresh mushrooms, and stir-fry for several minutes, or until the mushrooms begin to brown and start to release their juices.

4. Add the tomatoes, oregano, bay leaf, salt, pepper, porcini mushrooms, and strained soaking liquid to the skillet, and bring the mixture to a boil. Reduce the heat to low, cover, and simmer for 15 minutes, or until the sauce is thick and the flavors are well blended. Serve hot over your choice of pasta.

NUTRITIONAL FACTS (PER ½-CUP SERVING)

Calories: 59   Carbohydrates: 11.6 g   Cholesterol: 0 mg
Fat: 0.1 g   Fiber: 3.7 g   Protein: 3.5 g   Sodium: 167 mg

You Save: Calories: 60   Fat: 6.8 g

Savory Meat Sauce

1. Coat a large deep skillet with nonstick cooking spray. Add the garlic and beef, and place the skillet over medium heat. Cook, stirring to crumble, until the meat is no longer pink. (If the meat is 95% lean, there will be no fat to drain.)

2. Add the remaining ingredients, and bring to a boil over medium-high heat. Reduce the heat to low, cover, and simmer, stirring occasionally, for about 25 minutes, or until the vegetables are soft and the flavors are well blended. Serve hot over your choice of pasta.

Yield: 8 cups

2 teaspoons crushed fresh garlic

1 pound 95% lean ground beef

1 large Spanish onion, finely chopped

2 medium carrots, peeled and finely grated

2 stalks celery, finely chopped (include the leaves)

1 can (28 ounces) unsalted tomato purée

1 can (14½ ounces) unsalted tomatoes, crushed

¼ cup plus 2 tablespoons beef broth

2½ teaspoons instant beef bouillon granules

2 bay leaves

2 teaspoons dried oregano

2 teaspoons dark brown sugar

¼ teaspoon ground black pepper

¼ teaspoon ground nutmeg

NUTRITIONAL FACTS (PER ½-CUP SERVING)

Calories: 63 Carbohydrates: 7.2 g Cholesterol: 16 mg
Fat: 1.3 g Fiber: 1.7 g Protein: 6 g Sodium: 130 mg

You Save: Calories: 67   Fat: 6.9 g

Italian Sausage Sauce

Yield: *8 cups*

1 teaspoon crushed fresh garlic

1 pound Turkey Italian Sausage
(page 182)

2 medium yellow onions, finely
chopped

2 medium green bell peppers,
finely chopped

2 medium red bell peppers, finely
chopped

1 can (28 ounces) unsalted
tomato purée

1 can (14½ ounces) unsalted
tomatoes, crushed

½ cup chicken broth

1½ teaspoons dried Italian
seasoning

1½ teaspoons sugar

1. Coat a large deep skillet with nonstick cooking spray. Add the garlic and sausage, and place the skillet over medium heat. Cook, stirring to crumble, until the meat is no longer pink.

2. Add the remaining ingredients, and bring to a boil over medium-high heat. Reduce the heat to low, cover, and simmer, stirring occasionally, for 25 minutes, or until the vegetables are soft and the flavors are well blended. Serve hot over your choice of pasta.

NUTRITIONAL FACTS (PER ½-CUP SERVING)

Calories: 57   Carbohydrates: 6 g   Cholesterol: 14 mg
Fat: 0.7 g   Fiber: 1.7 g   Protein: 6.5 g   Sodium: 107 mg

You Save: Calories: 54   Fat: 6.1 g

Bolognese Mushroom Sauce

1. Coat a large nonstick skillet with olive oil cooking spray. Add the garlic and the turkey or beef, and cook, stirring to crumble, until the meat is no longer pink.

2. Add the mushrooms, onion or leek, carrot, and celery to the skillet, and stir to mix well. Increase the heat to medium-high, and add the wine. Cook, stirring frequently, for about 5 minutes, or until all of the wine has evaporated.

3. Add the milk to the skillet, and cook, stirring frequently, for about 5 minutes, or until all of the milk has evaporated.

4. Add the tomatoes, beef broth, tomato paste, bay leaf, and pepper to the skillet, and stir to mix well. Bring the mixture to a boil. Then reduce the heat to low, cover, and simmer, stirring occasionally, for about 20 minutes, or until the sauce is very thick. Serve hot over your choice of pasta.

Yield: *4 cups*

1 teaspoon crushed fresh garlic

$\frac{1}{2}$ pound ground turkey breast or 95% lean ground beef

2 cups chopped fresh mushrooms

$\frac{1}{2}$ cup finely chopped onion or leek

$\frac{1}{2}$ cup finely chopped carrot

$\frac{1}{2}$ cup finely chopped celery

$\frac{1}{2}$ cup dry red wine

$\frac{1}{2}$ cup skim milk

1 can (14$\frac{1}{2}$ ounces) unsalted stewed tomatoes, crushed

$\frac{1}{2}$ cup beef broth

2 tablespoons tomato paste

1 bay leaf

$\frac{1}{8}$ teaspoon ground black pepper

NUTRITIONAL FACTS (PER $\frac{1}{2}$-CUP SERVING)

Calories: 72   Carbohydrates: 7 g   Cholesterol: 18 mg
Fat: 0.8 g   Fiber: 1.7 g   Protein: 8.3 g   Sodium: 214 mg

You Save: Calories: 172   Fat: 19.7 g

Sun-Dried Tomato Pesto

Yield: *1 cup*

½ cup chopped sun-dried tomatoes (not packed in oil)

¾ cup boiling vegetable or chicken broth

½ cup (packed) fresh basil

¼ cup (packed) fresh Italian parsley

2 tablespoons pine nuts

2 tablespoons grated nonfat Parmesan cheese

2 teaspoons crushed fresh garlic

½ teaspoon coarsely ground black pepper

1 tablespoon extra virgin olive oil

Just 2 tablespoons of this savory sauce is enough to flavorfully coat up to 1½ cups of cooked pasta. The same amount of sauce will beautifully season a potful of steamed vegetables.

1. Place the sun-dried tomatoes in a small bowl, and pour the boiling broth over the tomatoes. Allow to sit for 10 minutes, or until the tomatoes have plumped. Drain well, reserving the broth.

2. Place the tomatoes, basil, parsley, pine nuts, Parmesan, garlic, and pepper in a food processor, and process until finely minced. (Be careful not to process too long, or you will make tomato paste.)

3. Transfer the tomato mixture to a small bowl, and stir in the olive oil and the reserved broth. Allow the mixture to sit for 5 minutes (it will thicken slightly upon standing). Serve at room temperature with your choice of pasta.

NUTRITIONAL FACTS (PER 2-TABLESPOON SERVING)

Calories: 40 Carbohydrates: 3 g Cholesterol: 0 mg
Fat: 2.6 g Fiber: 0.6 g Protein: 1.7 g Sodium: 146 mg

You Save: Calories: 141 Fat: 14.1 g

Light Pesto Sauce

Yield: *1⅛ cups*

1¼ cups (packed) fresh basil

½ cup (packed) fresh Italian parsley

½ cup grated nonfat Parmesan cheese

¼ cup pine nuts or walnuts

4 large cloves garlic, crushed

¼ teaspoon ground black pepper

½ cup chicken broth

1 tablespoon lemon juice

1 tablespoon extra virgin olive oil (optional)

Like Sun-Dried Tomato Pesto (above), this sauce is so flavorful that only 2 tablespoons or so is needed to season up to 1½ cups of pasta.

1. Place the basil, parsley, Parmesan, nuts, garlic, and pepper in the bowl of a food processor, and process until finely minced.

2. Add the broth, lemon juice, and, if desired, the olive oil to the food processor, and process for a few seconds, or just until well mixed. Let the mixture sit for 5 minutes (it will thicken slightly upon standing). Serve at room temperature with your choice of pasta or vegetables.

NUTRITIONAL FACTS (PER 2-TABLESPOON SERVING)

Calories: 40 Carbohydrates: 3.8 g Cholesterol: 2 mg
Fat: 1.7 g Fiber: 0.5 g Protein: 3.7 g Sodium: 127 mg

You Save: Calories: 111 Fat: 13.6 g

Time-Saving Tip

Although there's nothing quite like fresh pesto, this versatile sauce can be frozen for later use. Just make a double batch of Light Pesto Sauce, and freeze the sauce in an ice cube tray. Then transfer the cubes to plastic freezer bags. Whenever you need pesto, simply remove the desired number of frozen cubes, allow them to thaw, and use as desired.

White Clam Sauce

1. Coat a large nonstick skillet with olive oil cooking spray or with the olive oil, and preheat over medium heat. Add the garlic and mushrooms, and sauté for about 3 minutes, or until the mushrooms begin to brown and start to release their juices.

2. Add the clams with their juice, the lemon juice, and the pepper to the skillet. Cook, stirring frequently, for about 5 minutes, or until the clam juice is reduced by almost half.

3. Place the wine in a small bowl. Add the cornstarch, and stir to dissolve. Add the wine mixture to the skillet, and cook, stirring constantly, for about 2 minutes, or until the mixture comes to a boil and thickens slightly.

4. Remove the skillet from the heat, stir in the scallions and parsley, and serve hot over your choice of pasta.

Yield: *4 servings*

1 tablespoon extra virgin olive oil (optional)

2 teaspoons crushed fresh garlic

2 cups sliced fresh mushrooms

2 cans ($6\frac{1}{2}$ ounces each) chopped clams, undrained

1 tablespoon lemon juice

$\frac{1}{4}$ teaspoon coarsely ground black pepper

$\frac{1}{2}$ cup dry white wine

2 teaspoons cornstarch

$\frac{1}{2}$ cup thinly sliced scallions

$\frac{1}{4}$ cup plus 2 tablespoons chopped fresh parsley

NUTRITIONAL FACTS (PER $\frac{1}{2}$-CUP SERVING)

Calories: 114   Carbohydrates: 7.2 g   Cholesterol: 33 mg
Fat: 1.2 g   Fiber: 1 g   Protein: 14 g   Sodium: 155 mg

You Save: Calories: 104   Fat: 13.5 g

Red Clam Sauce

Yield: *4 servings*

1 tablespoon extra virgin olive oil (optional)

1½ teaspoons crushed fresh garlic

2 cans (6½ ounces each) chopped clams, undrained

1¼ pounds fresh plum tomatoes (about 6 to 8 medium), peeled and finely chopped

½ teaspoon dried Italian seasoning

¼ teaspoon ground black pepper

¼ teaspoon crushed red pepper

¼ cup finely chopped fresh parsley

1. Coat a large nonstick skillet with olive oil cooking spray or with the olive oil, and preheat over medium heat. Add the garlic, and sauté for about 30 seconds, or just until the garlic begins to turn color.

2. Drain the juice from the clams, and set the clams aside. Add the clam juice, tomatoes, Italian seasoning, and black and red pepper to the skillet. Increase the heat to medium-high, and let the mixture come to a boil. Then cook over medium heat, stirring frequently, for about 5 minutes, or until the liquid is reduced by about half, the tomatoes are soft, and mixture has cooked down into a sauce.

3. Add the clams and parsley to the skillet, and cook for another minute or 2, or until the mixture is heated through. Serve hot over your choice of pasta.

NUTRITIONAL FACTS (PER ½-CUP SERVING)

Calories: 104   Carbohydrates: 9.4 g   Cholesterol: 33 mg
Fat: 1.4 g   Fiber: 1.6 g   Protein: 14 g   Sodium: 162 mg

You Save: Calories: 113   Fat: 13.5 g

Almost Alfredo Sauce

Yield: *2½ cups*

½ cup evaporated skimmed milk

¾ cup grated nonfat Parmesan cheese

⅛ teaspoon ground white pepper

Pinch ground nutmeg

2 cups skim milk

1. Place the evaporated milk, Parmesan, pepper, and nutmeg in a small bowl, and stir to mix well. Set aside.

2. Place the milk in a 1½-quart pot, and bring to a boil over medium heat, stirring constantly. Add the evaporated milk mixture to the pot, and cook, still stirring, for about 2 minutes, or until the mixture is thickened and bubbly. Add a little more milk if the sauce seems too thick. Serve hot over pasta or vegetables, or use in casseroles as you would condensed cream soups.

NUTRITIONAL FACTS (PER ½-CUP SERVING)

Calories: 108   Carbohydrates: 15 g   Cholesterol: 9 mg
Fat: 0.2 g   Fiber: 0 g   Protein: 3.6 g   Sodium: 314 mg

You Save: Calories: 102   Fat: 16.4 g

11

Italian Home-Style Entrées

Many people believe that adopting a low-fat lifestyle means saying good-bye to the hearty home-style Italian dishes they love so much. But the truth is that you don't have to give up pot roast with gravy, Eggplant Parmesan, Chicken Cacciatore, or any of your other favorite dishes just because you're cutting down on fat. By replacing high-fat ingredients with no-fat and low-fat foods, and by using some very simple and innovative cooking techniques, you can still enjoy all of your Italian favorites.

How do you get maximum flavor with minimum fat? The entrées in this chapter begin with the freshest seafood or the leanest cuts of beef, pork, or poultry. Then fat is kept to an absolute minimum by using nonstick skillets and nonstick cooking sprays, and by replacing full-fat dairy products with their healthful nonfat and reduced-fat counterparts. Of course, fresh vegetables, a sprinkling of herbs, a few cloves of fresh garlic,

and a splash of wine play an important role in these dishes by adding their own great flavors and textures to these classic—but guilt-free—Italian dishes. The result? Satisfying home-style dishes, most of which have only 2 to 3 grams of fat per serving!

As you glance through the pages of this chapter, remember that these are just some of the delicious low-fat entrées that are within your reach. Palate-pleasing pasta entrées can be found in Chapter 7, crisp-crusted pizzas are presented in Chapter 8, and hearty risottos, polenta, and gnocchi are featured in Chapter 9. And, of course, many of your own family favorites can easily be "slimmed down" with the techniques and ingredients used within this chapter. You'll be delighted to find that even sausage-stuffed peppers and saucy meatball sandwiches can be part of a healthy, satisfying diet—once you learn the secrets of fat-free Italian cooking.

Braised Beef
With Hearty Mushroom Sauce

Yield: *8 servings*

3-pound top round roast

2 teaspoons crushed fresh garlic

½ teaspoon coarsely ground
   black pepper

2 medium yellow onions, chopped

2 medium carrots, chopped

2 stalks celery, sliced (include the
   leaves)

¾ teaspoon dried thyme

¾ cup dry red wine

½ cup water

2½ teaspoons instant beef
   bouillon granules

2 bay leaves

GRAVY

Meat drippings

2 cups sliced fresh mushrooms

One of the leanest beef cuts available, top round roast—sometimes sold as London Broil—substitutes nicely for fattier pot roast cuts.

1. Trim the meat of any visible fat, rinse with cool water, and pat dry. Spread the garlic over both sides of the meat, and sprinkle with the pepper.

2. Coat a large ovenproof skillet with nonstick cooking spray, and preheat over medium-high heat. Place the meat in the skillet, and brown for 2 to 3 minutes on each side. Remove the skillet from the heat.

3. Arrange the onions, carrots, and celery over and around the meat, and sprinkle the thyme over the top. Place the wine, water, and bouillon granules in a bowl, and stir to mix well. Pour the mixture over and around the meat. Drop 1 bay leaf into the liquid on each side of the roast. Cover the skillet tightly with foil, and bake at 325°F for 1 hour and 45 minutes to 2 hours, or until the roast is tender.

4. Remove the skillet from the oven and carefully remove the foil. (Steam will escape.) Transfer the meat to a serving platter, and cover to keep warm. Remove and discard the bay leaves.

5. To make the gravy, pour 1½ cups of the meat drippings into a heatproof bowl. (If there is extra broth, save it for another use.) Add 2 or 3 ice cubes to the broth, and let the cubes float in the broth for about 1 minute. (Any fat present in the broth will cling to the ice cubes.) Remove and discard the ice cubes.

6. Transfer the defatted broth to a blender. Transfer the vegetables from the skillet to the blender, and, leaving the lid slightly ajar to allow steam to escape, carefully process the mixture at low speed until smooth. Set aside.

7. Coat a large nonstick skillet with nonstick cooking spray, and preheat over medium-high heat. Add the mushrooms, and stir-fry for about 2 minutes, or just until the mushrooms start to brown and release their liquid. Add the puréed vegetable mixture to the skillet, and reduce the heat to medium. Cook, stirring constantly, for 2 minutes, or until the mixture begins to boil and is heated through.

8. Cut the meat into $\frac{1}{2}$-inch-thick slices, and arrange the slices slightly overlapping down the center of the platter. Spoon a little of the mushroom sauce over the meat, and serve the remaining sauce separately.

NUTRITIONAL FACTS (PER 3-OUNCE SERVING WITH SAUCE)

Calories: 173   Carbohydrates: 5.3 g   Cholesterol: 59 mg
Fat: 5 g   Fiber: 1.3 g   Protein: 26 g   Sodium: 282 mg

You Save: Calories: 146   Fat: 14.8 g

Steak Pizzaiola

1. Rinse the meat with cool water, and pat it dry with paper towels.

2. Place the flour, salt, and pepper in a shallow dish, and stir to mix well. Dip the steaks in the flour mixture, turning to coat each side. Set aside.

3. Coat a large nonstick skillet with nonstick cooking spray, and preheat over medium-high heat. Add the steaks to the skillet, and cook for about 3 minutes, or until nicely browned. Spray the tops of the steaks lightly with the cooking spray, turn them over, and cook for 3 additional minutes, or until nicely browned.

4. Place the tomatoes in a medium-sized bowl. Stir in the garlic and oregano, and pour the mixture over and around the steaks, lifting the steaks to allow the sauce to cover the bottom of the pan.

5. Let the sauce come to a boil. Reduce the heat to low, cover, and simmer for 8 minutes. Turn the steaks over, and simmer for 7 additional minutes, or until the sauce is thick and the steaks are tender.

6. Serve hot with your choice of pasta, topping each serving with a rounded teaspoon of Parmesan, if desired. Or use as a submarine-sandwich filling.

Yield: 4 servings

4 beef cube steaks, 4 ounces each

3 tablespoons unbleached flour

$\frac{1}{4}$ teaspoon salt

$\frac{1}{4}$ teaspoon ground black pepper

Nonstick cooking spray

1 can (14$\frac{1}{2}$ ounces) unsalted tomatoes, crushed

1$\frac{1}{2}$ teaspoons crushed fresh garlic

1 teaspoon dried oregano

2 tablespoons grated nonfat or reduced-fat Parmesan cheese (optional)

NUTRITIONAL FACTS (PER SERVING)

Calories: 183   Carbohydrates: 7.5 g   Cholesterol: 57 mg
Fat: 4.5 g   Fiber: 1.3 g   Protein: 25 g   Sodium: 191 mg

You Save: Calories: 119   Fat: 14.5 g

Sicilian Stuffed Peppers

Yield: *6 servings*

6 large green bell peppers

2¼ cups Basic Marinara Sauce (page 166) or bottled fat-free marinara sauce

¾ cup unsalted beef or vegetable broth

FILLING

¾ pound Turkey Italian Sausage (page 183)

1 cup chopped fresh mushrooms

3 cups cooked brown rice

¼ cup plus 2 tablespoons grated nonfat or reduced-fat Parmesan cheese

1. To make the filling, coat a large nonstick skillet with nonstick cooking spray, and preheat over medium heat. Add the sausage, and cook, stirring to crumble, until the meat is no longer pink. Add the mushrooms, and continue to cook and stir for 2 additional minutes, or until the mushrooms just begin to brown and release their juices. (Add a little broth or water to the skillet if it becomes too dry.) Remove the skillet from the heat, and stir in first the rice, and then the Parmesan. Set aside.

2. Cut the tops off the peppers, and remove the seeds and membranes. Divide the filling among the peppers, and replace the pepper tops.

3. Place the peppers upright in a 2½-quart casserole dish. Place the marinara sauce and broth in a small bowl, stir to mix well, and pour the mixture around the peppers. Cover the dish with aluminum foil, and bake at 350°F for about 1 hour, or until the peppers are tender. Serve hot.

NUTRITIONAL FACTS (PER SERVING)

Calories: 256   Carbohydrates: 40 g   Cholesterol: 38 mg
Fat: 2 g   Fiber: 6 g   Protein: 21.3 g   Sodium: 480 mg

You Save: Calories: 152   Fat: 18.1 g

Making Your Own Italian Sausage

Italian sausage is used to add richness and a distinctive flavor to a variety of Italian dishes. Fortunately, it's easy to make a sausage mixture that is as flavorful as a traditional one, but contains a fraction of the fat and calories.

This recipe gives you three different meat choices to use for the sausage base. Being 99-percent lean, ground turkey breast will produce the leanest sausage possible. Skinless turkey thigh meat will produce a mixture that is about 93-percent lean, while pork tenderloin will produce a mixture that is 95-percent lean. Italian sausage made from skinless turkey thigh meat or pork tenderloin will have a flavor and appearance that is most similar to full-fat pork Italian sausage. Sausage made from turkey breast meat will be lighter in color than traditional Italian sausage.

So let your taste buds and your fat budget be your guide, and stir Turkey Italian Sausage into sauces, add its savor to stuffings, or use it to spice up your favorite pizza, and enjoy an authentic taste of Italy.

Top Left: **Orange Burst Granita** (page 217)
Top Right: **Cassata Alla Siciliana** (page 200)
Bottom: **Fudge Marble Cheesecake** (page 199)

Left: Amaretto Baked Peaches (page 214)
Center: Tiramisu (page 212)
Right: Cherry-Almond Cheese Tarts (page 203)

Turkey Italian Sausage

1. Combine all of the ingredients in a medium-sized bowl, and mix thoroughly. Cover and refrigerate for several hours to allow the flavors to blend.

2. To precook for use in recipes, coat a large skillet with nonstick cooking spray and preheat over medium heat. Add the sausage, and cook, stirring to crumble, until the meat is no longer pink. Drain on paper towels. Use on pizzas, in pasta dishes, and in any way you would use pork Italian sausage.

Yield: 1 pound

1 pound skinless ground turkey breast, skinless ground turkey thigh meat, or ground pork tenderloin

2 teaspoons ground paprika

2 teaspoons crushed fresh garlic

1½ teaspoons whole fennel seeds

1 teaspoon dried Italian seasoning

¼ teaspoon crushed red pepper (or more to taste)

½ teaspoon salt

NUTRITIONAL FACTS (PER 2-OUNCE COOKED SERVING, MADE WITH TURKEY BREAST)

Calories: 65   Carbohydrates: 0 g   Cholesterol: 49 mg
Fat: 0.7 g   Fiber: 0 g   Protein: 17.1 g   Sodium: 165 mg

You Save: Calories: 118   Fat: 13.9 g

NUTRITIONAL FACTS (PER 2-OUNCE COOKED SERVING, MADE WITH TURKEY THIGH MEAT)

Calories: 106   Carbohydrates: 0 g   Cholesterol: 48 mg
Fat: 4 g   Fiber: 0 g   Protein: 16.2 g   Sodium: 178 mg

You Save: Calories: 77   Fat: 10.6 g

NUTRITIONAL FACTS (PER 2-OUNCE COOKED SERVING, MADE WITH PORK TENDERLOIN)

Calories: 93   Carbohydrates: 0 g   Cholesterol: 45 mg
Fat: 2.7 g   Fiber: 0 g   Protein: 16 g   Sodium: 165 mg

You Save: Calories: 90   Fat: 11.9 g

Mama's Meat Loaf

Yield: *8 servings*

LOAF

1½ pounds 95% lean ground beef

1 cup finely chopped fresh mushrooms

½ cup finely chopped onion

½ cup finely chopped green bell pepper

½ cup quick-cooking oats

¼ cup grated nonfat Parmesan cheese

3 egg whites

1½ teaspoons crushed fresh garlic

1½ teaspoons dried Italian seasoning

½ teaspoon ground black pepper

TOPPING

1 cup Basic Marinara Sauce (page 166) or bottled fat-free marinara sauce

1 tablespoon plus 2 teaspoons grated nonfat or reduced-fat Parmesan cheese

"Lean" meat loaf pans are great for low-fat cooking. These pans have a perforated inner liner that allows the fat to drain into the bottom of the pan instead of being reabsorbed into the meat.

1. Combine all of the loaf ingredients in a large bowl, and mix well. Coat a 9-x-5-inch meat loaf pan with nonstick cooking spray, and press the mixture into the pan to form a loaf.

2. Bake at 350°F for 35 minutes. Pour the marinara sauce over the loaf, and sprinkle the Parmesan over the top. Bake for 30 additional minutes, or until the meat is no longer pink inside.

3. Remove the loaf from the oven, and let sit for 10 minutes before slicing and serving.

NUTRITIONAL FACTS (PER SERVING)

Calories: 180 Carbohydrates: 10.3 g Cholesterol: 60 mg
Fat: 4.9 g Fiber: 1.4 g Protein: 24 g Sodium: 182 mg

You Save: Calories: 128 Fat: 14.8 g

Meatballs With Marinara

1. To make the meatballs, combine all of the meatball ingredients in a large bowl, and mix well. Shape the mixture into 24 (1½-inch) balls. Coat a large baking sheet with nonstick cooking spray, and arrange the meatballs on the sheet.

2. Bake at 350°F for about 25 minutes, or until the meatballs are no longer pink inside. Remove from the oven and set aside.

3. To make the sauce, coat a large nonstick skillet with olive oil cooking spray, and preheat over medium-high heat. Add the garlic, and stir-fry for about 30 seconds, or just until the garlic begins to turn color. Add the tomatoes, broth, Italian seasoning, bouillon granules, and red pepper, and stir to mix well. Bring the mixture to a boil; then reduce the heat to low.

4. Add the meatballs to the sauce, cover, and simmer, stirring occasionally, for 15 minutes, or until the flavors are well blended. Serve hot over your choice of pasta, or in Magnifico Meatball Sandwiches (page 186).

Yield: 6 servings

MEATBALLS

1 pound ground turkey breast or 95% lean ground beef

¾ cup finely chopped onion

½ cup oat bran or quick-cooking oats

¼ cup grated nonfat Parmesan cheese

2 egg whites, lightly beaten

1 teaspoon dried Italian seasoning

SAUCE

2 teaspoons crushed fresh garlic

1 can (28 ounces) unsalted crushed tomatoes or tomato purée

½ cup beef broth

2 teaspoons dried Italian seasoning

1 teaspoon beef bouillon granules

¼ teaspoon crushed red pepper

NUTRITIONAL FACTS (PER SERVING)

Calories: 179 Carbohydrates: 22 g Cholesterol: 49 mg
Fat: 1.7 g Fiber: 4.6 g Protein: 24.5 g Sodium: 330 mg

You Save: Calories: 186 Fat: 19.7 g

Magnifico Meatball Sandwiches

Yield: *6 servings*

1 recipe Meatballs With Marinara (page 185)

1 medium green bell pepper, cut into thin strips

1 medium yellow onion, cut into thin wedges

6 whole wheat submarine-sandwich rolls, each 6 inches long, or 6 pieces Italian bread, each 6 inches long

¼ cup plus 2 tablespoons shredded nonfat or reduced-fat mozzarella cheese

1. Make the Meatballs With Marinara as directed, and set aside to keep warm.

2. Coat a large nonstick skillet with olive oil cooking spray, and preheat over medium-high heat. Add the peppers and onions, and stir-fry for about 4 minutes, or until the vegetables are just tender. Add a little water or broth if the skillet becomes too dry.

3. To assemble the sandwiches, slice the rolls or Italian bread in half lengthwise, being careful to avoid cutting all the way through. Lay each roll open on an individual plate, and arrange 4 meatballs in each one. Top with ¼ cup of the sauce, a sixth of the peppers and onions, and a tablespoon of the mozzarella. Serve hot.

NUTRITIONAL FACTS (PER SERVING)

Calories: 369   Carbohydrates: 53 g   Cholesterol: 50 mg
Fat: 3.3 g   Fiber: 8 g   Protein: 36 g   Sodium: 638 mg

You Save: Calories: 168   Fat: 21.2 g

FAT-FREE COOKING TIP

Browning Without Fat

Great cooks know that browning enhances many foods by adding a deep color and a rich, full flavor. Unfortunately, the traditional method of browning often requires several tablespoons of oil, butter, or margarine. However, as the recipes in this chapter show, all that extra oil is simply not necessary.

To brown meat, chicken, or vegetables with virtually no added fat, spray a thin film of nonstick cooking spray over the bottom of a skillet. Then preheat the skillet over medium-high heat, and brown the food as usual. If the food starts to stick, add a few teaspoons of water, broth, or wine. If you use both a nonstick skillet and nonstick cooking spray, it should not be necessary to add any liquid at all.

When browning foods that have been breaded or floured, brown the bottom of the food as directed above. Then spray the top lightly with cooking spray before turning the food over and browning the second side.

Tuscan Roast Tenderloin

1. Trim the tenderloins of any visible fat and membranes. Rinse with cool water, and pat dry with paper towels.

2. Place the garlic, mustard, sage, rosemary, pepper, and salt in a small bowl, and stir together to form a paste. Spread the paste over the entire surface of the tenderloins.

3. Coat a 9-x-13-inch pan with nonstick cooking spray, and place the tenderloins in the pan, spacing them at least 2 inches apart. Bake uncovered at 350°F for about 45 minutes, or until an instant-read thermometer inserted in the center of a tenderloin registers 160°F and the meat is no longer pink inside.

4. Remove the pan from the oven, transfer the tenderloins to a cutting board, and cover loosely with aluminum foil to keep warm.

5. To make the sauce, pour the wine into the roasting pan, and, using a spatula, scrape up the glaze and the browned bits from the bottom of the pan. Pour the mixture into a $1\frac{1}{2}$-quart pot, and cook over medium heat, stirring frequently, for about 5 minutes, or until the mixture is reduced by half.

6. While the wine mixture is reducing, combine $\frac{1}{4}$ cup of the broth and the flour in a jar with a tight-fitting lid. Shake until smooth, and set aside. When the wine mixture is reduced by half, add the remaining $1\frac{1}{4}$ cups of broth to the pot, and bring to a boil over medium heat. Whisk in the flour mixture, and cook, stirring constantly, for about 2 minutes, or until the mixture is thickened and bubbly. Whisk in the mustard and vinegar, and remove the pot from the heat.

7. To serve, slice the tenderloins thinly at an angle, and arrange on a serving platter. Serve hot, accompanied by the sauce.

Yield: 8 servings

2 pork tenderloins, 1 pound each

1 tablespoon crushed fresh garlic

1 tablespoon Dijon mustard

$1\frac{1}{2}$ teaspoons dried sage

$1\frac{1}{2}$ teaspoons dried rosemary

$\frac{1}{2}$ teaspoon coarsely ground black pepper

$\frac{1}{4}$ teaspoon salt

SAUCE

$\frac{3}{4}$ cup dry white wine

$1\frac{1}{2}$ cups chicken broth, divided

2 tablespoons plus 2 teaspoons unbleached flour

1 teaspoon Dijon mustard

1 teaspoon balsamic vinegar

NUTRITIONAL FACTS (PER 3-OUNCE SERVING WITH SAUCE)

Calories: 159   Carbohydrates: 2.3 g   Cholesterol: 67 mg
Fat: 4.2 g   Fiber: 0.1 g   Protein: 24.3 g   Sodium: 275 mg

You Save: Calories: 147   Fat: 13.1 g

Chicken Cacciatore

Yield: *4 servings*

1 can (14½ ounces) unsalted tomatoes, crushed

2 tablespoons tomato paste

1 teaspoon dried Italian seasoning

¼ teaspoon crushed red pepper

4 boneless skinless chicken breast halves, about 4 ounces each

½ teaspoon salt

½ teaspoon ground black pepper

¼ cup dry white wine or chicken broth

1½ teaspoons crushed fresh garlic

1 medium yellow onion, cut into thin wedges

1 medium green pepper, cut into thin strips

1½ cups sliced fresh mushrooms

¼ cup grated nonfat or reduced-fat Parmesan cheese (optional)

1. Place the tomatoes, tomato paste, Italian seasoning, and red pepper in a medium-sized bowl, and stir to mix well. Set aside.

2. Rinse the chicken with cool water, and pat it dry with paper towels. Place the chicken pieces on a flat surface, and use a meat mallet to pound each piece to ¼-inch thickness. Sprinkle both sides of the chicken pieces with the salt and pepper.

3. Coat a large nonstick skillet with olive oil cooking spray, and preheat over medium-high heat. Arrange the chicken in the skillet, and cook for 3 to 4 minutes on each side, or until nicely browned and no longer pink inside. Transfer the chicken to a platter, and cover to keep warm.

4. Add the wine or broth to the skillet, and cook over medium-high heat for a minute or 2, or until most of the wine or broth has evaporated. Add the garlic, onions, peppers, and mushrooms to the skillet, and stir-fry for about 4 minutes, or until the vegetables are crisp-tender. Add a little more wine or broth if the skillet becomes too dry.

5. Move the vegetables to one side of the skillet, and return the chicken to the skillet. Arrange the vegetables over and around the chicken.

6. Pour the tomato mixture over the chicken and vegetables, and bring to a boil over medium-high heat. Reduce the heat to low, cover, and simmer for about 10 minutes, or until the flavors are well blended and the vegetables are tender. Serve hot with your choice of pasta, topping each serving with a tablespoon of Parmesan, if desired.

NUTRITIONAL FACTS (PER SERVING)

Calories: 199 Carbohydrates: 9.2 g Cholesterol: 82 mg
Fat: 2.2 g Fiber: 2.5 g Protein: 35 g Sodium: 358 mg

You Save: Calories: 247 Fat: 27.5 g

Tuna With Fresh Tomato Sauce

For variety, substitute other fish steaks such as grouper, salmon, or amberjack for the tuna.

Yield: *4 servings*

1. Rinse the tuna steaks with cool water, and pat them dry with paper towels. Sprinkle both sides of the steaks with the pepper.

2. Coat a large nonstick skillet with olive oil cooking spray, and preheat over medium-high heat. Arrange the tuna in the skillet, and cook for 3 to 4 minutes on each side, or until nicely browned. Transfer the tuna to a platter, and cover to keep warm.

3. Reduce the heat under the skillet to medium, and add the garlic. Sauté for about 30 seconds, or just until the garlic begins to turn color. Add the wine, and cook for about 5 minutes, or until the wine is reduced by half.

4. Add the tomatoes, olives, capers, oregano, red pepper, and, if desired, the anchovies to the skillet. Cover and cook, stirring occasionally, for about 5 minutes, or until the tomatoes soften and cook down into a sauce.

5. Return the tuna to the skillet, and reduce the heat to low. Cover and simmer for about 5 minutes, or until the flavors are well blended and the tuna steaks are no longer pink inside. Serve hot with your choice of pasta.

4 fresh tuna steaks, about 5 ounces each

½ teaspoon coarsely ground black pepper

1½ teaspoons crushed fresh garlic

½ cup dry white wine

1 pound fresh plum tomatoes, diced (about 6 medium)

3 tablespoons sliced black olives

1 tablespoon chopped capers

¾ teaspoon dried oregano

¼ teaspoon crushed red pepper

2 anchovy fillets, mashed (optional)

NUTRITIONAL FACTS (PER SERVING)

Calories: 206 Carbohydrates: 6 g Cholesterol: 63 mg
Fat: 2.4 g Fiber: 1.5 g Protein: 34 g Sodium: 270 mg

You Save: Calories: 108 Fat: 12.2 g

Chicken Rollatini

Yield: *4 servings*

4 boneless skinless chicken breast halves, about 4 ounces each

½ teaspoon ground black pepper

1 teaspoon crushed fresh garlic

3 tablespoons chicken broth

STUFFING

¼ cup finely chopped celery (include the leaves)

¼ cup finely chopped shallots or onions

¼ cup chopped golden raisins

1 cup soft whole wheat bread crumbs

¼ cup grated nonfat or reduced-fat Parmesan cheese

½ teaspoon poultry seasoning

¼ cup chicken broth

1. To make the stuffing, coat a large nonstick skillet with butter-flavored cooking spray, and preheat over medium-high heat. Add the celery and the shallots or onions, and stir-fry for about 3 minutes, or until the vegetables start to soften. Add a little chicken broth to the skillet if it becomes too dry. Remove the skillet from the heat, and set aside for a few minutes to cool slightly.

2. Add the raisins, bread crumbs, Parmesan, and seasoning to the skillet, and toss to mix well. Tossing gently, slowly add enough broth to make a moist, but not wet, stuffing that holds together. Set aside.

3. Rinse the chicken with cool water, and pat it dry with paper towels. Place the chicken pieces on a flat surface, and use a meat mallet to pound each piece to ¼-inch thickness.

4. Spread each piece of chicken with a fourth of the stuffing, extending the stuffing to within ½ inch of each edge. Starting at the short end, roll each piece of chicken up jelly roll-style, and tie in 3 places with string. Sprinkle each roll with some of the pepper.

5. Coat a large nonstick skillet with butter-flavored cooking spray, and preheat over medium-high heat. Arrange the chicken rolls in the skillet and cook for about 7 minutes, turning every few minutes, until nicely browned on all sides.

FAT-FREE COOKING TIP

Making Savory Fat-Free Stuffings

Savory stuffings add a down-home touch that makes any meal special. However, these flavorful mixtures of bread, seasonings, and vegetables are typically moistened with a liberal amount of butter or margarine, which can add an unhealthful amount of fat and calories to your diet. The good news is that you can make moist and delicious stuffings with absolutely *no* added fat. Simply substitute half as much broth or a liquid butter substitute such as Butter Buds for the butter or margarine called for in the recipe. For instance, if the recipe calls for 1 stick (½ cup) of butter, use ¼ cup of broth instead. Slowly pour the broth over the stuffing, tossing gently to mix, until all of the liquid has been incorporated. Then add a little more broth if the stuffing seems too dry. It should be moist, but not wet, and should hold together nicely.

Eggs are frequently added to stuffings to bind the mixture together. You can save more fat and cholesterol by replacing any eggs in the recipe with an equal amount of egg whites or fat-free egg substitute. And while you're modifying your stuffing recipe, boost its fiber and nutrition by substituting whole grain bread for refined white bread. With these modifications, you will have turned a high-fat, nutrient-poor food into a healthful and delicious dish.

6. Add the garlic and the 3 tablespoons of broth to the skillet. Reduce the heat to low, cover, and simmer for 5 minutes. Turn the rolls over, and simmer for 5 additional minutes, or until the chicken is no longer pink inside. Add a little more broth if the skillet becomes dry. Transfer the rolls to a serving platter, and cover to keep warm.

7. To make the sauce, increase the heat under the skillet to medium, and add the wine. Cook, stirring frequently, until the wine is reduced by half.

8. Place the chicken broth in a small bowl, and stir in the cornstarch. Add the cornstarch mixture to the skillet, and cook, stirring constantly, for about 2 minutes, or until the mixture begins to boil and thickens slightly.

9. Pour the sauce over the chicken rolls, and serve hot.

SAUCE

½ cup dry white wine

¼ cup plus 2 tablespoons chicken broth

1 teaspoon cornstarch

NUTRITIONAL FACTS (PER SERVING)

Calories: 226 Carbohydrates: 19 g Cholesterol: 69 mg
Fat: 2 g Fiber: 2.2 g Protein: 32 g Sodium: 328 mg

You Save: Calories: 168 Fat: 19 g

Italian Oven-Fried Scallops

1. Rinse the scallops and pat them dry with paper towels. Set aside.

2. Place the egg substitute in a shallow dish. Place the bread crumbs in another shallow dish. Dip the scallops in the egg substitute, and then roll them in the bread crumbs to coat all sides evenly. (Note that if the scallops are small, you may need extra crumbs, as there will be more surface area to coat.)

3. Coat a 9-x-13-inch pan with olive oil cooking spray, and arrange the scallops in a single layer in the pan. Spray the tops lightly with the cooking spray.

4. Bake at 500°F for 8 to 10 minutes, or until the scallops turn opaque and are nicely browned. Remove the pan from the oven and sprinkle with the parsley. Squeeze the lemon over the scallops, and serve hot.

Yield: 4 servings

1 pound fresh scallops

¼ cup plus 2 tablespoons fat-free egg substitute

½ cup Italian-style seasoned bread crumbs

Olive oil cooking spray

2 tablespoons finely chopped Italian parsley

4 fresh lemon wedges

NUTRITIONAL FACTS (PER SERVING)

Calories: 167 Carbohydrates: 13.7 g Cholesterol: 39 mg
Fat: 1.3 g Fiber: 0.6 g Protein: 23 g Sodium: 431 mg

You Save: Calories: 143 Fat: 15.8 g

Chicken With White Wine and Mushroom Sauce

Yield: *4 servings*

4 boneless skinless chicken breast halves, about 4 ounces each

3 tablespoons fat-free egg substitute

1/4 cup plus 2 tablespoons unbleached flour

1/2 teaspoon salt

1/4 teaspoon ground black pepper

Butter-flavored cooking spray

SAUCE

1/2 cup plus 2 tablespoons evaporated skimmed milk

1 teaspoon cornstarch

1/2 cup dry white wine, divided

2 teaspoons crushed fresh garlic

2 cups sliced fresh mushrooms

1. Rinse the chicken with cool water, and pat it dry with paper towels. Place the chicken pieces on a flat surface, and use a meat mallet to pound each piece to 1/4-inch thickness.

2. Place the egg substitute in a shallow dish. Place the flour, salt, and pepper in another shallow dish, and stir to mix well. Dip each chicken piece first in the egg, and then in the flour mixture, turning to coat each side. Set aside.

3. Coat a large nonstick skillet with butter-flavored cooking spray, and preheat over medium-high heat. Add the chicken and cook for about 3 minutes, or until nicely browned. Spray the top of the chicken lightly with cooking spray, turn, and cook for 3 additional minutes, or until nicely browned and no longer pink inside. Transfer the chicken to a serving platter, and cover to keep warm.

4. To make the sauce, place the evaporated milk and cornstarch in a jar with a tight-fitting lid, and shake to mix well. Set aside.

5. Add 1/4 cup of the wine to the skillet, and cook over medium-high heat, stirring frequently, until most of the wine has evaporated. Add the garlic and mushrooms, and stir-fry for about 3 minutes, or until the mushrooms begin to brown and release their juices. Add the remaining 1/4 cup of wine, and cook, stirring frequently, until the wine is reduced by half.

FAT-FREE COOKING TIP

Creamy Richness Without Cream

To make creamy sauces, soups, casseroles, and other dishes without the usual cream, simply replace this high-fat ingredient with an equal amount of evaporated skimmed milk. Or use 1 cup of skim milk mixed with 1/3 cup of instant nonfat dry milk powder for each cup of cream.

Replacing just 1 cup of heavy cream with either of these healthful alternatives saves you over 600 calories and 88 grams of fat. As a bonus, the substitute ingredients add calcium and other beneficial nutrients to your diet.

6. Reduce the heat under the skillet to medium, shake the evaporated milk mixture, and add it to the skillet. Cook, stirring constantly, until the mixture boils and thickens slightly. Pour the sauce over the chicken, and serve hot.

NUTRITIONAL FACTS (PER SERVING)

Calories: 220　Carbohydrates: 14.5 g　Cholesterol: 67 mg
Fat: 2 g　Fiber: 0.8 g　Protein: 32 g　Sodium: 407 mg

You Save:　Calories: 174　Fat: 22.4 g

Eggplant Parmesan

1. Trim the ends off the eggplants, but do not peel. Cut each eggplant crosswise into 9 rounds, each $\frac{1}{2}$-inch thick. Set aside.

2. Place the egg substitute in a shallow bowl. Place the bread crumbs, $\frac{1}{4}$ cup of the Parmesan, and the flour in another shallow bowl, and stir to mix well. Dip the eggplant slices first in the egg substitute, and then in the crumb mixture, turning to coat both sides.

3. Coat a large baking sheet with olive oil cooking spray, and arrange the eggplant slices in a single layer on the sheet. Spray the tops of the slices lightly with the cooking spray, and bake at 400°F for 15 to 20 minutes, or until the slices are golden brown and tender.

4. While the eggplant is baking, place the sauce in a medium-sized pot, and cook over medium heat, stirring frequently, until the sauce is heated through. Remove the sauce from the heat, and cover to keep warm.

5. Spoon a thin layer of sauce over the bottom of a 9-x-13-inch baking pan. Arrange the baked eggplant slices in the pan, slightly overlapping them to fit in a single layer. Pour the remaining sauce over the eggplant. Then sprinkle with the remaining Parmesan and the mozzarella.

6. Bake uncovered at 400°F for about 5 minutes, or until the cheese is melted. Serve hot with your choice of pasta.

Yield: 6 servings

2 large eggplants (1 pound each)

$\frac{1}{2}$ cup fat-free egg substitute

$\frac{1}{2}$ cup Italian-style seasoned bread crumbs

$\frac{1}{4}$ cup plus 2 tablespoons grated nonfat or reduced-fat Parmesan cheese, divided

2 tablespoons unbleached flour

Olive oil cooking spray

1 recipe Basic Marinara Sauce (page 166) or Arrabbiata Sauce (page 171), or $3\frac{1}{2}$ cups bottled fat-free marinara sauce

1 cup shredded nonfat or reduced-fat mozzarella cheese

NUTRITIONAL FACTS (PER SERVING)

Calories: 190　Carbohydrates: 31 g　Cholesterol: 6 mg
Fat: 1.1 g　Fiber: 6.6 g　Protein: 15.4 g　Sodium: 570 mg

You Save:　Calories: 134　Fat: 17.2 g

Almost Veal Parmesan

Yield: *4 servings*

4 turkey breast tenderloins, about 4 ounces each

¼ cup fat-free egg substitute

3 tablespoons unbleached flour

3 tablespoons grated nonfat or reduced-fat Parmesan cheese

¼ teaspoon ground black pepper

2 cups Basic Marinara Sauce (page 166) or bottled fat-free marinara sauce

2 tablespoons chicken broth or water

Olive oil cooking spray

¾ cup shredded nonfat or reduced-fat mozzarella cheese

Turkey breast has a taste and texture similar to that of veal, and substitutes nicely for the fattier meat in dishes like Veal Parmesan and Veal Marsala.

1. Rinse the turkey with cool water, and pat it dry with paper towels. Place the turkey pieces on a flat surface, and use a meat mallet to pound each piece to ¼-inch thickness.

2. Place the egg substitute in a shallow dish. Place the flour, Parmesan, and pepper in another shallow dish, and stir to mix well. Dip each turkey piece first in the egg, and then in the flour mixture, turning to coat each side. Set aside.

3. Combine the marinara sauce and the broth or water in a medium-sized bowl, and stir to mix well. Set aside.

4. Coat a large ovenproof skillet with olive oil cooking spray, and preheat over medium-high heat. Add the turkey pieces, and cook for about 3 minutes, or until nicely browned. Spray the top of the turkey lightly with the cooking spray, turn, and cook for 3 additional minutes, or until nicely browned and no longer pink inside.

5. Remove the skillet from the heat, and carefully pour the marinara sauce over and around the turkey pieces. (The sauce may splatter a little when it hits the hot skillet.) Lift the turkey pieces to allow the sauce to cover the bottom of the skillet.

6. Place the skillet in a 400°F oven, and bake uncovered for 10 minutes, or until the sauce is hot and bubbly. Sprinkle the mozzarella over the top, and bake for 5 additional minutes, or until the cheese is melted. Serve hot with your choice of pasta.

NUTRITIONAL FACTS (PER SERVING)

Calories: 257   Carbohydrates: 21 g   Cholesterol: 79 mg
Fat: 1.3 g   Fiber: 3.9 g   Protein: 39 g   Sodium: 471 mg

You Save: Calories: 177   Fat: 23.5 g

Almost Veal Marsala

1. Rinse the turkey with cool water, and pat it dry with paper towels. Place the turkey pieces on a flat surface, and use a meat mallet to pound each piece to $\frac{1}{4}$-inch thickness.

2. Place the egg substitute in a shallow dish. Place the flour, salt, and pepper in another shallow dish, and stir to mix well. Dip each turkey piece first in the egg, and then in the flour mixture, turning to coat each side. Set aside.

3. Place the chicken broth in a small bowl. Add the cornstarch, stir to dissolve, and set aside.

4. Coat a large nonstick skillet with butter-flavored cooking spray, and preheat over medium-high heat. Add the turkey pieces, and cook for about 3 minutes, or until nicely browned. Spray the top of the turkey lightly with the cooking spray, turn, and cook for 3 additional minutes, or until nicely browned and no longer pink inside. Transfer the turkey to a platter, and cover to keep warm.

5. Add the mushrooms to the skillet, and stir-fry for about 2 minutes, or until the mushrooms begin to brown and start to release their juices. (Add a little broth if the skillet becomes too dry.) Return the turkey to the skillet, and arrange the mushrooms over and around the turkey pieces.

6. Add the Marsala to the skillet, and bring to a boil. Reduce the heat to medium and cook uncovered for 2 minutes, or until the Marsala is reduced by half.

7. Stir the cornstarch mixture, and add it to the skillet. Increase the heat if necessary to bring the broth to a boil. Reduce the heat to medium-low, cover, and simmer for about 3 minutes, or until the sauce is slightly thickened and the flavors are well blended. Transfer the turkey to a serving platter, sprinkle with the parsley, and serve hot.

Yield: 4 servings

1 pound turkey breast tenderloins, cut into 8 equal pieces

$\frac{1}{4}$ cup fat-free egg substitute

$\frac{1}{4}$ cup plus 2 tablespoons unbleached flour

$\frac{1}{2}$ teaspoon salt

$\frac{1}{2}$ teaspoon ground black pepper

$\frac{1}{2}$ cup chicken broth

$\frac{3}{4}$ teaspoon cornstarch

Butter-flavored cooking spray

2 cups sliced fresh mushrooms

$\frac{3}{4}$ cup dry Marsala

2 tablespoons chopped fresh Italian parsley

NUTRITIONAL FACTS (PER SERVING)

Calories: 205 Carbohydrates: 12 g Cholesterol: 73 mg
Fat: 1.3 g Fiber: 0.9 g Protein: 29 g Sodium: 429 mg

You Save: Calories: 162 Fat: 19.4 g

Eggplant Rollatini

Yield: *6 servings*

2 large eggplants (1 pound each)

½ cup fat-free egg substitute

½ cup Italian-style seasoned bread crumbs

¼ cup plus 2 tablespoons grated nonfat or reduced-fat Parmesan cheese

⅓ cup unbleached flour

¾ cup nonfat ricotta cheese

1 tablespoon finely chopped fresh Italian parsley

Olive oil cooking spray

12 thin slices nonfat or reduced-fat mozzarella cheese, ½ ounce each

12 thin slices lean ham (at least 97% lean), ½ ounce each

1 recipe Basic Marinara Sauce (page 166) or Arrabbiata Sauce (page 171), or 3 ½ cups bottled fat-free marinara sauce

1. Peel and trim the ends off the eggplants. Cut each eggplant lengthwise into 6 slices, each ⅜-inch thick. Set aside.

2. Place the egg substitute in a shallow bowl. Place the bread crumbs, Parmesan, and flour in another shallow bowl, and stir to mix well. Dip the eggplant slices first in the egg substitute, and then in the crumb mixture, turning to coat both sides. Set aside.

3. Combine the ricotta and parsley in a small bowl. Stir to mix well, and set aside.

4. Coat a large baking sheet with olive oil cooking spray, and arrange the eggplant slices in a single layer on the sheet. Spray the tops of the slices lightly with the cooking spray, and bake at 400°F for about 15 minutes, or until the slices are golden brown and tender. Remove the slices from the oven, and let sit for a few minutes, or until cool enough to handle.

5. Coat a 9-x-13-inch baking pan with nonstick cooking spray. Lay 1 eggplant slice on a flat surface. Top the eggplant first with 1 slice of the mozzarella, and then with 1 slice of the ham. Spread a tablespoon of the ricotta mixture over the ham, and roll the eggplant up jelly roll-style. Place the roll seam side down in the prepared pan. Repeat with the remaining eggplant to make 11 more rolls.

6. Bake uncovered at 400°F for about 15 minutes, or until the rolls are heated through. While the eggplant is baking, place the sauce in a medium-sized pot, and cook over medium heat, stirring frequently, until the sauce is heated through. Serve the eggplant hot, topping each serving with some of the sauce.

NUTRITIONAL FACTS (PER SERVING)

Calories: 280   Carbohydrates: 38 g   Cholesterol: 26 mg
Fat: 1.6 g   Fiber: 7.1 g   Protein: 27 g   Sodium: 885 mg

You Save: Calories: 196   Fat: 24.4 g

12

Sweet Endings

In Italy, dessert is often a simple offering of fruit and, perhaps, some cheese. Things are very different here in America, though, where for many of us, a meal just isn't complete without a dish of ice cream or a wedge of cake or pie. Fortunately, Italian cuisine has no shortage of delectable confections—which the Italians eat at breaks throughout the day and after special-occasion dinners, but which you can enjoy after any meal.

Of course, like our own desserts, many Italian treats are high in fat and calories. A classic cheesecake, for instance, might include full-fat ricotta, whole eggs, and butter. Just as deadly is the popular tiramisu, which blends rich mascarpone cheese with egg yolks and whipping cream. Just a small portion of this extravagant creation can provide up to 25 grams of fat and 400 calories!

The good news is that it is possible to provide a sweet ending to a traditional Italian meal without watching your fat intake go sky high. Some Italian desserts, such as poached fruit, are already admirably low in fat. But even elaborate treats such as tiramisu can be dramatically slimmed down and made with much more wholesome ingredients. How? In the recipes that follow, fruit purées and juices, nonfat ricotta and cream cheese, evaporated skimmed milk, and other ingredients replace the high-fat foods traditionally used in desserts. Just as important, these desserts use 25 to 50 percent less refined sugar than is found in traditional recipes. Fruits and fruit juices; flavorings like vanilla extract and cinnamon; and mildly sweet flours like oat flour and whole wheat pastry flour have been used to reduce the need for sugar, and to add fiber and other nutrients as well.

But what about flavor? You'll be delighted to discover that the only thing missing from the low- and no-fat treats presented in this chapter is the fat. From Fudge Marble Cheesecake to Chocolate-Hazelnut Biscotti, these are truly great-tasting desserts. As you will see, you *can* have your cake and eat it too—once you know the secrets of fat-free Italian cooking.

Blueberry Cheesecake Supreme

Yield: *10 servings*

CRUST

5½ large (2½-x-5-inch)
   reduced-fat graham crackers,
   or 24 reduced-fat vanilla wafers

1 tablespoon sugar

1 tablespoon fat-free egg
   substitute

FILLING

3 blocks (8 ounces each) nonfat
   cream cheese, softened to
   room temperature

1 cup nonfat ricotta cheese

¾ cup plus 2 tablespoons sugar

¾ cup fat-free egg substitute

¼ cup unbleached flour

2 tablespoons lemon juice

2 teaspoons vanilla extract

TOPPING

2 tablespoons sugar

1 tablespoon plus 1 teaspoon
   cornstarch

¼ cup plus 1 tablespoon white
   grape juice

2 cups fresh or frozen blueberries

1. To make the crust, break up the crackers or vanilla wafers and place in the bowl of a food processor. Process into fine crumbs. Measure the crumbs. There should be ¾ cup. (Adjust the amount if necessary.)

2. Return the crumbs to the food processor, add the sugar, and process for a few seconds to mix. Add the egg substitute, and process until the mixture is moist and crumbly.

3. Coat a 9-inch springform pan with nonstick cooking spray, and use the back of a spoon to press the mixture against the bottom and ¼ inch up the sides of the pan, forming an even crust. (Dip the spoon in sugar periodically, if necessary, to prevent sticking.) Bake at 350°F for 8 minutes, or until the edges feel firm and dry. Set aside to cool.

4. To make the filling, place the cream cheese, ricotta, and sugar in a food processor, and process until well mixed. Add the egg substitute, flour, lemon juice, and vanilla extract, and process until smooth.

5. Spread the cheesecake batter evenly over the crust, and bake at 325°F for 1 hour, or until the center is set. Turn the oven off, and allow the cake to cool in the oven with the door ajar for 30 minutes. Remove the cake from the oven, and chill for at least 6 hours before adding the topping.

6. To make the topping, place the sugar and cornstarch in a small pot, and stir to mix well. Stir in the grape juice, and place the pot over medium heat. Cook, stirring constantly, until the mixture begins to boil. Add the blueberries, and cook for about 2 additional minutes, or until the mixture is thick and bubbly. Remove the pot from the heat, and set aside to cool to room temperature.

7. Spread the topping over the cheesecake, and chill the cake for at least 2 hours. Remove the collar of the pan just before slicing and serving.

NUTRITIONAL FACTS (PER SERVING)

Calories: 236   Carbohydrates: 42 g   Cholesterol: 5 mg
Fat: 0.6 g   Fiber: 1.2 g   Protein: 16 g   Sodium: 446 mg

You Save: Calories: 311   Fat: 33.8 g

Fudge Marble Cheesecake

1. To make the crust, break up the crackers and place in the bowl of a food processor. Process into fine crumbs. Measure the crumbs. There should be ¾ cup. (Adjust the amount if necessary.)

2. Return the crumbs to the food processor, add the walnuts and sugar, and process for a few seconds to mix. Add the egg substitute, and process until the mixture is moist and crumbly.

3. Coat a 9-inch springform pan with nonstick cooking spray, and use the back of a spoon to press the mixture against the bottom and ¼ inch up the sides of the pan, forming an even crust. (Dip the spoon in sugar periodically, if necessary, to prevent sticking.) Bake at 350°F for 8 minutes, or until the edges feel firm and dry. Set aside to cool.

4. To make the filling, place the cream cheese, ricotta, and sugar in the bowl of a food processor, and process until well mixed. Add the egg substitute, flour, and vanilla extract, and process until smooth.

5. To make the fudge filling, place ½ cup of the cheese filling in a small bowl. Add the cocoa, sugar, and vanilla extract, and stir to mix well.

6. Spread half of the plain cheesecake batter evenly over the crust. Spoon the fudge filling randomly over the batter; then top with the remaining batter. Draw a knife through the batter to produce a marbled effect.

7. Bake at 325°F for 1 hour, or until the center is set. Turn the oven off, and allow the cake to cool in the oven with the door ajar for 30 minutes.

8. Remove the cake from the oven, and chill for at least 8 hours. Remove the collar of the pan just before slicing and serving.

CRUST

5 large (2½-x-5-inch) reduced-fat chocolate graham crackers

2 tablespoons finely chopped walnuts

1 tablespoon sugar

1 tablespoon fat-free egg substitute

FILLING

2 blocks (8 ounces each) nonfat cream cheese, softened to room temperature

15 ounces nonfat ricotta cheese

¾ cup sugar

½ cup fat-free egg substitute

¼ cup plus 2 tablespoons unbleached flour

2 teaspoons vanilla extract

FUDGE FILLING

3 tablespoons Dutch processed cocoa powder

3 tablespoons sugar

¾ teaspoon vanilla extract

NUTRITIONAL FACTS (PER SERVING)

Calories: 232   Carbohydrates: 37 g   Cholesterol: 6 mg
Fat: 1.9 g   Fiber: 0.9 g   Protein: 16 g   Sodium: 335 mg

You Save: Calories: 217   Fat: 28.8 g

FAT-FREE COOKING TIP

Creamy Cheesecakes Without the Fat

Cheesecakes are definitely one of the most luscious desserts you can make, and are a favorite on the Italian dessert table. But with up to 500 calories and 40 grams of fat per slice, a piece of this popular confection can easily blow your fat budget for the entire day! Even worse, most of this fat is the saturated, artery-clogging type. But don't fear. Creamy, delicious, ultra-light cheesecakes can now be made using nonfat cream cheese.

To defat your favorite cheesecake recipe, substitute a block-style nonfat cream cheese like Philadelphia Free for the full-fat cream cheese on a one-for-one basis. For a lighter taste and texture, substitute nonfat ricotta cheese for up to half of the full-fat cream cheese. Both of these nonfat cheeses contain more water than full-fat products, so you will need to add a tablespoon of flour to the batter for each 8-ounce block of nonfat cream cheese or each cup of nonfat ricotta used. This should produce a firm, nicely-textured cake that is rich and creamy, yet remarkably low in fat and calories.

Cassata Alla Siciliana (Sicilian Cake)

Yield: *10 servings*

1 fat-free loaf cake (15 ounces)

¼ cup plus 2 tablespoons orange juice or amaretto liqueur

FILLING

15 ounces nonfat ricotta cheese

¼ cup sugar

1 teaspoon vanilla extract

¼ cup finely chopped dried cherries or apricots

¼ cup finely chopped semi-sweet chocolate chips

GLAZE

¾ cup powdered sugar

2 tablespoons Dutch processed cocoa powder

2 tablespoons skim milk

1. Using a bread knife, cut the cake horizontally to create 4 layers. Arrange the 3 bottom layers on a flat surface, and sprinkle each layer with 2 tablespoons of orange juice or liqueur. Set aside.

2. To make the filling, place the ricotta, sugar, and vanilla extract in a food processor, and process until smooth. Transfer the mixture to a bowl, and stir in the cherries or apricots and the chocolate chips.

3. To assemble the cake, place the bottom cake layer on a serving plate, and spread with a third of the filling. Repeat with the next 2 layers and the remaining filling. Top with the last layer, and cover the cake with plastic wrap or aluminum foil. Chill for 8 hours or overnight, or until the filling is firm.

4. To make the glaze, place the sugar and cocoa in a small bowl, and stir to mix well. Stir in enough of the milk to make a thick glaze. If using a microwave oven, place the glaze in a microwave-safe bowl, and heat at high power for 30 seconds, or until hot and runny. If using a conventional stove top, place the glaze in a small saucepan, and, stirring constantly, cook over medium heat for 30 seconds, or until hot and runny.

5. Spread the glaze over the top of the chilled cake, allowing some of the mixture to drip down the sides. Allow the glaze to cool for 5 minutes before slicing and serving, or return the cake to the refrigerator, and chill until ready to serve.

NUTRITIONAL FACTS (PER SERVING)

Calories: 223   Carbohydrates: 44 g   Cholesterol: 3 mg
Fat: 1.3 g   Fiber: 0.8 g   Protein: 8.8 g   Sodium: 169 mg

You Save: Calories: 211   Fat: 14.5 g

Crisp Almond Cookies

1. Place the cereal in a blender or food processor, and process into fine crumbs. Measure the crumbs. There should be $1\frac{1}{2}$ cups. Adjust the amount if necessary, and set aside.

2. Place the egg whites in a large bowl, and beat with an electric mixer until soft peaks form when the beaters are raised. Still beating, slowly add the sugar, a tablespoon at a time. Continue beating until all of the sugar is mixed in and the mixture is thick and glossy. Beat in the extracts.

3. Gently fold half of the cereal crumbs into the beaten egg whites. Then fold in the remaining crumbs.

4. Line cookie sheets with aluminum foil (do not coat with cooking spray). Drop rounded teaspoons of the egg white mixture onto the sheets, spacing them $1\frac{1}{2}$ inches apart. Sprinkle about $\frac{1}{3}$ teaspoon of the almonds over the top of each cookie.

5. Bake at 350°F for 15 minutes, or until the cookies are golden brown. Remove the cookie sheets from the oven, and allow the cookies to cool on the pan to room temperature. Peel the cookies from the foil, and serve immediately or store in an airtight container.

Yield: *36 cookies*

3 cups oat flake-and-almond cereal

2 egg whites, brought to room temperature

$\frac{3}{4}$ cup sugar

$1\frac{1}{2}$ teaspoons almond extract

1 teaspoon vanilla extract

$\frac{1}{4}$ cup sliced almonds

NUTRITIONAL FACTS (PER COOKIE)

Calories: 42   Carbohydrates: 8 g   Cholesterol: 0 mg
Fat: 0.8 g   Fiber: 0.4 g   Protein: 0.9 g   Sodium: 20 mg

You Save: Calories: 34   Fat: 4 g

Mocha Fudge Crumb Cake

Yield: *8 servings*

BATTER

¾ cup unbleached flour

½ cup whole wheat pastry flour

½ cup sugar

¼ cup Dutch processed cocoa powder

1 teaspoon baking soda

1½ teaspoons instant coffee granules

½ cup plus 2 tablespoons nonfat buttermilk

1½ cups finely chopped peeled pears (about 2 medium)

1 teaspoon vanilla extract

CRUMB TOPPING

3 tablespoons light brown sugar

2 tablespoons Dutch processed cocoa powder

2 tablespoons quick-cooking oats

2 tablespoons finely chopped walnuts

1 tablespoon chocolate syrup

GLAZE

½ cup powdered sugar

1 tablespoon Dutch processed cocoa powder

2½ teaspoons skim milk

¼ teaspoon instant coffee granules

1. To make the crumb topping, place the brown sugar, cocoa, oats, and walnuts in a small bowl, and stir to mix well. Add the chocolate syrup, and stir until the mixture is moist and crumbly. Set aside.

2. To make the batter, place the flours, sugar, cocoa, baking soda, and coffee granules in a medium-sized bowl, and stir to mix well. Add the buttermilk, pears, and vanilla extract, and stir just until the dry ingredients are moistened.

3. Coat an 8-inch round cake pan with nonstick cooking spray, and spread the batter evenly in the pan. Sprinkle the crumb topping over the batter. Bake at 350°F for about 30 minutes, or until the top springs back when lightly touched. Allow the cake to cool to room temperature.

4. To make the glaze, place all of the glaze ingredients in a small bowl, and stir to mix well. If using a microwave oven, place the glaze in a microwave-safe bowl, and heat at high power for 25 seconds, or until hot and runny. If using a conventional stove top, place the glaze in a small saucepan, and, stirring constantly, cook over medium heat for 25 seconds, or until hot and runny.

5. Drizzle the glaze over the top of the cake. Let the cake sit for at least 15 minutes to allow the glaze to harden before cutting into wedges and serving.

NUTRITIONAL FACTS (PER SERVING)

Calories: 220 Carbohydrates: 49 g Cholesterol: 0 mg
Fat: 2 g Fiber: 4 g Protein: 4.6 g Sodium: 183 mg

You Save: Calories: 117 Fat: 16.5 g

Cherry-Almond Cheese Tarts

1. To make the crust, place the cereal in the bowl of a food processor, and process into fine crumbs. Measure the crumbs. There should be 1 cup. (Adjust the amount if necessary.)

2. Return the crumbs to the food processor, add the sugar, and process for a few seconds to mix. Add the egg substitute, and process until the mixture is moist and crumbly.

3. Coat 12 muffin cups with nonstick cooking spray, and divide the crust among the cups. Using the back of a spoon, lightly press the crumbs against the bottom and $\frac{1}{4}$ inch up the sides of each cup, forming an even crust. (Dip the spoon in sugar periodically, if necessary, to prevent sticking.) Bake at 350°F for 7 minutes, or until the edges feel firm and dry. Set aside to cool.

4. To make the cheese filling, place the cream cheese, ricotta, and sugar in the bowl of a food processor, and process until well mixed. Add the liqueur, egg substitute, flour, and vanilla extract, and process until smooth.

5. Spoon the filling into the muffin cups over the crusts. Bake at 325°F for 30 minutes, or until the cheesecakes are puffed and the filling is set. Turn the oven off, and allow the cheesecakes to cool in the oven with the door ajar for 30 minutes. (The centers will fall slightly during cooling.)

6. Refrigerate the cheesecakes in the muffin cups for at least 4 hours, or until well chilled. Run a knife around the edge of each tart, and lift it out of the muffin cup. Arrange the tarts on a serving plate, and top each one with a slightly rounded tablespoon of the pie filling. Chill for at least 1 additional hour before serving.

Yield: 12 servings

CRUST

2 cups oat flake-and-almond cereal

1 tablespoon plus 1 teaspoon sugar

1 tablespoon fat-free egg substitute

FILLING

2 blocks (8 ounces each) nonfat cream cheese

1 cup nonfat ricotta cheese

$\frac{2}{3}$ cup sugar

2 tablespoons amaretto liqueur

$\frac{1}{2}$ cup fat-free egg substitute

$\frac{1}{4}$ cup unbleached flour

$1\frac{1}{2}$ teaspoons vanilla extract

TOPPING

1 cup light (reduced-sugar) cherry pie filling

NUTRITIONAL FACTS (PER SERVING)

Calories: 170 , Carbohydrates: 28 g Cholesterol: 3 mg
Fat: 0.8 g Fiber: 0.7 g Protein: 10.7 g Sodium: 260 mg

You Save: Calories: 189 Fat: 24.7 g

LOW-FAT COOKING TIP

Chocolate Flavor With a Fraction of the Fat

For rich chocolate flavor with minimum fat, substitute cocoa powder for high-fat baking chocolate. Simply use 3 tablespoons of cocoa powder plus 1 tablespoon of water or another liquid to replace each ounce of baking chocolate in cakes, brownies, puddings, and other goodies. You'll save 111 calories and 13.5 grams of fat for each ounce of baking chocolate you replace!

For the deepest, darkest, richest cocoa flavor, use Dutch processed cocoa in your chocolate treats. Dutching, a process that neutralizes the natural acidity in cocoa, results in a darker, sweeter, more mellow-flavored cocoa. Look for a brand like Hershey's Dutch Processed European Style cocoa. Like regular cocoa, this product has only half a gram of fat per tablespoon—although some brands do contain more fat. Dutched cocoa can be substituted for regular cocoa in any recipe, and since it has a smoother, sweeter flavor, you may find that you can reduce the sugar in your recipe by up to 25 percent.

Chocolate-Raspberry Torte

Yield: *16 servings*

BATTER

1 cup unbleached flour

¾ cup oat flour

1½ cups sugar, divided

½ cup Dutch processed cocoa powder

1 teaspoon baking soda

¼ teaspoon salt

1¼ cups coffee, cooled to room temperature

1 tablespoon distilled white vinegar

2 teaspoons vanilla extract

6 large egg whites, brought to room temperature

For variety, substitute apricot or cherry jam for the raspberry jam, and use apricot or cherry yogurt instead of raspberry yogurt.

1. To make the cake, place the flours, ¾ cup of the sugar, and the cocoa, baking soda, and salt in a large bowl. Stir to mix well, and set aside.

2. Place the coffee, vinegar, and vanilla extract in a medium-sized bowl. Stir to mix well, and set aside.

3. Place the egg whites in a large bowl, and, using an electric mixer, beat at high speed until soft peaks form when the beaters are raised. Still beating, gradually add the remaining ¾ cup of sugar, and continue beating until stiff peaks form when the beaters are raised. Set aside.

4. Add the coffee mixture to the flour mixture, and mix with a wire whisk until the batter is smooth. Using a rubber scraper or a large spoon, gently fold a third of the whipped egg whites into the batter. Then fold in the remaining whipped egg whites.

5. Divide the batter between two ungreased 9-inch round cake pans, and bake at 325°F for 25 to 30 minutes, or until the top springs back when lightly touched. Remove the cakes from the oven, and allow to cool to room temperature in the pans.

6. To make the filling, place the pudding mix and skim milk in a small bowl, and beat with a wire whisk or electric mixer for 2 minutes, or until the mixture is smooth and starts to thicken. Cover and chill until ready to assemble the torte.

7. To assemble the torte, run a knife around the sides of the cake pans to loosen the cakes. Turn the cakes out onto a flat surface, and use a bread knife or piece of string to cut each cake into 2 layers.

8. Place 1 layer on a serving plate, and spread with half of the pudding. Place a second layer over the pudding, and spread with the jam. Place a third layer over the jam, and spread with the remaining pudding. Place the fourth layer over the pudding.

9. To make the frosting, place the whipped topping in a medium-sized bowl, and gently fold in the yogurt. Swirl the frosting over the sides and top of the cake. Cover the cake, and refrigerate for at least 2 hours before slicing and serving. If desired, sprinkle the almonds or raspberries over the top just before serving.

FILLING

1 package (4-serving size) instant chocolate pudding mix (sugar-free or regular)

1½ cups skim milk

½ cup raspberry jam

FROSTING

2 cups fat-free or light whipped topping

½ cup nonfat raspberry yogurt

3 tablespoons toasted sliced almonds (page 207) or ½ cup fresh raspberries (optional)

NUTRITIONAL FACTS (PER SERVING)

Calories: 199 Carbohydrates: 45 g Cholesterol: 1 mg
Fat: 0.9 g Fiber: 2 g Protein: 4.9 g Sodium: 241 mg

You Save: Calories: 177 Fat: 17.9 g

Time-Saving Tip

To save time when preparing Chocolate-Raspberry Torte, use a reduced-fat chocolate cake mix instead of making the cake from scratch. Then simply whip up the pudding and the frosting, and assemble the cake.

Frozen Mocha Pie

Yield: *8 servings*

1½ quarts coffee ice cream, slightly softened

CRUST

8 large (2½-x-5-inch) reduced-fat chocolate graham crackers

2 tablespoons sugar

2 tablespoons tub-style nonfat margarine

FUDGE TOPPING

½ cup sugar

¼ cup Dutch processed cocoa powder

1 tablespoon plus 1½ teaspoons cornstarch

¾ cup skim milk

1 teaspoon vanilla extract

For variety, substitute different flavors of ice cream for the coffee. Try nonfat raspberry ripple, cherry vanilla, or cookies and cream.

1. To make the crust, break up the crackers and place in the bowl of a food processor. Process into fine crumbs. Measure the crumbs. There should be 1¼ cups. (Adjust the amount if necessary.)

2. Return the crumbs to the food processor, add the sugar, and process for a few seconds to mix. Add the margarine, and process for about 30 seconds, or until the mixture is moist (but not wet) and crumbly, and holds together when pinched. If the mixture seems too dry, add more margarine, ½ teaspoon at a time, until the proper consistency is reached.

3. Coat a 9-inch pie pan with nonstick cooking spray, and use the back of a spoon to press the mixture over the bottom and sides of the pan, forming an even crust. (Dip the spoon in sugar periodically, if necessary, to prevent sticking.) Bake at 350°F for about 9 minutes, or until the edges feel firm and dry. Set aside to cool.

4. To make the fudge topping, place the sugar, cocoa, and cornstarch in a 1-quart pot, and stir to mix well. Slowly stir in the milk, and cook over medium heat, stirring constantly, for about 5 minutes, or until the mixture comes to a boil. Cook, still stirring, for an additional minute or 2, or until the mixture is thick and bubbly.

5. Remove the pot from the heat, and stir in the vanilla extract. Transfer the topping to a covered container, and refrigerate for at least 2 hours, or until well chilled.

6. Spread the ice cream in the cooled crust, mounding the top slightly. Cover the pie loosely with aluminum foil, and freeze for at least 2 hours, or until firm.

7. Stir the fudge topping, and spread it evenly over the top of the pie. Cover the pie, return it to the freezer, and freeze for at least 2 hours before slicing and serving.

NUTRITIONAL FACTS (PER SERVING)
Calories: 263 Carbohydrates: 56 g Cholesterol: 2 mg
Fat: 1.5 g Fiber: 1.1 g Protein: 8.4 g Sodium: 137 mg

You Save: Calories: 259 Fat: 29 g

Chocolate-Hazelnut Biscotti

For variety, substitute chopped almonds for the hazelnuts and amaretto liqueur for the Frangelico.

Yield: *24 biscotti*

1. Place the flour, sugar, cocoa, and baking powder in a large bowl, and stir to mix well. Stir in the nuts and chocolate chips.

2. Add egg substitute, chocolate syrup, liqueur, and vanilla extract to flour mixture, and stir just until dry ingredients are moistened and dough holds together. Add a little more egg substitute if mixture seems too dry.

3. Turn dough onto lightly floured surface, and shape into two 8-x-2-inch logs. Coat a baking sheet with nonstick cooking spray, and place logs on sheet, spacing them 4 inches apart to allow for spreading. Bake at 350°F for about 25 minutes, or until lightly browned and firm to the touch.

4. Transfer the logs to a wire rack, and allow to cool for 15 minutes. Then place on a cutting board, and use a serrated knife to slice the logs diagonally into $1/2$-inch slices.

5. Reduce oven temperature to 300°F. Return slices to baking sheet, arranging them in a single layer, cut side down. Bake for 10 minutes. Then turn the slices, and bake for 10 additional minutes, or until dry and crisp.

6. Transfer the biscotti to wire racks, and cool completely. Serve immediately or store in an airtight container.

$1 2/3$ cups whole wheat pastry flour

$2/3$ cup sugar

$1/4$ cup Dutch processed cocoa powder

2 teaspoons baking powder

$1/3$ cup chopped toasted hazelnuts (below)

$1/3$ cup semi-sweet or white chocolate chips

$1/4$ cup plus 2 tablespoons fat-free egg substitute

$1/4$ cup chocolate syrup

2 tablespoons Frangelico liqueur

1 teaspoon vanilla extract

NUTRITIONAL FACTS (PER BISCOTTI)
Calories: 87   Carbohydrates: 16.5 g   Cholesterol: 0 mg
Fat: 1.9 g   Fiber: 1.6 g   Protein: 2 g   Sodium: 42 mg

You Save: Calories: 40   Fat: 5.4 g

LOW-FAT COOKING TIP

Getting the Most Out of Nuts

Nuts add crunch, great taste, and essential nutrients to all kinds of baked goods. Unfortunately, nuts also add fat. But you can halve the fat—without halving the taste—simply by toasting nuts before adding them to your recipe. Toasting intensifies the flavor of nuts so much that you can often cut the amount used in half.

Simply arrange the nuts in a single layer on a baking sheet, and bake at 350°F for about 10 minutes, or until lightly browned with a toasted, nutty smell. (For sliced almonds or chopped nuts, bake for only 6 to 8 minutes.) To save time, toast a large batch and store leftovers in an airtight container in the refrigerator for several weeks, or keep them in the freezer for several months.

Cherry Risotto Pudding

Yield: *6 servings*

$\frac{1}{2}$ cup plus 1 tablespoon arborio rice

3 cups skim milk

$\frac{1}{4}$ cup plus 1 tablespoon dried cherries

$\frac{1}{4}$ cup plus 2 tablespoons evaporated skimmed milk

$\frac{1}{4}$ cup plus 2 tablespoons fat-free egg substitute

$\frac{1}{4}$ cup plus 2 tablespoons sugar

1 teaspoon vanilla extract

1. Place the rice and milk in a heavy 2-quart pot, and place over medium heat. Cook, stirring frequently, until the mixture comes to a boil. Reduce the heat to low, cover, and simmer, stirring occasionally, for about 25 minutes, or until most of the milk has been absorbed and the rice is tender.

2. Add the dried cherries to the rice mixture, cover, and cook for about 2 minutes, or until the cherries start to soften.

3. Place the evaporated milk, egg substitute, sugar, and vanilla extract in a small bowl, and stir to mix well. Slowly stir the evaporated milk mixture into the rice mixture. Cook and stir for 3 to 5 minutes, or until the mixture is thick and creamy.

4. Remove the pot from the heat, and allow to cool for 10 minutes. Stir the pudding, and spoon into dessert dishes. Serve warm.

NUTRITIONAL FACTS (PER $\frac{3}{4}$-CUP SERVING)

Calories: 199 Carbohydrates: 40 g Cholesterol: 3 mg
Fat: 0.5 g Fiber: 0.6 g Protein: 8.5 g Sodium: 107 mg

You Save: Calories: 98 Fat: 12.4 g

Sicilian Ice Cream Sundaes

Yield: *6 servings*

2 cups fresh or frozen (thawed) raspberries

2 tablespoons sugar

2 tablespoons Chambord, amaretto, or Frangelico liqueur

12 ladyfingers

1 quart nonfat vanilla ice cream

3 tablespoons chocolate syrup

1. Place the raspberries, sugar, and liqueur in a medium-sized bowl, and mash them together. Set aside.

2. Crumble 1 ladyfinger into the bottom of each of six 10-ounce balloon wine glasses. Spoon $1\frac{1}{2}$ tablespoons of the raspberry mixture over the ladyfinger in each glass, and top with $\frac{1}{3}$ cup of the ice cream. Repeat the ladyfinger, raspberry, and ice cream layers.

3. Drizzle $1\frac{1}{2}$ teaspoons of chocolate syrup over the top of each sundae, and serve immediately.

NUTRITIONAL FACTS (PER SERVING)

Calories: 244 Carbohydrates: 51 g Cholesterol: 25 mg
Fat: 0.9 g Fiber: 2 g Protein: 7 g Sodium: 35 mg

You Save: Calories: 177 Fat: 17.9 g

Polenta Pudding

1. Scrub the orange and remove the peel, reserving half of the peel. Cut the orange in half, and discard any seeds. Coarsely chop the orange and the reserved peel. Place the orange, orange peel, and brown sugar in a food processor, and pulse several times to mince the orange and peel.

2. Place the minced orange mixture and the honey in a $2\frac{1}{2}$-quart pot, and bring to a boil over medium heat. Cook, stirring constantly, for 8 to 10 minutes, or until the mixture is thick and syrupy.

3. Add the milk, evaporated milk, and cornmeal to the orange mixture. Cook, stirring constantly, for 10 to 12 minutes, or until the mixture comes to a boil. Reduce the heat to low, and cook, still stirring constantly, for 2 additional minutes, or until slightly thickened.

4. Place the egg substitute in a small bowl. Remove 1 cup of the hot cornmeal mixture from the pot, and stir it into the egg substitute. Slowly stir the egg mixture back into the pudding. Cook and stir for 2 minutes, or until slightly thickened. Remove the pot from the heat, and stir in the vanilla extract and the apricots or raisins.

5. Coat a $1\frac{1}{2}$-quart round casserole dish with nonstick cooking spray. Pour the pudding mixture into the dish, sprinkle lightly with the nutmeg, and place the dish in a pan filled with 1 inch of hot water.

6. Bake uncovered at 350°F for 50 minutes, or until set. When done, a sharp knife inserted midway between the center of the pudding and the rim of the dish should come out clean. Remove the pudding from the oven, and allow to cool for 30 minutes. Serve warm or at room temperature, refrigerating any leftovers.

Yield: 8 servings

1 medium orange

3 tablespoons light brown sugar

$\frac{1}{4}$ cup honey

$2\frac{1}{2}$ cups skim milk

1 cup evaporated skimmed milk

$\frac{1}{4}$ cup plus 2 tablespoons coarsely ground cornmeal or polenta

1 cup fat-free egg substitute

$1\frac{1}{2}$ teaspoons vanilla extract

$\frac{1}{3}$ cup chopped dried apricots or golden raisins

Ground nutmeg

NUTRITIONAL FACTS (PER $\frac{2}{3}$-CUP SERVING)

Calories: 153   Carbohydrates: 30 g   Cholesterol: 2 mg
Fat: 0.5 g   Fiber: 1.2 g   Protein: 9 g   Sodium: 130 mg

You Save: Calories: 128   Fat: 16.4 g

Orange-Almond Biscotti

Yield: *24 biscotti*

1 cup whole wheat pastry flour

1 cup unbleached flour

½ cup sugar

2 teaspoons baking powder

¼ cup chilled reduced-fat margarine or light butter, cut into pieces

⅓ cup chopped toasted almonds or pecans (page 207)

⅓ cup chopped golden raisins or dried cherries

¼ cup plus 2 tablespoons fat-free egg substitute

2 tablespoons frozen orange juice concentrate, thawed

1 teaspoon vanilla extract

1. Place the flours, sugar, and baking powder in a large bowl, and stir to mix well. Using a pastry cutter, cut in the margarine or butter until the mixture resembles coarse meal. Stir in the nuts and the dried fruit.

2. Add the egg substitute, juice concentrate, and vanilla extract to the flour mixture, and stir just until the dry ingredients are moistened and the dough holds together. Add a little more egg substitute if the mixture seems too dry.

3. Turn the dough onto a lightly floured surface, and shape into two 8-x-2-inch logs. Coat a baking sheet with nonstick cooking spray, and place the logs on the sheet, spacing them 4 inches apart to allow for spreading. Bake at 350°F for about 25 minutes, or until lightly browned and firm to the touch.

4. Transfer the logs to a wire rack, and allow them to cool for 15 minutes. Then place on a cutting board, and use a serrated knife to slice the logs diagonally into ½-inch slices.

5. Reduce the oven temperature to 300°F. Return the slices to the baking sheet, arranging them in a single layer, cut side down. Bake for 10 minutes. Turn the slices, and bake for 10 additional minutes, or until dry and crisp.

6. Transfer the biscotti to wire racks, and cool completely. Serve immediately or store in an airtight container.

NUTRITIONAL FACTS (PER BISCOTTI)

Calories: 79   Carbohydrates: 14.5 g   Cholesterol: 0 mg
Fat: 1.8 g   Fiber: 1 g   Protein: 2 g   Sodium: 46 mg

You Save: Calories: 28   Fat: 3.4 g

LOW-FAT COOKING TIP

Baking With Reduced-Fat Margarine and Light Butter

Contrary to popular belief, you *can* bake with reduced-fat margarine and light butter. These products make it possible to reduce fat by more than half, and still enjoy light, tender, buttery-tasting cakes; crisp cookies and biscotti; and other goodies that are not easily made fat-free.

Creamy Cappuccino Mousse

1. Place the liqueur in a blender. Sprinkle the gelatin over the liqueur, and set aside for 2 minutes to allow the gelatin to soften. Pour the boiling coffee over the gelatin, and, with the lid slightly ajar, blend at low speed for about 1 minute, or until the gelatin is completely dissolved.

2. Add the ricotta, sugar, cocoa, cinnamon, and vanilla extract to the blender, and blend for about 1 minute, or until the mixture is smooth.

3. Pour the ricotta mixture into a medium-sized bowl, cover, and chill for at least 1 hour, or until the mixture is set. Stir the chilled mixture well with a whisk for about 30 seconds, or until it has a pudding-like consistency. If the mixture is too soft, chill it for a little longer; then stir again.

4. When the ricotta mixture has reached the proper consistency, place the chilled evaporated milk in a medium-sized bowl. Using an electric mixer, beat the milk at high speed for about 2 minutes, or until stiff peaks form when the beaters are raised. Immediately fold the whipped milk into the ricotta mixture. Then gently fold in the whipped topping.

5. Spoon the mousse into six 8-ounce wine glasses or dessert dishes, and chill for at least 3 hours, or until set. If desired, when ready to serve, top each serving with a tablespoon of the crushed graham crackers.

Yield: *6 servings*

¼ cup Tiramisu liqueur or coffee liqueur

1 envelope (¼ ounce) unflavored gelatin

¼ cup boiling hot coffee

1¼ cups nonfat ricotta cheese

¼ cup plus 2 tablespoons sugar

2 tablespoons Dutch processed cocoa powder

¼ teaspoon ground cinnamon

1½ teaspoons vanilla extract

¼ cup evaporated skimmed milk, chilled

1½ cups fat-free or light whipped topping

1½ large (2½-x-5-inch) reduced-fat chocolate graham crackers, coarsely crushed (optional)

NUTRITIONAL FACTS (PER ⅞-CUP SERVING)
Calories: 171   Carbohydrates: 31 g   Cholesterol: 4 mg
Fat: 0.3 g   Fiber: 0.6 g   Protein: 9.7 g   Sodium: 127 mg

You Save: Calories: 94   Fat: 18.3 g

Because reduced-fat margarine and light butter are diluted with water, they cannot be substituted for their full-fat counterparts on a one-for-one basis. To compensate for the extra water, substitute three-fourths of the light product for the full-fat butter or margarine. For instance, if a cake recipe calls for 1 cup of butter, use ¾ cup of light butter. Be sure to use a brand that contains 5 to 6 grams of fat and 50 calories per tablespoon. (Full-fat brands contain 11 grams of fat and 100 calories per tablespoon.) Brands with less fat than this should be used only in recipes specifically designed for these products.

Be careful not to overbake your reduced-fat creations, as they can become dry. Bake cakes and quick breads at 325°F to 350°F, muffins at 350°F, and biscuits and scones at 375°F to 400°F, and check the product a few minutes before the end of the usual baking time. Bake cookies at 325°F until golden brown. Then enjoy!

Tiramisu

Yield: *6 servings*

18 ladyfingers (about 4$\frac{1}{2}$ ounces)

2 teaspoons Dutch processed cocoa powder

$\frac{3}{4}$ cup fat-free or light whipped topping (optional)

CUSTARD

3 cups skim milk, divided

$\frac{1}{2}$ cup instant nonfat dry milk powder

3 tablespoons cornstarch

$\frac{1}{4}$ cup plus 2 tablespoons sugar

$\frac{1}{2}$ teaspoon dried grated orange rind

Pinch ground nutmeg

$\frac{1}{4}$ cup plus 2 tablespoons fat-free egg substitute

1$\frac{1}{2}$ teaspoons vanilla extract

COFFEE MIXTURE

$\frac{1}{2}$ cup espresso or strong black coffee, cooled to room temperature

2 tablespoons brandy or orange liqueur

2 tablespoons Dutch processed cocoa powder

A creamy custard replaces the traditional high-fat mascarpone cheese and egg filling in this luscious Italian dessert.

1. To make the custard, place $\frac{1}{2}$ cup of the milk and all of the milk powder and cornstarch in a small jar with a tight-fitting lid. Shake the mixture until smooth, and set aside.

2. Place the remaining 2$\frac{1}{2}$ cups of milk in a 2-quart pot. Add the sugar, orange rind, and nutmeg, and cook over medium heat, stirring constantly, until the mixture just begins to boil. Add the cornstarch mixture, and cook, still stirring, for about 2 minutes, or until the mixture returns to a boil and thickens slightly. Reduce the heat to low.

3. Place the egg substitute in a small bowl. Remove $\frac{1}{2}$ cup of the hot milk mixture from the pot, and stir into the egg substitute. Return the mixture to the pot, and cook, stirring constantly, for 2 to 3 minutes, or until the mixture thickens slightly. Remove the pot from the heat, stir in the vanilla extract, and, stirring every 10 minutes, allow the custard to cool for about 30 minutes.

4. To make the coffee mixture, place the coffee, brandy or liqueur, and cocoa in a small bowl, and stir until smooth. Set aside.

5. To assemble the desserts, coarsely crumble 1$\frac{1}{2}$ ladyfingers into the bottom of each of six 10-ounce balloon wine glasses. Top the ladyfingers with 1 tablespoon of the coffee mixture, and $\frac{1}{4}$ cup of the custard. Repeat the layers. Then sift a little cocoa over the top of each dessert.

6. Cover the desserts, and refrigerate for at least 2 hours. If desired, top each serving with 2 tablespoons of the whipped topping just before serving.

NUTRITIONAL FACTS (PER SERVING)

Calories: 221   Carbohydrates: 41 g   Cholesterol: 40 mg
Fat: 1.6 g   Fiber: 1.2 g   Protein: 10 g   Sodium: 151 mg

You Save: Calories: 311   Fat: 39 g

Italian Trifle

1. To make the custard, place $\frac{1}{2}$ cup of the milk and all of the milk powder and cornstarch in a small jar with a tight-fitting lid. Shake the mixture until smooth, and set aside.

2. Place the remaining $2\frac{1}{2}$ cups of milk in a 2-quart pot. Add the sugar and lemon rind, and cook over medium heat, stirring constantly, until the mixture just begins to boil. Add the cornstarch mixture, and cook, still stirring, for about 2 minutes, or until the mixture returns to a boil and thickens slightly. Reduce the heat to low.

3. Place the egg substitute in a small bowl. Remove $\frac{1}{2}$ cup of the hot milk mixture from the pot, and stir into the egg substitute. Return the mixture to the pot, and cook, stirring constantly, for 2 to 3 minutes, or until the mixture thickens slightly.

4. Remove the pot from the heat. Stir in the vanilla extract, and, stirring every 10 minutes, allow the custard to cool for about 30 minutes, or until it is lukewarm. Transfer the custard to a covered container and refrigerate for several hours, or until well chilled.

5. To assemble the trifle, arrange the cake slices on a flat surface, and sprinkle with the amaretto. Then spread each slice with a thin layer of the marmalade. Set aside.

6. Spread a thin layer of the chilled custard over the bottom of a 3-quart glass bowl, and arrange half of the cake slices over the custard. Top the cake slices with half of the remaining custard, all of the apricots, the remaining cake slices, and, finally, the remaining custard.

7. To make the topping, place the whipped topping in a medium-sized bowl, and gently fold in the yogurt. Swirl the topping over the trifle, and chill for at least 2 hours. If desired, sprinkle the almonds over the top just before serving.

Yield: 12 servings

1 fat-free loaf cake (15 ounces), cut into $\frac{1}{2}$-inch slices

$\frac{1}{4}$ cup amaretto liqueur

$\frac{1}{4}$ cup orange marmalade

1 can (1 pound) apricot halves in juice, drained and chopped

CUSTARD

3 cups skim milk, divided

$\frac{1}{3}$ cup instant nonfat dry milk powder

2 tablespoons plus 1 teaspoon cornstarch

$\frac{1}{4}$ cup plus 2 tablespoons sugar

1 teaspoon dried grated lemon rind, or 1 tablespoon freshly grated lemon rind

$\frac{1}{2}$ cup fat-free egg substitute

1 teaspoon vanilla extract

TOPPING

$1\frac{1}{2}$ cups fat-free or light whipped topping

$\frac{1}{2}$ cup nonfat vanilla yogurt

3 tablespoons toasted sliced almonds (optional) (page 207)

NUTRITIONAL FACTS (PER SERVING)

Calories: 211   Carbohydrates: 44 g   Cholesterol: 1 mg
Fat: 0.3 g   Fiber: 0.9 g   Protein: 6 g   Sodium: 120 mg

You Save: Calories: 115   Fat: 15.1 g

Amaretto Baked Peaches

Yield: 6 servings

3 extra-large peaches (8 ounces each)

½ cup amaretto liqueur

2 tablespoons water

3 cups nonfat vanilla ice cream (optional)

TOPPING

1½ cups oat flake-and-almond cereal

¼ cup light brown sugar

3 tablespoons sliced almonds (optional)

2 tablespoons plus 1½ teaspoons amaretto liqueur

1. To make the topping, place the cereal in a blender or food processor, and process into crumbs. Measure the crumbs. There should be ¾ cup. (Adjust the amount if necessary.)

2. Place the cereal crumbs, brown sugar, and, if desired, the almonds in a small bowl, and stir to mix well. Add the amaretto, and stir until the mixture is moist and crumbly. Set aside.

3. Peel the peaches. Then cut each in half lengthwise, and remove the pit. Using a spoon, scoop a thin layer out of the cavity of each peach to form a more pronounced depression. Cut a thin slice off the bottom of each peach half so that it will sit upright.

4. Place a heaping tablespoon of the filling in the cavity of each peach half, mounding it slightly. Pour the amaretto and water into the bottom of a 9-inch square pan, and arrange the peaches in the pan. Bake uncovered at 375°F for 25 to 30 minutes, or until the peaches are tender and the topping is golden brown. Cover loosely with aluminum foil during the last few minutes of baking if the topping starts to brown too quickly.

5. Drizzle a little of the pan juices over and around each peach, and serve warm, accompanying each half with a scoop of the ice cream, if desired.

NUTRITIONAL FACTS (PER SERVING)
Calories: 173   Carbohydrates: 35 g   Cholesterol: 0 mg
Fat: 1.5 g   Fiber: 2.6 g   Protein: 1.6 g   Sodium: 93 mg

You Save: Calories: 148   Fat: 16.3 g

Plums Poached in Wine

Poached fruits are a naturally fat-free dessert. This recipe also has about half the sugar of most poached-fruit recipes.

Yield: *6 servings*

1. Place the wine, juice, and sugar in a large nonreactive skillet.* Place the skillet over medium-high heat, and cook, stirring frequently, until the sugar dissolves and the mixture comes to a boil.

2. Add the cloves, cinnamon sticks, and plums to the skillet, and return the mixture to a boil. Reduce the heat to medium-low, cover, and simmer for 3 minutes. Turn the plums over and simmer for 2 additional minutes, or until just tender.

3. Using a slotted spoon, transfer the plums to a medium-sized bowl. Increase the heat under the pot to medium, and cook, stirring frequently, for about 5 minutes, or until the wine mixture is reduced by half and is slightly syrupy.

4. Pour the syrup over the plums, cover, and refrigerate for several hours, or until the plums are well chilled. Remove and discard the cinnamon sticks and cloves, and spoon the plums into serving dishes, pouring some of the syrup over each serving. Serve chilled.

¾ cup dry red wine

¾ cup orange juice

½ cup sugar

3 whole cloves

2 sticks cinnamon, each 2 inches long

9 medium unpeeled plums, pitted and quartered

NUTRITIONAL FACTS (PER SERVING)
Calories: 139 Carbohydrates: 32 g Cholesterol: 0 mg
Fat: 0.6 g Fiber: 2 g Protein: 0.9 g Sodium: 1 mg

You Save: Calories: 65 Fat: 0 g

*Pans made from aluminum, cast iron, and unlined copper can react with acidic ingredients such as wine and fruit juice to create an unpleasant taste and color. When recipes contain a large amount of acidic ingredients, as the poached plum recipe does, always use a nonreactive pan—one made of stainless steel, enameled steel, anodized aluminum, or glass. Or use a pan coated with a nonstick surface.

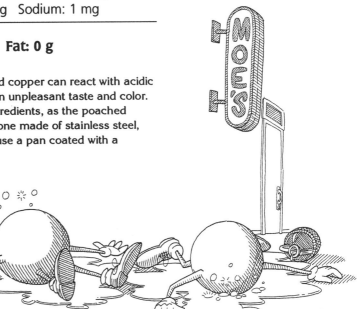

Baked Pears With Walnut Crunch Stuffing

Yield: *6 servings*

3 large pears (8 ounces each)

3 tablespoons apple or orange juice

3 cups nonfat vanilla ice cream (optional)

FILLING

¼ cup barley nugget cereal

¼ cup light brown sugar

3 tablespoons whole wheat flour

2 tablespoons finely chopped walnuts

¼ teaspoon ground cinnamon

1 tablespoon plus ½ teaspoon frozen apple or orange juice concentrate, thawed

1. To make the filling, place the cereal, brown sugar, flour, walnuts, and cinnamon in a small bowl, and stir to mix well. Add the juice concentrate, and stir just until the mixture is moist and crumbly. Set aside.

2. Peel the pears. Then cut each in half lengthwise. Cut a thin slice off the bottom of each pear half, so that it will sit upright. Using a spoon, remove the seeds to create a small cavity in the pear. Then cut away the fibrous line leading from the core to the stem end. Spoon a sixth of the filling into the cavity of each pear half, mounding it slightly.

3. Pour the apple or orange juice into the bottom of a 9-inch square pan, and arrange the pears in the pan. Bake uncovered at 375°F for 25 to 30 minutes, or until the pears are tender and the topping is golden brown. Cover loosely with aluminum foil during the last few minutes of baking if the topping starts to brown too quickly.

4. Serve the pears warm, accompanying each half with a scoop of the ice cream, if desired.

NUTRITIONAL FACTS (PER SERVING)

Calories: 136 Carbohydrates: 30 g Cholesterol: 0 mg
Fat: 1.9 g Fiber: 3.6 g Protein: 2.1 g Sodium: 35 mg

You Save: Calories: 69 Fat: 9.7 g

FAT-FREE COOKING TIP

Getting the Fat Out of Crumb Toppings

Most crumb toppings are high in fat—usually because of the butter or margarine used to hold the crumbs together and to promote browning. But you can easily reduce the fat in your favorite crumb or crumble topping by moistening the mixture with juice concentrate instead of the usual shortening.

Start by replacing the butter or margarine in your recipe with half as much thawed frozen fruit juice concentrate. Then mix up the topping. If the mixture seems too dry, add a little more juice concentrate. To prevent the topping from being overly sweet, reduce the sugar by the amount of juice concentrate used.

To save even more fat in crumb toppings, replace part of the nuts with a barley nugget cereal like Grape-Nuts. You will still get a crunchy nutty taste, but with none of the fat of nuts. Toasted wheat germ is another excellent substitute for nuts in baking. Rich in vitamins and minerals, wheat germ has a sweet and nutty taste, and, cup-for-cup, contains 90 percent less fat than nuts.

Orange Burst Granita

Granita—an icy Italian confection—is always fat-free. This version has the added virtue of using no refined sugar, and is bursting with orange flavor.

1. Pour the orange juice and juice concentrate into an 8-inch square pan, and stir to mix well.

2. Place the pan in the freezer, and freeze for 25 minutes, or until ice crystals begin to form around the sides of the pan. Using a spoon, stir the frozen crystals from around the edges and bottom of the pan back into the liquid portion.

3. Repeat the scraping process every 20 minutes for about 2 hours, or until the mixture is icy and granular. Spoon the granita into four 10-ounce balloon wine glasses, and serve immediately.

Yield: *4 servings*

3 cups freshly squeezed orange juice

¼ cup plus 2 tablespoons frozen orange juice concentrate, thawed

---

NUTRITIONAL FACTS (PER ⅞-CUP SERVING)
Calories: 126 Carbohydrates: 29.5 g Cholesterol: 0 mg
Fat: 0.3 g Fiber: 0.6 g Protein: 2 g Sodium: 3 mg

You Save: Calories: 55   Fat: 0 g

Time-Saving Tip

To make Orange Burst Granita with less fuss, pour the juice into 2 ice cube trays, and freeze for at least 3 hours, or until frozen solid. (Remove the cubes from the trays, and transfer them to freezer bags if you want to partially prepare the granita several days ahead of time.) Just before serving, place the ice cubes in the bowl of a food processor, and process for several minutes, pulsing and scraping the mixture down the sides of the bowl until small crystals are formed. Spoon the granita into serving dishes, and serve immediately.

Resource List

Most of the ingredients used in the recipes in this book are readily available in any supermarket, or can be found in your local health foods store or gourmet shop. But if you are unable to locate what you're looking for, the following list should guide you to a manufacturer who can either sell the desired product to you directly or inform you of the nearest retail outlet.

Meat Substitutes

Harvest Direct, Inc.
PO Box 988
Knoxville, TN 37901-0988
(800) 835-2867

Texturized vegetable protein (TVP).

Nondairy Cheeses

Sharon's Finest
PO Box 5020
Santa Rosa, CA 95402
(800) 656-9669

Almondrella Cheese, Tofurella Cheese, and Veganrella Cheese.

Whole Grains and Flours

Arrowhead Mills, Inc.
Box 2059
Hereford, TX 79045
(800) 749-0730

Whole wheat pastry flour, oat flour, and other flours and whole grains.

King Arthur Flour
PO Box 876
Norwich, VT 05055
(800) 827-6836

White whole wheat flour, whole wheat pastry flour, unbleached pastry flour, and other flours, whole grains, and baking products.

Mountain Ark Trading Company
PO Box 3170
Fayetteville, AR 72702
(800) 643-8909

Whole grains and flours, unrefined sweeteners, dried fruits, fruit spreads, and a wide variety of other natural foods.

Walnut Acres
PO Box 8
Penns Creek, PA 17862

(800) 433-3998

Baking and cooking aids, whole grains, whole grain flours, unrefined sweeteners, dried fruits, and a wide variety of other natural foods.

Sweeteners

Advanced Ingredients
331 Capitola Avenue, Suite F
Capitola, CA 95010
(408) 464-9891

Fruit Source granulated and liquid sweeteners.

Sucanat North America Corporation
26 Clinton Drive #117
Hollis, NH 03049
(603) 595-2922

Sucanat granulated sweetener.

Vermont Country Maple, Inc.
76 Ethan Allen Drive
South Burlington, VT 05403
(800) 528-7021

Maple sugar, maple syrup, and other maple products.

Index